The Remnant Spirit

The Remnant Spirit

Conservative Reform in Mainline Protestantism

DOUGLAS E. COWAN

Foreword by Irving R. Hexham

Westport, Connecticut
London

o51886480

Library of Congress Cataloging-in Publication Data

Cowan, Douglas E.
    The remnant spirit : conservative reform in mainline Protestantism / Douglas E.
    Cowan ; foreword by Irving R. Hexham.
      p. cm.
    includes bibliographical references and index.
    ISBN 0–275–97449–9 (alk. paper)
    1. Protestant churches—North America.   2. Church renewal.   I. Title.
    BR510.C69   2003
    280′.4′0973090511—dc21   2003046390

British Library Cataloguing in Publication Data is available.

Library of Congress Catalog Card Number: 2003046390
ISBN: 0–275–97449–9

First published in 2003

Praeger Publishers, 88 Post Road West, Westport, CT 06881
An imprint of Greenwood Publishing Group, Inc.
www.praeger.com

Printed in the United States of America

The paper used in this book complies with the
Permanent Paper Standard issued by the National
Information Standards Organization (Z39.48–1984).

10 9 8 7 6 5 4 3 2 1

For Jeffrey K. Hadden (1936–2003)
mentor, colleague, and friend

Contents

Foreword

In *The Remnant Spirit*, Douglas E. Cowan has written an extraordinary book dealing with the rise, effectiveness, and future prospects of renewal movements within four of the mainline Protestantisms in North America. Since such movements are to be found in all mainline denominations, both in North America and abroad, where a vibrant conservative evangelicalism constantly challenges the prevailing liberal establishment, this book speaks to issues that concern a great number of people. Its lessons reach out far beyond the boundaries of the particular groups that provided Cowan with his source material.

Because he is one of those rare academics who writes with both insider insights and the impartial candor of an outside observer, he is uniquely situated to tell this story in this way. As a minister in the United Church of Canada, he worked for more than 10 years as a pastor. Add to that his previous involvement as a lay member and later as a theological student, and we have nearly 20 years of experience within the mainline Protestant church. Equally important, though, is the fact that for the past several years Cowan has worked as first a graduate student and then an academic with a growing reputation as an astute sociologist of religion. His first major work, *Bearing False Witness?*, was on the evangelical Christian countercult movement in North America, and is also published by Praeger.

The study of renewal and revitalization movements in any religious tradition is of vital importance both to members of living religions and to academics studying religion. Out of such renewal movements new religions are often born, old religious traditions take on new life, and estab-

lished groups reform themselves to meet the various challenges to their
authority presented by the leaders of revival groups.

Of course, groups that deliberately set out to revive or revitalize an old
tradition are not the same as revival movements that occur spontaneously
within a society or religious organization. Revivals like the Great Awak-
ening have provided historians and other scholars with a wealth of material that has been studied and restudied over the past hundred years.
The study of groups that set out deliberately to revive or revitalize an
established religious tradition, however, have received very little attention
except where they became schismatic and lapsed into independent fundamentalist movements.

Thus, Cowan's work addresses several of the more neglected aspects of
the sociology of religion, theology, and the history of religions that deserve
far closer study than they have received to date. Although written primarily by a sociologist of religion, the book is also authored by a trained
theologian with extensive pastoral experience and a gift for writing born
in his undergraduate years at the University of Victoria as a student of
literature. The unique combination of a truly multidisciplinary approach
with a natural gift for writing makes this book not only enlightening but
very enjoyable to read.

Irving R. Hexham
University of Calgary
Advent 2003

Acknowledgments

There are a number of people I would like to thank for their specific contributions in terms of books, magazines, journals, and historical documents. The Reverend Brian Nicholson, pastor of Christ Presbyterian Church in Savannah, Georgia, very kindly shared copies of both church and court documents concerning Eastern Heights and Mary Elizabeth Blue Hull Memorial Presbyterian Churches. Jennifer Smith provided copies of original material on her great-grandfather, the Burnsite preacher, Albert Truax. Jennifer Peters, archivist for the Episcopal Church, provided copies of the Walter Righter trial documents. Susan Cyre, executive director of Presbyterians for Faith, Family and Ministry, sent me numerous back issues of their journal, *Theology Matters,* as did James Heidinger of *Good News.* Thanks also to Diana Henderson for back issues of the Prayer Book Society's journal, *Mandate,* and to John Trueman for material related to the Community of Concern. Many others sent documents and pieces of information, and my heartfelt gratitude to you all.

Conversations stretching back over many years have contributed greatly to both my interest in and understanding of conservative reform and renewal movements. For these times, I would like to thank especially Joanne Carlson Brown, Don Collett, Bob Harper, Lynne Hubbard, Mike Jones, Sandra Severs, and Chris Sykes.

I would like to thank the anonymous reviewers contacted by my editor at Praeger, Suzanne Staszak-Silva, for their many perceptive critiques and all but uniformly helpful suggestions.

Penultimately, for his encouragement and support over many years, I would like to thank my teacher, Irving Hexham, who in the midst of a busy schedule of his own, very kindly contributed the foreword.

And, as always, my wife Joie is my first reader, first critic, and first fan.

PART I

Precipitous Moments and the Crisis of the Mainline Church

For the record, please note who is screaming the loudest—the punditocracy. The members of the Confessing Churches, on the other hand, don't care about the conventional wisdom. Instead, following as the Spirit leads, they are trying to preserve that peace, purity and unity by proclaiming Jesus Christ alone as the way, the truth and the life.

—Craig M. Kibler, Presbyterian Lay Committee

What a pity. We have been led slowly but inevitably to the tragic conclusion that since 1988 harassment of both dissenting clergy and laity has been, and continues to be, the questionable distinction of the United Church. The last four Moderators have denied its existence outright, or have been unable or unwilling to end it.

—John Trueman, The Community of Concern

Basic sociology teaches that institutions are in a constant state of change. It also teaches that people who reject new paradigms are most often those who administer the institution. "Institutionalists" frequently deny the need for reform, delay the reform, or manage it in ways that do not truly reform. As such, when "reformers" appear, they are often treated with disdain, viewed with suspicion, or manipulated with stonewalling tactics.

—Steve Harper, A Foundation for Theological Education

CHAPTER 1

Reform and Renewal in the Mainline Church: An Introduction to the Precipice

TWO GLIMPSES OF THE PRECIPICE

The picture was disturbing, to say the least: rotting banana peels and brown lettuce, moldy muffin wrappers, possibly a used diaper or two, and a stench you can almost smell with your eyes. But that wasn't all, for there, nestled in the midst of the garbage, splattered with coffee grounds and soiled by heaven-knows-what, lay the *Book of Order*, the constitution of the Presbyterian Church (USA). No mistake by an inattentive cleaning staff, however; this was the picture that greeted readers on the cover of the December 2002 issue of *The Layman*, a bimonthly conservative broadsheet mailed to nearly half a million PC(USA) homes. To say that the Presbyterian Lay Committee, the oldest evangelical reform movement in the church and *The Layman*'s publisher, believes that its denomination is in trouble would be an understatement. In its eyes, the PC(USA), with its more than 11,000 congregations and 2.5 million members, is standing on the edge of a precipice, staring chaos in the face. This time, the issue was constitutional defiance.

As it has so often in recent years, the problem for conservative members of the church turns on one particular section of the *Book of Order*: G-6.0106b, the so-called fidelity and chastity clause from the list of "Gifts and Requirements" for those called to ministry in the church. More specifically, the provision declares for members of the order of ministry "the requirement to live either in fidelity within the covenant of marriage between a man and a woman, or chastity in singleness." Even more than that, though, the constitution states that "persons refusing to repent of any self-acknowledged practice which the confessions call sin shall not be ordained and/or installed as deacons, elders, or ministers of the Word and Sacrament." And therein lies the current rub. According to *The Layman*, the fact that "hundreds of local and regional Presbyterian leaders have declared that they are willfully defying the standard that prohibits the ordination of people who are sexually active outside of marriage" had effectively thrown the constitution into the trash (Adams 2002), and threatened to do the same with the entire church.

In response to the crisis, one California congregation petitioned its local presbytery to order another congregation "to apologize for a resolution stating its intention to ignore the ordination standard" (Adams 2002). On the other coast, a New York congregation complained that adverse publicity about these "defiant churches" had so seriously damaged its own local mission that funds to complete a family life center were jeopardized, and this congregation petitioned to leave the denomination along with all its property ("Summary of Cases" 2002).

While this section of the *Book of Order* speaks rather broadly of fidelity and chastity, those who invoke the passage clearly view it as the constitutional means to prevent gay men and lesbians from serving as ordained elders or ministers in the Presbyterian Church (USA). However, according to Adams (2002:1), the actions of "constitutional defiers and violators" are not limited merely to open contempt of G-6.0106b, but also include the "brazen invitation" of non-Christians to PC(USA) communion tables, the designation of same-sex union services as marriages, and the incipient idolatry of worship services that include any religious references other than Christian.

However abstract issues such as these may seem to those who are not directly affected by them, whose congregations are not in immediate danger of closing, and whose churches either welcome the presence of gay men and lesbians or who are so staunchly opposed to it that the possibility of a homosexual minister is rendered an absurdity, it is worth remembering from the start that there *are* real people involved in these disputes, and that real families *are* affected—some permanently.

The Reverend Donald Collett is a thoughtful, articulate minister, a trained family therapist, and a man of deep pastoral concern. In 1988, when he was chosen by his presbytery of The United Church of Canada to represent them at the church's biennial General Council, he knew that he carried with him the weight of expectation—of his family, his congregation, and many of his professional colleagues. After years of seemingly interminable debate, denominational studies and reports, and growing suspicion and rancor, the United Church would finally decide whether homosexuality, in and of itself, could serve as a barrier to ministry. Collett had been elected as the ordained commissioner from South Alberta Presbytery on the strength of a conservative viewpoint that would say "No!"

to any possibility of gay ordination or commissioning. His task was to defeat, in no uncertain terms, the recommendations of a report known as *Toward a Christian Understanding of Sexual Orientation, Lifestyles and Ministry (SOLM)* (National Coordinating Group 1988). And many might have thought Collett uniquely positioned to do just that, for he had also been chosen to serve on Sessional Committee 8, the group charged with facilitating discussion of the contentious document. While numerous other issues loomed before the Council, few commissioners or denominational members doubted that the *SOLM* report and its implications for the church were the crux of the meeting.

And *SOLM* was defeated—soundly. But, to the dismay of conservatives across Canada's largest Protestant denomination, the church did not say, specifically and unequivocally, that gay men and lesbians could not serve in ministry. On balance, it was something of a Pyrrhic victory for both sides, and news of the Council spread like a prairie fire across the country. Building on the newsworthiness of ultraconservative outrage, newspaper articles and broadcast commentary from coast to coast trumpeted that the pulpits of the United Church were no longer the sole domain of the straight, but that gay men and lesbians were now welcomed with open arms and blessed in their ministries. That wasn't what happened, of course, but that's the way the story was told.

When he returned to the small farming community of Taber in late August, though, and stood in the pulpit of Knox United Church, Collett knew his parishioners would want to hear little but what happened at General Council. They already knew what the media were saying. Now, what would the man they sent "to beat back the forces of darkness" say? Surprisingly, even if they were not entirely supportive of the decision the church had made, Collett found that not a few of his friends and colleagues were sympathetic about the grueling days and nights he had spent wrestling with The Issue. Their respect for his integrity as a minister prevented them from blaming him directly.

That Sunday morning, Collett stared out at a full church. People shifted nervously, expectantly, as the invocatory prayers were offered, the opening hymns sung, and the children safely shuttled off to church school. Departing from the prepared text of his sermon, he simply told them what had happened: how he had traveled to the Council three days ahead of most other delegates in order to deal with the more than 1,800 petitions that had been sent regarding the *SOLM* report. How he and his fellow committee members had gone back and forth between the various interest groups that were competing for control of the church's agenda—conservative reform groups like the Community of Concern, which wanted the discussion buried forever, and AFFIRM, which sought an even more active role for gay men and lesbians in the church. And how Sessional Committee 8 had worked into the wee hours of the morning more times than once trying to forge a compromise with which both sides could live in peace.

Of all those in the sanctuary that morning, though, the person whose face Collett remembers most was his wife, Jane, who sat like stone in the pew as he talked. Collett finished his message and bowed his head for the pastoral prayer. When he raised it again, less than a minute later, his wife was gone, her seat in the church empty. When they finally spoke that afternoon, she told him that she felt betrayed by his part in the decisions made at General Council, and that she was leaving. She moved out of their home that day, and they were divorced two years later.

INTRODUCTION

This is a book about church fights, fights the combatants believe will shape the future of their respective denominations, fights that affect not only the large, often unwieldy religious institutions within which they take place, but individual families as well. Church conflict, of course, is nothing new. In fact, the history of the Christian Church is arguably the history of the different ways in which devout men and women have understood the nature of their relationship with God, how they have argued about the relative merits of those different understandings, and how they have resolved—or failed to resolve—the tensions inherent in the disputes. From the Council at Jerusalem where Paul argued that Gentiles could not be excluded from Jesus' vision of the commonwealth of God to the ecumenical councils of the Church that gradually decreed that only those who believed according to the tenets of Athanasian theology could be included, from the *filioque* split of the great Eastern and Western Churches over the nature of Christ to congregational splits at First Baptist, Grace Methodist, or St. Andrew's Presbyterian, Christianity has been caught for most of its history in the ebb and flow of schism and reunion, of conflict, debate, and reconciliation.

Specifically, though, this book is about some of the church fights that have taken place since the end of World War II in what is known colloquially as mainline North American Protestantism. While both Robert Wuthnow (1988, 1989) and James Davison Hunter (1991) have examined the larger arena of religious liberals versus religious conservatives in, as Hunter puts it, "the struggle to define America," for the most part their analyses have considered broader interdenominational conflicts—evangelical Protestants versus mainline Protestants, for example. In this book, I would like to take their discussion to the intradenominational level, for the larger battles that they so aptly describe are being played out in very similar ways on these much smaller fields. These are the struggles to define, in the United States, the Presbyterian Church (PC[USA]), the United

Methodist Church (UMC), and the Episcopal Church (ECUSA); and in Canada, the United Church (UCCan).

Sometimes, at both the congregational and denominational levels, the conflict revolves around a particular event in the life of a church: the publication of a new hymnbook, a new prayer book, a new church school curriculum. Those opposed to these new resources contest what they often regard as skewed visions of the faith, visions largely unauthorized by the constituencies on which they have been allegedly foisted. For example, in order to bring his congregation in line with something called "inclusive language," a young minister has developed the annoying habit of announcing changes to the lyrics of favorite hymns. "He" becomes "they," "Father" becomes "Creator"—both regardless of their effect on the poetics or the theology of the piece. Likewise, treasured prayers are rewritten, ostensibly to reflect new (and by implication, better) understandings of the faith. Or, just a week after the annual church school Christmas pageant, a guest preacher from the local seminary tells the same congregation that no thinking Christian has believed in a literal Virgin Birth for more than a century. More than a few are caught off guard by these comments, and grumble angrily in their pews. These are common examples of instances when the pace at which theology and doctrine evolve in the church collides with the cherished beliefs of those who populate (and, as is so often pointed out in the ensuing arguments, pay for) its sanctuaries.

Other times, though, church members interpret these particular events more as warning signs, as symptoms of much larger, more deeply rooted systemic problems. Rather than a mere Sunday morning irritant, traditionalists contend that the introduction of inclusive language represents a decisive shift in basic theological positioning. Rewritten prayers are regarded as attempts to change the very nature of God, rather than simply the dominant metaphors for God. Liturgical experimentation, such as altering the established baptismal formula of "Father, Son, and Holy Spirit" to something like "Creator, Redeemer, and Sustainer," raises concerns that such practices will place the denomination outside the pale of legitimate ecumenical participation. And, finally, to take one of the most trenchant recent examples, proposed changes in ordination standards that would permit gay men and lesbians to serve in the church openly and honestly are regarded by denominational conservatives as part of an ongoing attack on the authority of the Bible, an abandonment of traditional or historic Christian mores, and the perpetuation of a pattern of hegemonic governance that has increasingly alienated denominational authorities from their grassroots constituencies.

In the midst of these debates, congregations split, and it is not uncommon for family members to come down on different sides of the conflict. Clergy protest their billet assignments at denominational conferences, proclaiming indignantly that they will not share a room with one of "those"—whoever "those" are. Indeed, in the wake of significant denominational conflict over such issues as inclusive language or homosexual ordination, especially when it has been reported in (and often aggravated by) mass media, more than one mainline clergyperson has been asked to yield his or her seat at the local ministerial group. At this end of the conflict continuum, disputants often believe that the very nature of their identity as Christians is at stake.

These issues are among many that have been regarded by traditionalists as clear signs of the need for *reform* in the mainline Protestant denominations. Many consider them evidence that clerical freedom of speech has been effectively rescinded, that ministers are no longer permitted to preach as their hearts direct, but must adhere to some politically correct party line. Most often, issues such as the revision of theology and liturgy, the use of inclusive language, denominational support for various kinds of social action, and the ongoing debate over homosexuality in the church are among the reasons traditionalists give to explain the drastic decline in mainline membership, participation, and financial commitment since the late 1960s. That there are other reasons for this decline does not go entirely unnoticed by denominational conservatives, but that the effects of these issues remain in the eyes of conservatives largely unacknowledged by denominational elites only increases the alienation felt by those who disagree with changes in church doctrine, polity, and practice. The well-known gospel chorus, "Gimme that old-time religion," may not be heard often in the sanctuaries of mainline Protestant churches, but the desire to recover that religion, which traditionalists regard as a more authentic and legitimate Christianity, is what motivates conservative reform and renewal movements.

Their fight is to see the Christian Church returned to the state of grace for which they believe God created it, and from which they insist it has fallen. And, in this fight, they contend that they manifest the remnant spirit of faithful resistance.

REFORM AND RENEWAL GROUPS IN DENOMINATIONAL PERSPECTIVE

As with so many topics, this book could easily have been expanded to fill several volumes. Many of the conservative reform groups I discuss, as well as the denominational conflicts that brought them into being, warrant entire books devoted to their social histories. The Good News Movement within United Methodism, the Presbyterian Lay Committee, and the Prayer Book Society of the Episcopal Church (USA) have all been active for nearly four decades. While many of the original founders and movement leaders no longer play active roles, the movements themselves have continued as a new generation of traditionalists has risen in their place.

In some churches, reform groups have institutionalized over time, and now occupy well-established (if not universally beloved) places on the denominational landscape. And, over that same time, the range of issues with which reform movements have felt compelled to deal has broadened considerably. Indeed, far more has happened in the course of their involvement with denominational politics, theology, and ecclesiology than could possibly be discussed in the brief space of one book.

I am interested here in the public face of reform and renewal, what Ron Eyerman and Andrew Jamison would call its *cognitive praxis* (1991). That is, I wanted to understand the ways in which specific events in the life of a church are perceived and interpreted by those who are in staunch disagreement with them, what ideas inform and shape those perceptions and interpretations, and what concrete responses have emerged from the interaction between construal and explanation. In brief, then, I have let my analysis be guided by the popular persona of the various reform and renewal movements as it is presented in public or semipublic documents: newsletters, magazines, occasional papers, books, Internet Web sites, as well as a variety of audio and video materials. These I regard as the *documentary artifacts* of the social movement. Where other voices are included—interviews, conversations, and anecdotes—they are offered to fill in the canvas, to add color to the larger issues with which reform and renewal movements are concerned.

This approach allows us a broader picture of the various denominational issues with which reform and renewal movements are concerned without being tied only to those movements themselves. As well, it shows us something of the organizational trajectory of various reform groups, of the complex of issues they have regarded as significant over the course of their emergence, development, and decline. This career path, if you will, particularly highlights the dialectical relationship that exists between reform and renewal movements and the denominational Others with whom they compete. This is especially true in terms of the development of the different statements of position or movement manifestos that appear as the various conflicts mature. Internal histories of most reform and renewal indicate varying degrees of tension within the movements themselves. Different persons have different reasons for their participation in reform praxis; different problems draw different participants to the cause. Using official or quasi-official documents—the public persona as presented in publications such as *The Layman, Mandate, Fellowship Magazine,* or *Concern, reNEWS,* or *Theology Matters*—reveals what and how issues have been privileged by the groups themselves. How are issues treated as emerging reform movements develop and evolve? Are particular issues omitted, avoided, or minimized? Is it possible to talk of a coherent reform agenda? I think so. Even some denominational conservatives believe there is a "reform agenda," and are, in fact, dissatisfied with more established reform and renewal movements on the basis of this "agenda." What is-sues, then, does the hierarchy within these movements—what we might call the established movement intellectuals—privilege in their presenta-tion of reform and renewal concerns?

Despite their shared concerns for denominational reform and renewal, for example, the perspective of lay movement participants is often very different from that of clerical movement leaders and intellectuals—bear-ing in mind that, while the majority of these leaders *are* clergy, this is certainly not always the case. Generational differences as well cloud the issue. In the United Methodist Church, for example, a new generation of traditionalist clergy regard the institutionalized Good News Movement and its entrenched bureaucracy as hopelessly out of touch with the con-servative grass roots of the church and see little future for themselves within that more established movement. As well, not all issues concern all members. Indeed, members of reform and renewal groups frequently participate based on their opposition to very specific denominational po-sitions or decisions, and are just as often uninterested in other issues ad-dressed by the group. In The United Church of Canada, for example, once the *Sexual Orientation, Lifestyles and Ministry* report was defeated in 1988, many denominational members who had joined the nascent Community of Concern saw little reason to remain. Indeed, as the Community of Con-cern began to evolve into a more general theological and doctrinal watch-dog, these members found themselves increasingly at odds with the conservative positioning of the movement and chose to leave.

That said, however, it is most often the institutionalized advocacy of established reform and renewal movements with which denominational authorities must deal. It is groups like Good News, the Voices of Orthodox Women, the Presbyterian Forum, the Community of Concern, the Prayer Book Society, and the Institute on Religion and Democracy—to name just a few—that set up information tables at denominational conferences, or-ganize pre- and postconference caucuses on controversial issues, and pub-lish their views in a wide variety of media. And, it is these organized (and, in some cases, institutionalized) reform groups, those that have achieved and maintained a recognizable public persona through their actions, to which mass media often turn in search of a controversial sound bite, a trenchant comment, the human interest controversy that lies at the heart of modern mass media-making.

This approach shows us three things: (1) what issues are regarded as the *legitimate* or *authoritative concerns* for traditionalist members; (2) how these authoritatively regarded problems are *defined* and, more impor-tantly, how they are *explained* to their various constituencies; and (3) what the *organizationally authoritative solutions* to them are.

For example, the fact that membership in Anglican churches has de-clined precipitously in recent decades, to the point where a number of parishes are on the verge of bankruptcy, is less of an issue to Prayer Book Society director Peter Toon than what he calls "the corporate selfish autonomy of individual provinces/national churches" (2001a, 3). Unpacked a bit, this means that the inability of St. Swithin's-on-the-Green to pay its skyrocketing heating bill is understood as an inevitable consequence of the "selfish innovation" of the ordination of women or "the claimed right of an individual province ... to go its own way and to stay within the Anglican Communion without any penalty." Now, for some, these reasons are clearly accurate; members *have* left over the possibility of the ordination of women, of gay men, or of the creation of autonomous Episcopal provinces. In the ongoing construction of a social movement's cognitive praxis, though, the accuracy of these reasons or the percentage of decline for which they account really don't matter. They *become* the authoritative reasons because they are offered to and accepted by the movement constituency as such. They name the problem authoritatively regardless of their accuracy.

Thus, the decline at St. Swithin's is not due to urban migration that decimated the previous two generations of farming families—a migration inextricably linked to the decline of the family farm and the concomitant growth of transnational agribusiness; it is not due to the undeniable effects of an open religious economy and an increasing apathy toward institutional religion in mainstream culture; it is not due to the fact that the parish has a deteriorating physical plant and has been poorly served pastorally for the past two decades. No. It is due to the abandonment of the *Book of Common Prayer* (*BCP*) and the other Anglican Formularies, the modern disregard for proper Anglican identity, and the host of doctrinal and ecclesiastical aberrations these circumstances admit into the church. For Toon, the established ecclesiology and morality that Anglican traditionalists contend are anchored in the doctrinal composition of the *BCP* and the Formularies are "in danger of collapsing, and if [they do] so then the Anglican Way will be judged by many to have failed as an expression of the catholic Church" (2001a, 6). Conversely, once the problem has been authoritatively defined, especially if that definition can successfully exclude competing explanations for the problem, the solution readily presents itself. In this case, this means a wholesale return to the tradition of the *BCP*.

COMPETING VOICES

As Eyerman and Jamison point out, however, it is important to remember that "all activists do not participate equally in the cognitive praxis" of a social movement (1991, 94). That is, not all participants have equal access to publication in the pages of *Mandate*, *The Layman*, or *Good News*; their profile as denominational traditionalists is not such that journalists seek them out for commentary on the latest church conflict; and, as noted, many consider themselves outside the structure of established reform and renewal organizations. Through *The Layman*, though, editor-in-chief Parker Williamson is able to engage in what he calls advocacy journalism, an explicit attempt to persuade members of the PC(USA) of the correctness of the traditionalist position. Issues are chosen and framed with this perspective in mind. Similarly, when it first began to publish *Concern*, the United Church of Canada's Community of Concern called its newsletter "An Alternative Voice at General Council." "This Council is going to discuss matters fundamental to the faith of the United Church," *Concern*'s statement of purpose announced. "It would be tragic, then, if only a one-sided presentation was made to both commissioners and the public. There *is* another side. Read on. The truth will make you free" (Community of Concern 1992).

As in all situations of conflict, in the context of reform and renewal movements there are a number of voices competing for dominance and authority. These include, but are not necessarily limited to (a) voices within the various reform and renewal movements themselves, including their movement intellectuals, both lay and professional; (b) denominational hierarchies against which reform and renewal movements are most often arrayed; (c) oppositional advocacy groups—for example, peace groups, feminist organizations, or groups that argue in support of homosexual ordination; (d) what we might call collateral participants—that is, the people in the pews, whose interest in any particular conflict can range from extreme to nonexistent (cf. Hoge, Johnson, and Luidens 1994; Johnson, Hoge, and Luidens 1993); (e) reform and renewal movements in other mainline denominations, which often take the material produced by one group, modify it to suit their needs, and then use it in their own situation; and (f) media, both secular and religious, both of which function no differently if the conflict is a church fight over gay men and lesbians in the pulpit than they do over bodies pulled from an upscale mansion in Rancho Santa Fe. That is to say, controversy is most often the engine that drives the production of "news."

It is these discourses—the public faces each movement wears, the ways in which the struggle for and against domination is managed by conservative reform and renewal movements within mainline Protestantism, the attempts to persuade the various denominational publics of the righteousness of the conservative cause—that I would like to engage here.

First, though, I readily admit that there is something of a problem with using the term "mainline" to describe the denominations included in this study. Wade Clark Roof (1987), for example, suggests that in the current social climate—what he calls "the church in the centrifuge"—any talk of a Christian mainline is increasingly anachronistic, less and less useful in the context of a religious pluralism that continues to add new factors to the religious equation. How helpful is it, after all, to talk about denominations such as the United Methodist Church, the Presbyterian Church (USA), the Episcopal Church (USA), and The United Church of Canada as mainline, when the largest Protestant denomination in North America, the Southern Baptist Convention, claims more members than all these four others combined? As denominations historically viewed as the mainline polarize into conservative and liberal factions over precisely the issues discussed here and elsewhere (for example, Hunter 1991; Roof and McKinney 1987; Wuthnow 1988), and, as some of these factional elements come more and more to resemble the evangelical branch of North American Protestantism than the historical tradition of their own denominations, the concept of a coherent mainline loses any descriptive power it might once have had. Coalter, Mulder, and Weeks (1996, xii–xiv) also critique the often ambiguous fashion in which the term mainline Protestantism has been used since its first postwar appearance in the 1950s. For example, "mainline Protestantism" has been used to describe certain denominations associated with the National Council of Churches as well as denominations that "have exercised a dominant influence on American culture because of the size of their membership" (Coalter, Mulder, and Weeks 1996, xii). The mainline has been defined theologically, that is, denominations with a more liberal approach to matters of doctrine, polity, and practice. Corbett (1999) terms them "consensus Protestants," while Quebedeaux (1976) defines them as "ecumenical liberals."

None of these make the current problem any easier. However, accepting Roof's critique of the term, I will continue to use "mainline" in this work for two reasons: first, it describes an array of churches that have historically held themselves separate from conservative, evangelical Protestant denominations; and second, it is still the language used by members of many of these churches to describe themselves today—a circumstance we cannot easily ignore.

My goal in this work is not to provide an intensive or exhaustive analysis of one particular reform or renewal group, or even all the reform and renewal groups in one denomination. That road, it seems to me, runs the risk of a deductive inference that does not sufficiently consider broader denominational, theological, cultural, and social contexts. Lewis Daly's *A Moment to Decide* (2000b), which is a more thorough examination of the reform and renewal groups in the Presbyterian Church (USA), is a good example of this problem. While interesting for some of the detail that it provides about the groups in question, his analysis is fraught with vaguely rendered conspiracy theories, guilt by association, and innuendo. In the end, Daly's critique makes the group that sponsored its publication, the Institute for Democracy Studies, seem little more than the religious left's version of the mainline right's Institute on Religion and Democracy. Because he approaches these groups as a threat to democracy, rather than as one collection of actors in the larger democratic drama, as legitimate if often unpopular competitors in the marketplace of mainline religious ideas, any discernible patterns of ideation or behavior—the cognitive praxis of reform and renewal as a denominational concept—become part and parcel of the conspiracy that constitutes the threat.

I am more interested in the broader phenomenon of conservative reform itself. That is, the question of why traditionalist members remain within denominations that are clearly and increasingly inhospitable to their theological needs and desires, and that are unlikely to alter course any time soon. It is true that, in many cases, denominational change comes slowly, far too slowly for advocates of whatever change is under way. But, that reality notwithstanding, mainline denominations have become increasingly polarized around real and perceived differences in theology, doctrine, and practice. While there may be attempts at dialogue, the question is often framed as, How do we learn to live with our (often irreconcilable) differences? rather than, How do we create a denomination in which we all agree? So, one of my central questions is, Why stay?

The answer, I believe, or at least a significant part of the answer, has to do with identity and meaning. Reform as a concept only exists in the context situation that requires change, that demands reformation. Reform and renewal groups belong to that class of social movements that only exist in the presence of a reciprocal, adversarial Other. Indeed, it is in the adversarial relationship that both sides often locate their collective senses of meaning and identity. Thus, for denominational conservatives, to give up the fight, to surrender the field of theological battle, is to abandon one's identity as the remnant faithful.

In the four denominations that I discuss at length, and recognizing that within denominations many reform and renewal organizations have shared memberships, more than 50 such groups exist—and that does not include other mainline denominations such as the Disciples of Christ, the American Baptists, and the Lutheran Church in America. Space quite simply prohibits the thick description of each that one might want. Rather, by considering a greater number of groups (approximately 15) to a somewhat lesser degree, those broad patterns of meaning and action, the cognitive praxis of conservative reform, become more visible.

This approach, however, means that many reform and renewal movements have either been omitted entirely or relegated to the position of bit players on the denominational stage. Numerous other movement participants could have been included: The Baxter Institute, A Foundation for Theological Education, and ReNew (UMC); Knox Fellowship, One by One, Presbyterian Elders in Prayer, Presbyterians Pro-Life (PC[USA]); Forward-in-Faith, the Episcopal Synod of America, Concerned Clergy and Laity of the Episcopal Church, Anglican Essentials (ECUSA and the Anglican Church of Canada). I chose the ones I did, however, because they represent the most established and public of the conservative reform movements in their respective denominations, and as such ground the movement's conservative agenda.

Of course, the question is often raised whether any of these groups are, in fact, legitimate players on that mainline denominational stage. Many liberal opponents of conservative or traditionalist groups very clearly believe not. Robert Bohl, for example, former moderator of the PC(USA), wonders openly, often antagonistically, why groups like these simply won't go away. In ways virtually identical to the religious right, the mainline religious left often characterizes reform groups as acting in direct contravention to the principles and beliefs upon which mainline Protestantism was founded. Others have chosen more infantile means to express their disapproval. At the 1997 meeting of The United Church of Canada's General Council, opponents of conservative reform groups put canine feces in plastic bags filled with the groups' logo buttons. While both liberals and conservatives within the church deplored the incident, it illustrates the lengths to which some, at least, will go to express their displeasure.

Denominational liberals who wonder why traditionalists won't simply go away, however, tend to miss the point of the argument in one significant regard. The conservative church members they oppose *are*, in fact, members of that denomination. They love their church no less than liberals, and are certainly no less committed to it. They support what they believe their church stands for—or ought to stand for—and are willing to fight for its integrity on those grounds. To suggest otherwise is to impute motives clearly unsupported by the available data.

Another question—legitimately raised, although the answers provided by reform and renewal groups are clear—is whether denominational institutions are willing to include all interested or affected stakeholders in decision-making processes that affect the church as a whole. And if not, why not? Are denominational structures set up to enable the hard discussions, discussions which many stakeholders believe to be fundamentally theological, to take place? Again, if not, why not? Part of the initial problem in denominational conflicts such as the ones considered here is that affected stakeholders very often do not recognize adversarial Others as legitimate parties in particular dialogues. Often, liberals acknowledge the legitimacy of conservative voices no more than those of liberals. In many cases, each regards the other as acting in bad faith, and history suggests that each is unlikely to change its opinion.

Many traditionalist reform groups, however, are vocal about their intention not to split the church or otherwise effect denominational schism. They are clear that their commitment is to the integrity of the denomination and to working within its structures. Other conservatives, though, regard denominational hierarchies as so irredeemably corrupt that no rapprochement is possible. To leave the denomination in protest, however, would be to invite, even demand, dissolution of one's identity as a reformer.

If traditionalists question the authority of liberals to control denominational direction, then where do conservative reform groups and movements claim their authority to control those directions? The recent emergence of a variety of traditionalist confessing movements (in the UMC, the PC[SA], and implicitly in the UCCan, through such actions as the 1997 Christmas Confession) raises the question of whether conservative reform groups any longer acknowledge that there are sincere Christians on the other side of the debate. The invocation of such terms as heretic, apostate, and blasphemer by some of the most strident traditionalists suggests that the line has been crossed, perhaps irrevocably. Since neither side is likely to give in on either the primary issues that divide them, or on the meta-issues that constellate around them, what is the future of mainline denominations polarized by these kinds of conflicts and fractures? How will they continue? Indeed, will they continue? Or is the denominational decline that is so patently clear destined finally to relegate the great mainline Protestant Churches of the twentieth century to a footnote in Christian history?

In an effort to avoid what might be called the chimera of objectivity, as Eyerman and Jamison point out, "at some level, the sociologist must identify—either positively or negatively—with her object of investigation" (1991, 40). This is my moment for disclosure.

I was ordained in 1989 in The United Church of Canada and served pastoral charges in southern Alberta for 11 years. In the midst of a denominational firestorm over the 1988 decision known as Membership, Ministry, and Human Sexuality (MMHS), in which Donald Collett was involved and which many church members to this day regard as an open door for the ordination and commissioning of gay men and lesbians, I watched at a wide variety of denominational venues as church members—both lay and clergy, on both sides of The Issue—acted out a hostility I found hard to comprehend. Presbytery members refused to sit at table with other members, or pass the peace during the celebration of Communion; clergy walked out on worship services at presbytery and conference meetings. Families divided over The Issue—some, like the Colletts, permanently. Under the leadership of a conservative evangelical minister, 80 percent of the congregation that had sponsored my own candidacy for ordination left the United Church two months after the MMHS decision. And, while I had known about the more established reform and renewal movements for some time, during this period I watched the emergence of the Community of Concern with fascination.

For at least a couple of reasons, as the research progressed, this has been a more and more difficult book to write. On the one hand, there is the

rigid theological, doctrinal, and social positioning of the conservative reform movements themselves, and the often ungracious manner in which
they seek to make their case to the rest of the church. Like the eminent
Northwestern University religious studies scholar, Charles Braden, theologically I am "an unrepentant liberal"—a situation that is unlikely to
change. On the other hand, however, in each of the churches I discuss,
there is a similarly ungracious rhetoric and behavior among the denominational left, and the never far from the surface implication that by ex-
ercising the rights accorded them under denominational constitutions and
statutes, conservative reform movements are somehow acting conspira-
torially, unfaithfully, or, in the opinion of critics such as Lewis Daly
(2000b), antidemocratically. While I can espouse neither the social nor the
theological positions of the reform and renewal movements I discuss in
this book, as a former minister in The United Church of Canada, I often
found myself dismayed (even ashamed, at times) at the naïveté and malice
with which these groups are regarded by more liberal members of their
denominations.

The Remnant Spirit is organized in three parts, each of which considers
the question of conservative reform and renewal from a slightly different
angle. In the rest of part 1, chapter 2 discusses the postwar decline of
mainline Protestantism in North America and reviews some of the explanations that have been advanced for it. This is followed by a brief consideration of the concept of the precipitous moment—a pivotal event or event
process in the life of a denomination that catalyzes latent dissatisfaction
into manifest dissent. Chapter 3 examines three different modes of dissent,
which I am calling the three responsive domains of reform and renewal:
the ecclesiological domain (the legalist response); the experiential domain
(the charismatic response); and the theological domain (the evangelical or
fundamentalist response).

Part 2 expands consideration of the third domain, the evangelical or
fundamentalist response, and discusses conservative reform movements
in four mainline Protestant denominations. One chapter each is devoted
to (a) the Presbyterian Church (USA), which came into being in 1983 when
the Presbyterian Church in the United States (the so-called southern
church) merged with the United Presbyterian Church in the United States
of America (the northern church), and which, with approximately 2.5 million members, is the largest Presbyterian denomination in North America.
(b) The United Methodist Church, created in 1968 by the union of the
Evangelical United Brethren Church and the Methodist Church, stood at
the time as one of the largest Protestant denominations in the world. Now,
the UMC claims over 8 million members. (c) With 2.3 million baptized
members, the Episcopal Church in the United States of America is the
largest North American denomination in the Anglican communion. And
(d) The United Church of Canada, which came into being in 1925 with

the merger of the Presbyterian Church in Canada, the Methodist Church, and the Congregational Churches of Canada, is the largest mainline denomination in that country.

Part 3 presents these conservative reform movements as emergent denominational spaces within which the politics of religious identity are contested. Reform movements follow an identifiable pattern in their development, and, as this happens, they often come to understand themselves as defenders of a particular religious identity, rather than simply opponents of specific church decisions or proposals. As this development takes place, the manner in which that identity is named and articulated also changes. For example, denominational conservatives insist that, rather than maintaining fidelity to traditional theology, reform movements are actually defending Christian orthodoxy. Finally, and wanting to approach the question of What will happen? with some care, chapter 9 concludes the study with a discussion of reform and renewal teleology, that is, the place of conservative reform movements in the midst of mainline churches that seem, at this stage anyway, unlikely to change their denominational courses.

CHAPTER 2

Precipitous Moments: The Platform of Reform and Renewal

"THERE IS A HELL, MR. PHIPPS": THE ALLEGED BOOM AND INDISPUTABLE DECLINE IN MAINLINE PROTESTANTISM

He had "disheartened and weakened our Church," one minister is quoted as saying in a local newspaper (Enman 1997). Another said that attendance at Sunday worship had dropped off by more than 75 percent. A third feared that one of the two rural churches he served would be forced to close its doors. The issue? Remarks made by then-Moderator of The United Church of Canada (UCCan), William F. Phipps, in a metropolitan newspaper that Jesus was not the only way to God, that the physical resurrection of Jesus was not a scientific fact, that Christ was not God, and that he "had no idea" if there is a heaven or a hell. In response, messages appeared on church signs across the country: "Jesus is the ONLY way"; "We still believe that Jesus is God"; and, almost inevitably, "There is a hell, Mr. Phipps."

In late October 1997, when newly elected moderator Bill Phipps, a lawyer, minister, and now leader of Canada's largest mainline Protestant denomination, was invited for an interview by the *Ottawa Citizen*, he thought he was going to talk about the church's position on a variety of social and political issues. Instead, Phipps found himself the target of what could only be described as a carefully orchestrated set of theological questions designed to test what many came to see as his personal doctrinal orthodoxy. When the interview was published, the controversy it generated raged across the country, headlining national newspapers and even finding its way into the *Washington Post* (Schneider 1997).

Responding to some of his comments—specifically his denial of Jesus as the ontological Son of God—one of Phipps's colleagues, the Reverend Alan Schooley, a minister in Phipps's adopted hometown of Calgary, Alberta, preached to his congregation that the moderator was guilty of heresy, apostasy, and the abandonment of his ordination vows. Schooley, an often blunt critic of liberal directions in the church, called on the moderator either to repent or to resign (cf. Cunningham 1997; Schooley 1997; Walker and Legge 1997). Because of Phipps's remarks in the interview, Schooley told both his colleagues and his congregation, "the church is haemorrhaging," a sentiment echoed in sanctuaries across the country. Graham Scott, then-president of the conservative reform group Church Alive, opined that "Moderator Phipps's denials, unbelief and agnosticism are not good news. They seem to me to be an invitation to [denominational] suicide" (1997). While, in the weeks and months that followed, Phipps and Schooley did come to some manner of reconciliation, the rift begun by the *Ottawa Citizen* interview did not close, and the widespread perception that the United Church was in decline deepened.

Few researchers, professional clergy, interested church watchers, or those who occupy the pews on Sunday morning doubt the now decades-long membership decline in mainline Protestant denominations. While the reasons for the decline in each denomination may vary, and however churches may argue about the relative pitch of the slope, the plain fact of decline is not in serious dispute. Some factors mask or mitigate aspects of the decline: migration from inner-city residential areas to suburbs, for example, has depopulated urban congregations and forced a variety of congregational responses ranging from outright closure to amalgamation. Until the advent of gentrification in those urban cores, there are few new people to replace those who have left. Built in the boom years of postwar church construction, many of these inner-city churches are impressive physical structures, but they are now unwieldy and difficult to maintain. Often poorly insulated, large, labyrinthine church plants drain the resources from congregations that are both aging and dwindling, a situation that does little to ease migration away or encourage migration in.

For example, during the 1960s "Sunny Hills Church" celebrated two full worship services every Sunday. There were over 1,200 children in Sunday School, and more than 120 Sunday School teachers. An adult choir, 70 voices strong, was led by one of only a few Casavant Freres pipe organs in the city. So many people attended the church that in the early 1970s a daughter church was born—St. Martin's, a congregation now considered a flagship church in the region. Today at Sunny Hills however, there is only one service and it is considered full if 200 people attend with a score of children in Sunday School.

In the decades between the 1960s and the first part of the 1990s, Sunny Hills employed two full-time ministers, a secretary, and at times a paid

Christian education coordinator. As attendance declined, though, the financial strain on the builder generation of the church increased. Fiscal responsibility became the priority item at church council meetings. Following a series of less-than-successful ministry team situations, the Sunny Hills congregation decided to move from two clergy to one. While some may contend that this decision was made to bring an end to intrateam conflicts, the root cause of the decision was clearly financial. One minister was considerably less expensive than two, and was what the church felt it could afford at that point in its life.

Several issues have contributed to the decline in membership in congregations like Sunny Hills, for its story is repeated in congregations across mainline denominations and across North America. Some of these issues have been well documented in the scholarly and professional literature (cf., for example, Becker 1999; Coalter, Mulder, and Weeks 1990, 1996; Daly 2000b; Finke and Stark 1992; Hadaway and Roozen 1995; Hillis 1991; Hoge 1976; Hoge and Roozen 1979; Hutcheson and Shriver 1999; Hutchinson 1989; Kelley 1977; Leas and Kittlaus 1973; Leith 1997; Oden 1995; Reeves 1996; Roof and McKinney 1987; Wilke 1986). Others, such as those raised in this book, less so. At both academic and congregational levels, various reasons for the decline have been advanced: (a) an aging builder generation, coupled with (b) the church's inability in large measure to retain the children of that generation (see Hoge, Johnson, and Luidens 1994); (c) the abandonment of exclusive Christian religious claims by liberal churches (cf. Cowan 2000; Johnson, Hoge, and Luidens 1993); and (d) the vastly expanded social and cultural opportunities that are available to the children, grandchildren, and sometimes great-grandchildren of the builder generation, opportunities that no longer suffer the religious proscription and social censure of earlier decades. Sunday shopping is now a regular feature in all major North American cities and few bat an eye; athletic leagues that at one time prohibited play on Sundays—or at least play before noon—now begin their schedules early Sunday morning. Where once church attendance was considered a positive social value, concerns are now raised about its relevance in a late modern society.

In terms of generational retention, for example, a common question asked of ministers during church council meetings and job interviews is, What will you do to bring back the young people? Ministers who are, in many cases, younger than the young people under discussion are at a loss to answer. The simple fact is that, at Sunny Hills Church and any number of demographically similar mainline Protestant congregations, the vast majority of those 1,200 Sunday Schoolers no longer attend the church in which they were raised, and many no longer attend church at all. While members of the builder generation remember with pride the days when they had a "very successful Sunday School," the inability of mainline churches to retain these members as adults calls into serious question how

successful the religious socialization processes of the 1960s and 1970s actually were.

The first major work that sought to explain the membership decline in
mainline denominations was Dean Kelley's *Why Conservative Churches Are
Growing* (1977). Using membership statistics drawn both from denominational sources and from the standard reference work on the subject, the
Handbook of American and Canadian Churches (published annually by the
National Council of Churches, the group for which he worked), Kelley
demonstrated what appeared to be an increase in membership among
mainline denominations in the immediate postwar period. This increase
peaked in the early- to mid-1960s and was followed quickly by various
degrees of decline in each of the denominations he considered. According
to Kelley's figures, for example, in the decade between 1966 and 1975, the
Episcopal Church went from just over 3.4 million members to less than 3
million (1977, 22)—a drop of nearly half a million members. The United
Presbyterian Church (USA) did not decline quite so sharply, but still lost
more than 300,000 members in that same period. With just over 11 million
members, the two denominations that formed the United Methodist
Church peaked in composite membership in the few years immediately
preceding union; that figure had declined to just under 11 million by the
time union actually took place. And, by 1975, it had dropped a full million
to just under 10 million members—a net loss of over 100,000 members per
year (1977, 21).

During those same years, noted Kelley, more conservative denominations such as the Seventh-day Adventists, the Church of the Nazarene,
and the Salvation Army were posting membership gains that averaged
three times the U.S. population growth at the time. While the Salvation
Army gained nearly 100,000 members between 1964 and 1974, the
Seventh-day Adventists added nearly half again that many. The Jehovah's
Witnesses, considered a cult by many conservative Christians (cf. Cowan
2003; Martin 1985; Martin and Klann 1974), increased from about 330,000
in 1968 to 560,000 in 1975 (Kelley 1977, 25). And the Church of Jesus Christ
of Latter-day Saints—the Mormons—had posted such impressive gains
that by 1984 sociologist Rodney Stark considered it the most likely candidate for a new world religion since the time of the prophet Muhammad
(see Stark 1984).

Kelley's work drew its share of criticism, both from scholarly colleagues
who recognized his achievement but questioned his methodology and his
interpretations (see Finke and Stark 1992, 245–50) and from many of his
liberal coreligionists who denounced his assertions not only that mainline
denominations were losing members but that conservative denominations, which Kelley labeled "the 'wrong' churches" (1977, 25), were growing. If Kelley was right, this growth confounded much of the accepted
wisdom among the mainline denominations. As Kelley put it, these

"wrong" churches "contradict the contemporary notion of an acceptable religion. They are not 'reasonable,' they are not 'tolerant,' they are not ecumenical, they are not 'relevant.' " "Quite the contrary!" he concluded.

Kelley's basic position was fairly simple. Known now as the strict church hypothesis, conservative churches were growing because they maintained a theological traditionalism that had been gradually abandoned in mainline denominations. While mainline denominations relaxed membership requirements and proved reluctant to demand either practical or theological commitment of their members, conservative churches obligated their membership to higher levels of service, contribution, and doctrinal confession. Whereas in the mainline, church attendance and involvement had become simply one more option to be weighed in the balance of any given Sunday morning, in more conservative denominations church life maintained significant influence as the social center around which members organized their lives.

In the wake of interest generated by Kelley's work, sociologists struggled both to test his conclusions and to wrestle with their implications. Hoge and Roozen (1979) challenged some of the fundamental assumptions of Kelley's work, concluding that demographic and social factors played far more important roles in the growth of conservative churches than did their theological or ethical strictness. (However, see Iannaccone 1994 for a positive revisiting of Kelley's thesis.) While most of the debate swirled around the cogency and accuracy of the strict church hypothesis, little research challenged the underpinning message of mainline decline.

Canadian sociologist Reginald Bibby was among the first to note that, contrary to Kelley's conclusions, mainline membership did not really skyrocket after World War II. Rather, it crossed a broad plateau prior to a steep decline beginning in the mid- to late-1960s, a decline made all the more precipitous when factored against the postwar baby boom. Bibby challenged the notion that there was a spectacular growth period, a "golden age for religion" following the Second World War (1989, 12). Numbers were up denominationally, at least in terms of raw figures, but the proportion of the overall population represented by those numbers, the market share, was and had been dropping steadily for some time. "The statistical truth of the matter," writes Bibby, "is that most of Canada's religious groups were essentially standing still when they thought they were enjoying tremendous growth" (1989, 13). With the exception of growth spikes that occurred as a result of denominational mergers, similar dynamics obtain for mainline Protestant denominations in the United States.

Roger Finke and Rodney Stark (1992) concur. Using the same sources as Kelley, they conclude that in the postwar period mainline Protestant churches had lost between 38 percent and 70 percent of their religious market share. One of the problems was that Kelley and others had been

working from membership figures provided by the denominations themselves, which in turn derived their figures from congregational self-
reporting. Membership rolls and denominational census data are rarely
reliable indicators of either religiosity or institutional religious commitment. Churches seeking financial support for a capital building project,
for example, have been known to inflate membership statistics in an effort
to demonstrate congregational growth and avail themselves of denominational funding. Churches are often loath to remove from their rolls long-
term members who are now housebound, and who no longer attend
worship nor actively participate in congregational life. Occasionally, as
Hadaway and Marler report (1998), inactive or partially active members
often misreport their own church involvement to poll takers because they
do not want to be characterized as "unchurched." In many cases, this is
not a calculated deception on their parts, but a function of the way in
which the information is gathered. For example, the survey question may
have asked whether they attended church in the *past* week, when that was
the *only week* in the month they did not attend, or one of the two weeks
per month they do not. They recognize that the question is designed to
test their religious commitment, and they exaggerate their answer to avoid
being categorized as unchurched or not religious. "We may not be in
church all the time," goes the refrain, "but we're still Presbyterian!"

Indeed, in many mainline denominations, the concept of membership
is sufficiently ambiguous to include, on the one hand, those who attend
worship every week and are actively involved in their congregations, and,
on the other, men and women who know they are Methodist or Presbyterian only because they know they are *not* Mormon or Buddhist (see
Cowan 2000). Whatever the reasons, Hadaway and Marler's research,
which tested the survey data by actually counting the number of persons
in attendance at worship, points to a significant overreporting of church
attendance by congregational and denominational sources.

MAINLINE DECLINE: SOME GENERAL EXPLANATIONS

In the four decades bracketing the first printing of Kelley's landmark
book, various theories have been proposed to account for the decline in
North American mainline Protestantism. Some have found minimal support in the research; others, because there was an intuitive correctness to
their explanations, maintained a more robust presence in the literature.
These theories have broken out into two major and three derivative categories. Among the major causes suggested were: (a) *secularization*, that is,
religious nonparticipation as a result of belief that has been discarded or
abandoned in the face of modernization and (b) *liberalization*, nonparticipation as a result of the perceived irrelevance of the church, but without,

necessarily, the abandonment of personal belief itself. Three other possibilities derive from these as a way of explaining what happened to those members who chose not to participate in mainline churches: (c) *true secularization* and *practical secularization,* the situation in which religious belief is discarded either completely or for all intents and purposes; (d) *conservatization,* in which mainline denominations declined because members migrated to more conservative denominations; and (e) *individualization,* decline in mainline adherence because members intentionally invested themselves in more individualized modes of "self-spirituality" (Heelas 1996), the New Age, or some other part of what Bibby calls the "selective consumption of religion" (1989, 111–149).

Secularization

In its April 1966 cover story, *Time* magazine asked, "Is God Dead?" a question to which church lore has it that evangelist Billy Graham is said to have responded, "No, he's not, I talked with him this morning." *Time's* declaration, however, was hardly new. Voltaire predicted the demise of religion by the end of the eighteenth century. A century after that, Nietzsche boldly declared that "God was dead. God remains dead. And we have killed him" (1974, 181). Graham's rejoinder to the Divine obituary notwithstanding, well into the 1970s and early 1980s *secularization,* the theoretical progeny of Voltaire, Nietzsche, and the *Time* statement, was the reigning academic and professional theory of church decline. Some commentators, however, (for example, Bellah 1967; Greeley 1972; Hadden 1989; Stark and Bainbridge 1987) were not so quick to call the time of death. Sociologist Jeffrey Hadden, for example, contended that secularization was more a *"doctrine* than a theory . . . an *ideology* that is taken for granted rather than a systematic set of interrelated propositions" (1989, 4; emphasis in the original).

At its most basic level, and holding in plain view the "inexcusable looseness" with which the term came to be used (Greeley 1972, 136), secularization theory argued that people were less religious in the 1970s than they were a century earlier because of the changes brought about by the collision between religion and modernity. Operationally, it held that the rise of the scientific worldview had reduced the need for a religious explanation of natural phenomena and had diminished popular reliance on the notion of God; the separation of church and state had removed religion from the social foreground and exiled it to the private sphere of life; and the evolution of the modern bureaucratic state had assumed (some argued usurped) many of the functions typically relegated to religion and religious communities. As a result of these countervailing pressures against both a religious worldview and institutional religious commitment, religious adherents (and their offspring) gave less priority to their involvement in faith communities. A wide range of other activities were taking religion's place in the calendar of everyday life. Not unlike their Enlightenment forerunners, secularization theorists such as Berger (1967), Dobbelaere (1981, 1984, 1989, 1999), Fenn (1978), Lenski (1961), and Wilson (1966, 1975, 1985) declared that religion in the modern period was little more than a rapidly fading echo of a less sophisticated human past.

This seemed to explain the decline in mainline denominational membership until researcher after researcher began both to challenge the theoretical foundation of secularization theory and to point out the fact that empirical data on religious involvement did not appear to support the theory's main proposition. That is, people were not becoming *less* religious, they were becoming *differently* religious.

In his 1986 presidential address to the Southern Sociological Society, Jeffrey Hadden summarized the historical underpinnings of secularization theory, and then laid out "four important challenges" to its utility (Hadden 1989, 13). Hadden argued that, first, secularization was "a hodgepodge of loosely employed ideas rather than a systemic theory." So many researchers had used the term in so many different ways that, citing Dobbelaere (1981, 1984), "'secularization means whatever I say it means'" (Hadden 1989, 14). However, because it had been treated as a theory, indeed a paradigm in the Kuhnian sense (Kuhn 1970), it "dominated our assumptions about religion and guided the types of research questions scholars have asked" (Hadden 1989, 14). In the words of anthropologist Clifford Geertz, it had "a vague and unexamined notion of emotive resonance" that seemed to fill the explanation gap (1973, 207). Second, Hadden pointed out that the existing empirical data simply did not support the theory of secularization. Despite whatever faults particular data sets may have, "their most important message is that the data cannot confirm the historical process predicted by secularization theory" (1989, 15; cf. Greeley 1972; Stark 1999). Religion may be changing; it may mean something different than it did 50, 100, or 200 years ago; but it was far from dead. Third, Hadden regarded the "effervescence of new religious movements in the very locations where secularization appears to cut deeply into established institutional religion" as evidence that religious consciousness, commitment, and allegiance are perhaps shifting, but not disappearing (1989, 13). Finally, the mainline situation in North America could hardly be extrapolated to all other countries in the world, and from there somehow universalized as a theory of religion qua religion rather than a theory about particular religious traditions in certain places at specific times. Among other examples, the rise of Islamic states in the Middle East, the emergence of Buddhist fundamentalism as an expression of Sri Lankan nationalism, and the continuing growth of African Independent Churches all challenge the basic thesis of the secularization theory.

The important point here is that religious vitality is not globally relegated to the private sphere of life; in many parts of the world, including North America, it continues to animate social life and political involvement, in some places underpinning the fight for civil rights and social equality, in others aiding and abetting their suppression (cf., for example, Glock and Stark 1965; Gualtieri 1989; Hadden 1969; Hadden and Longino 1974; Hutchinson 1971). As an explanation for the alleged decline in religious commitment, secularization had shown itself too anemic to survive. And, as Rodney Stark notes: "After nearly three centuries of utterly failed prophecies and misrepresentations of both present and past, it seems time to carry the secularization doctrine to the graveyard of failed theories, and there to whisper 'requiescat in pace' " (1999, 270).

Liberalization

While the decline in the religious consciousness of North Americans was not as precipitous as the most vocal of secularization theorists proposed, that there was an ongoing decline in mainline Protestant Christianity, however, could not be denied. Others observers, especially theological conservatives, argued that the liberalization of theology and church doctrine had resulted in the irrelevance of the institutional, mainline church and its subsequent decline in membership numbers. The primary, secondary, and now tertiary literature on the development of liberal theology from the latter half of the nineteenth century to the present is vast (for various viewpoints, cf. Ahlstrom 1972; Averill 1967; Baulmer 1996; Cauthen 1962; Coleman 1972; Deck 1995; Hoge, Johnson, and Luidens 1994; Marshall 1992; Novak 1978; Oden 1995; Roof and McKinney 1987; Wuthnow 1988, 1989). While I have no intention of rehearsing its history here, there are a few points about the rise of liberalism, especially as they are interpreted to affect the decline in mainline denominationalism at the close of the twentieth century, that ought to be made.

First, understood as countervailing pressure against a more entrenched or dominant form of belief or ideology, liberalism is hardly new. Indeed, any movement that seeks to establish the primacy or authority of one's own beliefs against those decreed either by state or by church is a liberalism of sorts. The assertion of *choice* in the face of established orthodoxy or orthopraxy, the freedom to believe in a manner different from the dominant, is the liberalizing process of *hairesis*, or heresy. Pelagius (ca. 360–420) arguing against the theological constraints of Augustine's doctrines of free will and original sin; Abelard (ca. 1079–1142) asserting the rational grounds for Christian belief in the face of ecclesiastical authority and mandate; the medieval heretical complex of the Albigenses, the Bogomils, and the Cathars teaching a Manichaean dualism and rejecting the sacraments of the Church—all are examples of this liberalizing intention toward choice. And, as Greeley points out, even "Thomas Aquinas was condemned for being far too modern and . . . his books were burned at Oxford University shortly after his death on the grounds that he was so advanced that he must be considered heretical" (1972, 22). As we will see in many of the conservative reform movements discussed in this book, the connection between liberalism and heresy has not gone unnoticed.

In this sense, then, any attempt to expand the permitted range of religious, political, economic, or cultural discourse can be interpreted as a liberalizing trend. However wide ranging, or however narrow that trend ultimately turns out to be at any particular moment in history, at its inception the liberalizing intention represents a willingness to consider viewpoints other than those traditionally (often inflexibly) held in the particular culture.

As it contributes to our current discussion, theological liberalism finds its roots in the Enlightenment and the French Revolution, the rise of the scientific method (particularly the appearance of Darwin's *On the Origin of Species* in 1859), the development of historico-literary criticisms of the Bible in Germany and later the United States, and the shift in theological positioning that resulted from that critical hermeneutic movement. With this diverse array of influences, it is easy to see that there is no set system of doctrines or beliefs that could be used to define liberalism. In the spirit of its etymology, it is more on the order of a mind-set, a worldview oriented toward freedom of human action and belief, confidence in the merits of human reason and development, and a willingness to exchange the certainty of an objectively imposed dogmatism for the unsteady independence that comes with subjectively apprehended modes of being and believing.

Objectivism, in the sense of an externally imposed doctrinal authority, and supernaturalism, the incursion into the mechanisms of time and space by forces not bound by those mechanisms, were two of the main theoretical foundations of traditional theology weakened by the advent of modernism and the attendant rise of liberal theology. In the Protestant context, the notion that the different books of the Bible had specific and varying sociohistoric contexts out of which they arose and particular problems of practical life to which they were addressed challenged the objective authority not only of Holy Scripture, but of the multivariate layers of doctrine that had been built upon the Protestant commitment to that authority. For Roman Catholics, on the other hand, various movements (exemplified, for example, in the Vatican II documents *Sacrosanctum Concilium* and *Dignitatis Humanae*) were seen as forsaking the dogmatic timelessness of the Church's authoritative magisterium; among other things, these movements challenged the ontological status of the Catholic economy of salvation, shearing believers loose from both their ecclesiastical and their soteriological moorings. In both cases, with its emphasis on human dignity, freedom, and reason, liberalism challenged the nature of the exclusive religious

claims on which both streams of Christianity had established their soteriological authority. Whether their particular soteriology rested on an objectivist interpretation of the Bible or an objectivist reliance on the
ecclesiastical magisterium, the openness to other forms of belief implicit
in the concept of liberalism represented a serious threat to the exclusive
nature of Christianity. If there was no compelling soteriological reason for
being a Christian, what compelling reason was there at all?

For example, in The United Church of Canada, the Twenty Articles of
Faith of the Basis of Union comprise the main doctrinal statement of the
denomination. When individuals are preparing for ordination or commissioning in the UCCan, these articles are used to evaluate the candidate's doctrinal position. However, because there is no requirement for
credal subscription by candidates, it is at precisely this juncture that the
liberal rejection of theological objectivism becomes most evident. In its
sections on ministry, the *Manual of The United Church of Canada* states:
"These candidates shall be examined on the statement of doctrine of The
United Church, and shall, before ordination, satisfy the examining body
that they are *in essential agreement* therewith, and that as ministers of the
Church they accept the statement as *in substance agreeable* to the teachings
of the Holy Scriptures" (United Church of Canada 1928, 46; emphases
added). Despite repeated calls by denominational conservatives for the
introduction of credal subscription, this requirement has not changed
since church union in 1925. It is the conceptual (and consequently doctrinal) elasticity built into the phrases "in essential agreement" and "in
substance agreeable" that has created problems for the denomination. For
many within its conservative reform and renewal groups, the Articles of
Faith have been imbued with an objectivist authority in some cases rival-
ing that of the Bible itself. In the midst of calls for more biblical preaching,
there are also demands that pulpit ministers, theology professors, and
even Sunday School teachers subscribe to the Articles of Faith as a test of
doctrinal orthodoxy. For these members of the church, the range of interpretation permitted by essential agreement is fairly limited. On the other
hand, despite his more liberal views on the person of Christ, former moderator Phipps is clear that he too stands well within the range of essential
agreement allowed for by the Basis of Union.

Whether objectivist authority is lost through theological attrition or outright abandonment, many interpreted that loss as contributing to the decline in mainline Protestantism. If denominational statements of doctrine
do not provide a clear and unambiguous boundary between those who
are members of the Church and those who are not, how are members to
know where they stand? Or who they are? Put theologically, if there is no
distinct soteriological advantage to membership in one particular church
over another, why seek membership in any? In these cases, because there
is no clear grounding for the exclusive nature of Christianity's truth

claims, there are few criteria by which to evaluate the truth claims made by any other religion. This results in a liberal trend toward theological relativism, syncretism, and an often uncritical universalism.

In testing variations on the themes raised by Dean Kelley, however, numerous researchers (for example, Hoge, Johnson, and Luidens 1994; Hoge and Polk 1980; Iannaccone 1994; Johnson, Hoge, and Luidens 1993) have noted the relationship between the exclusiveness of religious claims, which is often expressed in terms of the commitment required of individuals to maintain those claims, and the active involvement of individuals in faith communities. That is, the further one moves in the direction of exclusivity (that is, away from the position of theological liberalism), the stronger religious communities will be, in terms of both membership numbers and active involvement. When Hoge and Polk (1980) tested a number of theories of church participation and commitment, they found that the one most strongly supported was the doctrinal beliefs theory; they determined that "if the members hold orthodox beliefs, their participation will be relatively high" (1980, 316). More than a decade later, Johnson, Hoge, and Luidens (1993; cf. Hoge, Johnson, and Luidens 1994) reiterated this finding, stating the case with even less ambiguity. "In our study," they write, "the single best predictor of church participation turned out to be *belief,* orthodox Christian belief, and especially the teaching that a person can be saved only through Jesus Christ" (Johnson, Hoge, and Luidens 1993; cf. Hoge, Johnson, and Luidens 1994). Iannaccone (1994) operationalized part of Kelley's thesis about strong churches and describes the strength of these communities as the result of a reduction in "free riding"; strict requirements for membership, which in Iannaccone's analysis were distilled to a single variable—"the degree to which a group limits and thereby increases the *cost* of nongroup activities" (Iannaccone 1994, 1182)—"[screen] out members who lack commitment and [stimulate] participation among those who remain" (1994, 1204).

The concomitant of this is that the further one moves along the theological continuum toward the liberal pole—the end of which could be described theologically as either an unqualified universalism or a functional agnosticism—the less commitment to any one religious position we can expect. When the theological stance of the religious institution tends toward this pole, there is little reason for members to belong, especially if the collateral political, economic, and social stances taken by the denomination are at odds with values held by constituents. The resulting generational trajectory becomes clear: members leave; they see no compelling reason to socialize their children into the faith; those children, who would be the replacement generation for their parents, feel neither social obligation nor religious need to commit to the church. The denomination declines. Likewise, because there is held to be no compelling soteriological or theological reason to belong to one denomination (or one faith) over another, proselytization and conversion of the unchurched loses meaning. The decline continues.

However, in the same manner that secularization theory falters and ultimately fails, the thesis that theological and social liberalization is depleting the mainline is one that can only be asked to carry so much freight. The question remains: If people are leaving the mainline church, and their children and now grandchildren are not replacing them, where are they going? After all, while organized institutional religion on the mainline model is on the decline, other forms of religious organization and commitment clearly are not.

The Cracks and Between

In the face of a declining relevance of the mainline church, for those who do leave at least three alternative directions have appeared: (1) true and practical secularization, (2) conservatization, and (3) individualization.

First, not all those who leave the institutional mainline church find spiritual homes in other places. Some, whom we might call the true secularists, do abandon the church altogether. Whether through considered action or simple lack of interest and no compelling reason to do otherwise, they forsake any formal religious commitment at all. It no longer occupies any portion of their lives. Others, those I am calling the practical secularists, what Hoge, McGuire, and Stratman (1981) referred to as "dropouts," remain nominal members who have left all but the most rudimentary aspects of religious commitment behind. Well known to any number of clergy, these are the men and women whose sole commitment to the church, apart from the occasional appearance at a Christmas Eve service, is as a venue for weddings, baptisms, and funerals.

The second group underpins Kelley's argument: members who, because of perceived or actual liberalization, leave liberal Protestant churches for denominations they consider more theologically correct (which usually means conservative). In some instances, they move within their own denomination or denominational domain, a variation on what Bibby and Brinkerhoff call "the circulation of the saints" (cf. Bibby 1999; Bibby and Brinkerhoff 1973, 1983, 1994). That is, rather than abandoning the United Methodist Church because they disapprove of a current position taken on social issues and moving to a Southern Baptist or a nondenominational community church, dissatisfied members might migrate to a more conservative Methodist, Presbyterian, Episcopalian, or Lutheran congregation. For these, the offense is not enough to warrant a clear denominational break from the mainline to the evangelical-conservative. And, once time has mitigated whatever trauma caused the breach and people begin to miss friends and family, many of these members find their way back to their original denominational or congregational homes. In other cases, however, the breach is deemed sufficiently egregious to push members from the mainline into a more conservative denominational tradition. In both instances, the parent denomination is perceived either to have abandoned principal religious or moral tenets, or to have diluted or modified them in a manner the adherents consider offensive and unforgivable. Rather than stagnate in what they see as theological error or ecclesiastical irrelevance, these members seek firmer religious ground in churches that offer clearly defined, expressed, and maintained doctrinal statements and ethicomoral stances.

In contrast to the conservatization process, the third direction actually takes liberalization of the mainline further. These are people who have left the mainline and often no longer describe themselves as "religious," but as "spiritual." Though liberalized mainline theology has ceased to meet their faith needs, those needs still maintain some level of primacy in their lives. Individualization, however, does not mean that they now walk their spiritual paths in some shell of existential isolation; rather they have stepped beyond the bounds of organized religion as it has been presented to them, and drawn instead on a wider variety of spiritual options. For many, this could be called the path of polyspiritual syncretism— the "Sheilaism" coined in Robert Bellah's seminal *Habits of the Heart* (1996). Members who may preserve nominal ties to mainline Christianity construct what is for them a more suitable personal faith by drawing on a diverse range of traditions, practices, and spiritual novelties, including Celtic, Native American, or Goddess spirituality; feminist or masculinist spiritualities; Buddhism, yoga, or even kabala; nonspecific meditative practices (for example, labyrinths); and psychotherapeutic practices that have been spiritualized in some way (for example, the Myers-Briggs Type Indicator and the Enneagram).

However realistic each of these decline processes turns out to be in terms of sheer numbers that move from mainline denominations into each category, many denominational members—particularly supporters of conservative reform and renewal movements—regard them as eminently authoritative in terms of the major problems facing their churches. Indeed, they represent the fallout from precipitous moments in denominational history.

PRECIPITOUS MOMENTS

While scholars pondered the causes of mainline denominational decline, proposing theories, debating hypotheses, and conducting research, thousands of members of those faith communities had little difficulty addressing the problem and conceptualizing it in clear, unambiguous terms. This is the denominational segment with which we are concerned in this book. For these members, the problem is obvious. While, as John Wilson notes, "there is a fund of issues over which conflict can legitimately take place" (1971, 6), in situations of actual or potential schism, these members maintain that certain precipitous moments in each denomination's history have driven people out of the church and steepened the rate of decline. It could be controversy over issues that appear as simple as the introduction of a new denominational hymnbook or church school material, to what is perceived as the wholesale shift of denominational policy regarding the nature of professional ministry, social (especially sexual) mores, and theological orthodoxy.

It is important to emphasize here that social scientific research has demonstrated that declines in the mainline do not really evidence these precipitous moments. In fact, the issues most often cited by conservative reformers are precisely the issues Johnson, Hoge, and Luidens (1993) found to be least supported in terms of explaining denominational decline. Rather than the polarization that is often the organizing concept of both conservative reform rhetoric and mass media portrayal of mainline church conflicts, they "suspect that today's culture war within the mainline Protestant denominations is waged mainly by national elites and only rarely engages the attention and passions of ordinary church members" (Johnson, Hoge, and Luidens 1993; cf. Hoge, Johnson, and Luidens 1994, 175–202). As a general statement, I agree with this; the public persona of denominational conflict *is* often polarized between statements by church officials on the one hand, and those of self-appointed opposition movements on the other. Indeed, in many cases, it is only when an issue is sufficiently contentious that it engages the attention of the secular media that "ordinary church members" become aware of it at all. Not unlike a political election, however, it is this largely uncommitted denominational center that both poles seek to mobilize in support of their position. Arguments over whether irreconcilable differences exist within the PC(USA) is a good example of this. While conservative reform groups ask for a clear declaration that such differences do exist, denominational officials resist any such statement as fundamentally opposed to the notion of an open and inclusive church. Rather than convince each other of their position, each attempts to persuade the denominational center that they have the best interests of the church at heart.

Sociologists and other rabble-rousers notwithstanding, in the context of groups that form the subject of this study—conservative reform and renewal movements—these precipitous moments *are* the reasons for the decline in mainline Protestant denominations. It doesn't matter what the demographic reality is, or what the survey data say, or what researchers interpret the message of sample interviews to be, or what denominational officials predict. What matters is the perceived reality of the individuals who comprise these groups, and the ways in which they name and construct that reality in order to explain the problems and conflicts experienced by their denominations.

What I am calling a *precipitous moment*—as opposed, for example, to Neil Smelser's "precipitating factor" (1962)—is a pivotal event or event process in the life and health of a particular denomination. These moments embody sufficient tension to generate some manner of breach within the social structure of the church. They are the crises that generate structural conflict and provide the medium in which reform and renewal movements emerge and develop. The particulars of each precipitous moment give content to the problem of practical life to which reform and renewal movements respond. In terms of the church organizational structures, precipitous moments can manifest themselves in a variety of ways.

First, they can be *intracongregational*, limited to a specific portion of a particular congregation. For example, in congregations that require some measure of membership commitment on the part of the parents before an infant can be baptized, the refusal either by the minister or the church council to sanction a particular baptism can create *intracongregational* strain. Perhaps the grandparents of the child are part of the church's builder generation, and regard the refusal of the church council to permit the baptism as a personal affront to the years of commitment they have given to the congregation—the utter nonparticipation of the child's parents notwithstanding. Such an event could precipitate the departure of the grandparents, as well as some of their supporters in the congregation. In this case, movement would normally be circular, intercongregational as opposed to interdenominational. Rather than seek an entirely different religious denomination (although this is not outside the realm of possibility), discontented members simply move from one congregation of their own denomination to another. In cases like this, the precipitous moment concerns personal, not denominational conflict. As well, in cases like this, various modes of resolution are possible. Those who are upset can choose to resolve their differences and remain within the congregation, leave the congregation and renounce their church membership and commitment altogether, or transfer their allegiance and migrate to a different congregation either within the denomination or within a different denomination. Church conflict literature is filled with examples of these sorts of cases, and with various processes for dealing with them (cf., for example, Becker 1999; Boers 1999; Haugk 1988; Leas and Kittlaus 1973; Rediger 1997; Shelley 1994). At this level, though, the precipitous moment itself is confined to a particular congregation.

Second, precipitous moments can be *intradenominational*. In these cases, the problem is viewed as sufficiently serious to catalyze a breach across the denomination, one that crosses and transcends the boundaries of individual congregations. The decision not to forbid the ordination and commissioning of gay men and lesbians generated such a breach in The

United Church of Canada. Within that denomination and others that have dealt with similar issues, few if any congregations are left entirely unaffected. Intradenominational conflicts also present a variety of possibilities for either resolution or ongoing conflict. For those who are upset, for whom the precipitous moment represents a clear problem of practical life, there is the option to remain within the denomination and seek to change the conditions that resulted in the breach. Put simply, these are the reform and renewal movements with which we are concerned here. In chapter 8, I will discuss how this contributes a process of *protosectarianism*. Like the second and third options above, members upset by denominational decisions can choose either to leave the denomination and not take up church membership elsewhere, or to leave the denomination for one they believe more congenial to their particular beliefs. Respectively, these are the options for *renunciation* and *migration*.

Finally, there is the most serious option: *sect formation*. Protesting denominational policy and practice, disgruntled members leave the denomination and form a new worshiping community. Organizationally, these new communities range from a new, nondenominational congregation constituted largely by the departed members, to a loose collection of similarly oriented congregations, to entirely new denominational bodies.

REFORM AND RENEWAL: RESPONSES TO THE PRECIPICE

In this study, we are concerned with the second of these organizational responses: conservative reform and renewal that occurs both within a particular denomination, and across different denominations as they experience similar precipitous moments. It bears repeating that, for the time they remain as reform and renewal movements within the denomination, these groups claim to be intentionally nonsecessionist. They want to save the church, not leave it behind. Throughout this book I will use concepts such as traditionalist movements, conservative reform movements, and reform and renewal movements as rough-and-ready equivalents. Within their denominational contexts, there is often little functional or practical difference between them. In addition to the leadership services of significant movement intellectuals, a number of these groups share both lay and clergy membership.

At this point, however, I would like to make a brief conceptual distinction between reform and renewal—again, bearing in mind that many denominational traditionalists operate with a foot in both camps. When used as a distinct category, which Finke and Stark refer to as the "new Holy Clubs" (2001), I understand *reform movements* to comprise groups whose cognitive praxis is theologically evangelical, noncharismatic, and oriented specifically toward changing or preventing something within the doc-

trinal, political, or practical contexts of their denomination that they regard as erroneous or in breach of traditional doctrine, polity, or practice.
I recognize that not all participants in these movements would necessarily
regard themselves as evangelical. In mainline Protestantism that label often has a distinctly derogatory nuance. Indeed, out of the fund of issues
over which denominational conflicts can ignite, members from across the
theological spectrum can and often do agree on issues worth fighting. For
example, not all church members who have opposed the various proposals regarding human sexuality in the UMC, PC(USA), or the UCCan—
whether the issue before the church was gay ordination or denominational
sanction for same-sex covenanting services—would consider themselves
evangelicals; many have been very clear that on most if not all other issues, they are thoroughgoing liberals. They support the use of inclusive
language, see ecumenical and interfaith cooperation as beneficial to all
parties, and have no problem with most of the stands taken by their denomination on a wide range of other social and political issues. On this
issue, however, and for whatever reason, liberals find themselves aligned
with conservatives. Church members who would disagree on virtually
everything else find themselves signing the same petitions, sending the
same letters of protest, and praying for the same outcome.

As reform movements evolve, however, and as movement intellectuals
define the knowledge space that these movements come to occupy in the
mainline landscape, the cosmology that is most often articulated *is* evangelical in nature. It is bounded by theologically conservative understandings of such doctrines as the Virgin Birth, the ontological divinity of Christ,
a theory of substitutionary atonement, the infallibility (and not infrequently
the inerrancy) of the Bible, and, more and more often, the need for personal
conversion as a necessary condition of salvation. Over time, this positioning
results in a kind of theological feedback loop that forces reform movements
further and further to the right. Movement intellectuals define the nature
of their opposition in evangelical terms. This definition resonates with and
attracts other evangelicals within the denomination, while at the same time
dissuading less theologically conservative members from participating.
This reinforces the movement's evangelical position, and as the process
continues, conservative reform movements that might initially have included a much broader theological spectrum gradually become narrower
and narrower.

As I will elaborate throughout the book, reform movements emerge as
a reaction to particular problems of practical life, precipitous moments
that catalyze latent dissatisfaction into manifest dissent. Their objective is
to change the denomination, to re-form it in line with their theological
perspective as well as the social, ethical, and moral values that are in
dialectic with that perspective. This notion of dialectic is important because one of the liberal criticisms of conservative reform movements is

that they simply clothe retrograde social positions in the evangelical language of faith. A pietistic appeal to the few scriptures that can be interpreted as condemning homosexuality, for example, is regarded as nothing more than a cloak for politically incorrect homophobia. Indeed, Daly's (2000b) argument implies that conservative reform movements in the PC(USA) are so inextricably linked to extreme right-wing political and economic interests that any consideration of the theology with which those interests are in conversation is unnecessary.

I want to suggest, however, that any analysis of conservative reform movements must attend to the particular professions of faith made by reform groups (that is, what it is they say they believe), their interpretations of the denominational situation (that is, what it is they say they are responding to and how are they responding), and, finally, the manner in which these groups have evolved over the course of that response. While one may not agree with their positions, these movements do constitute legitimate competing voices, and do contribute to the ongoing creation of mainline Protestantism at the beginning of the twenty-first century.

Understood as a discrete category of conservative mainline Protestantism, reform movements are also not charismatic. That is, they do not normally include in their cognitive praxis neo-Pentecostal manifestations of the Holy Spirit, such as glossolalia, ecstatic prophecy, or faith healing. Indeed, many evangelical reform groups regard their charismatic coreligionists with a mixture of suspicion and disdain—not unlike many liberals in the same denomination. Largely in keeping with the kinds of names they choose for themselves—for example, the Aldersgate Renewal Ministries (UMC) or the United Church Renewal Fellowship—I label these neo-Pentecostal manifestations of the remnant spirit *renewal movements.* While critics often refer to such groups as "holy rollers," gatherings of overly emotional believers whose antics range from the mildly disconcerting to the manifestly alarming, these are more akin to the holiness revivals that swept through American Methodism in the latter half of the nineteenth century. But, as with evangelical reform groups, these are also legitimate social actors who share the denominational stage and whose contributions to the way in which churches develop cannot be ignored. While their theological positioning is very often identical to that of non-charismatic evangelicals, renewal movements *do* include in their cognitive praxis an understanding that these neo-Pentecostal manifestations will serve to renew and regenerate the spirit of the church.

The distinction here between *reform* and *renewal* is for conceptual purposes only, helpful to discriminate between movements when necessary. Renewal movements, for example, need not be adversarial. The Aldersgate Movement in the United Methodist Church maintains that it is more concerned with "lighting candles than cursing the darkness" (Aldersgate Renewal Ministries n.d.). On the other hand, the core identity of reform movements is located precisely in its active opposition to denominational policies and proposals. What *reform* and *renewal* share is a concern that mainline Protestantism in North America has reached a crisis point, that the precipitous moment has arrived, and that some manner of faithful response is required.

CHAPTER 3

Precipice and Response: The Three Domains of Reform and Renewal

INTRODUCTION

The battle for reform and renewal is fought in a number of different ways. Dissatisfied church members, both clergy and lay, adopt a variety of strategies to encourage or to force what they regard as recalcitrant denominations back onto acceptable religious paths. They implement those strategies through tactics that range from silent prayer at the entrance to denominational meetings, to broadsheet publication of the "truth" about upcoming church proposals and debates, to leafleting general conferences, councils, and synods. Some propose to take denominational authorities to court, to force a legal resolution onto the problem at hand. Others regard litigation as only slightly less problematic than the crisis in the church itself. Many feel that the most appropriate response is the rediscovery of the gifts of God's spirit in the midst of the church. Manifesting such charismatic gifts as speaking in tongues, prophecy, ecstatic trance, and healing leavens the denominational dough, as it were. Still other traditionalists, who may hold the option for litigation in reserve, and who may find themselves uncomfortable with the more demonstrative character of their charismatic colleagues, believe that the best way to reform the denomination is by maintaining an active, often adversarial conservative witness in the midst of the denomination.

These examples are drawn from the three major domains of response in which reform and renewal strategies are enacted in mainline Protestantism: the legal, the charismatic, and the evangelical-fundamentalist. When we consider these responses, however, it is important to bear in mind that they are social arenas within which particular individuals and groups press their cause; they are not discrete categories that bound out the possibility of other response options. As I have indicated, there are shared affinities between reform and renewal movements in terms of theological conservatism and basic conceptualizations of the problem. And there are crossovers in terms of organizational commitment and affiliation; that is, the lines between reform and renewal become somewhat blurred when members of the United Church Renewal Fellowship or the Aldersgate Movement are also members of the Community of Concern or the Coalition for United Methodist Accountability. Nevertheless, it is possible to elucidate the three principle responsive domains of conservative reform and renewal.

ECCLESIOLOGY AND JURISPRUDENCE: THE LEGAL RESPONSE

Bob Harper is an affable, seasoned minister in The United Church of Canada. A trained spiritual director, Harper has dedicated himself to ministries of prayer and meditation. He is also an accomplished bagpiper, and for many years has piped in retirees at the annual meetings of his denominational conference. Like most church conferences, though, there are times when tempers flare and heated, often bitter words are exchanged. In 1993, Harper's church conference met in Edmonton, on the campus of the University of Alberta. On the agenda were a series of motions regarding acceptable liturgical wording for services of baptism. Specifically, when performing baptisms, could ministers use language other than the traditional Trinitarian formula of Father, Son, and Holy Spirit? Because issues such as these cut to the quick of Christian belief and identity, the debate was vigorous and, at times, acrimonious. More than once, words like "heresy" and "blasphemy" were hurled across the conference floor. Rather than debate the motions on theological grounds, though, conservative members of the conference often sought to forestall discussion of the issue entirely, arguing that it contravened a specific section in the *Manual of The United Church of Canada,* the denomination's ecclesiastical rule book.

Voice after voice pointed to the same section: V.24.2(a). That is, all matters related to changes in church doctrine and practice—especially something as significant as a modification of the traditional baptismal formula (which, admittedly, could seriously strain interdenominational relations)—have to be made through the office of the church's General Council, the highest conciliar body in the denomination. Even then, the General Council can only make such changes if the majority of pastoral charges approved them by remit. Opponents not only of the motion to amend the baptismal formula, but of the very discussion itself, invoked this statute in an effort to have the entire debate declared *ultra vires*. Eventually, incensed by what he regarded as the parliamentary avoidance of key issues in the church's life, Harper stood and denounced those who would stifle the debate as "moral cowards," who insisted on "hiding behind some stupid book."

More than one voice in the large room wondered aloud, "Does he mean the *Bible?*"

Harper's response notwithstanding, this debate illustrates an important point in the social processes of identity construction, boundary maintenance, and denominational control when traditionalists feel that foundational elements of the faith are at risk. If biblical arguments will not prevail, as many believed they would not have in this case, given that the opposing sides were as far apart on issues of biblical interpretation and authority as they were on the theology of baptism, then recourse is often made to denominational polity and legal canons. While civil litigation between Christians is for many precluded by Paul's injunction that believers ought not take one another to court (1 Cor. 6:1–11), church investigations and tribunals have been a part of the ecclesial landscape since the early years of the Christian faith. In many ways, the ecumenical councils of the early Church were incipient tribunals called to consider the various competing "Christianities" and to establish the dividing line between the emergent theological domains of orthodoxy and heresy.

When it happens, the church in the dock takes two major forms and operates in two distinct arenas. On the one hand, there is the church court. Throughout the Middle Ages and into the Renaissance, church agencies— for example, the Holy Office of the Inquisition or the Geneva Consistory under John Calvin—have acted, often with the blessing of the state, to suppress dissident belief (cf., for example, Bauer 1971; Boyer and Nissenbaum 1974; Briggs 1996; Demos 1982; Kieckhefer 1979; Lüdemann 1995; Midelfort 1972; Starkey 1949; Wakefield and Evans 1991; Walker 1981). In the context of these proceedings, heresy is very often the conceptual order of the day. Individuals and groups are perceived to have so egregiously contravened the basic principles of Christian belief that the public censure of a heresy trial is warranted. As late as the end of the nineteenth century, in fact, among others, church historian Phillip Schaff (1819–1893), as well as biblical scholars Crawford Howell Toy (1836–1919) and Charles Augustus Briggs (1841–1913) were brought before ecclesiastical courts for charges ranging from an incipient "popery" to advocating higher criticism of the Bible (cf. Briggs 1893; Hatch 1969; McCook 1893; Rogers 1964; Shriver 1966).

On the other hand, in more open social contexts and more expansive religious economies, the Church itself may be called to account in civil court for complaints ranging from child and adolescent sexual abuse by clergy either in the parish or in religious residential schools (cf. Berry and

Greeley 2000; Shupe, Stacey, and Darnell 2000) to disputes over the ownership of church property in the event of a church split (see below), from complaints by clergy who believe they have been discriminated against by church institutions (Ellenby 1996; Ogilvie 1996; Outerbridge et al. 1994) to various issues related to the operation of separate religious schools (cf. Dwyer 1998; Mawdsley 2000) and the option not to participate in certain aspects of public education (see Bates 1993). To illustrate the legal domain of church response to denominational crises, I would like to consider two brief examples drawn from each of these major arenas of conflict.

THE CHURCH COURT: HERESY THEN AND NOW

Recent attempts to develop an explicit sociology of orthodoxy and heresy all lament the scholarly inattention paid to this important domain of religious interaction and development (cf. Berlinerblau 2001; Henderson 1998; Kurtz 1983; Weber 1951; Zito 1983). Progress to date, however, has been somewhat limited. In any sociology of orthodoxy and heresy, one of the most fundamental issues is that of historical and theological precedence. Put simply, does orthodoxy precede heresy, and heresy then merely deviate from the established orthodoxy, or does what becomes orthodoxy develop out of contested interactions between what are later declared competing heresies? The well-known Bauer thesis (see Bauer 1971), lately expanded by Bart Ehrman (1993) and Gerd Lüdemann (1995; cf. Kraft 1975; Lüdemann and Janssen 1997; Robinson 1988), contends the latter: early Christianity did not comprise an established orthodoxy that later spawned rival heresies. Rather, in the first centuries of the Church, numerous understandings of the Jesus event competed for dominance, and orthodoxy depended in large measure upon where one lived, in whose apostolic lineage the church in that region was founded, and to which texts that lineage had access and considered authoritative. Critics of the Bauer thesis (cf., for example, Brown 1998; House 1997) argue that there has always been an established orthodoxy, one which often closely resembles modern evangelicalism, and one from which these heretics strayed.

While the debate over precedence continues, once the Christian Church did establish a canon of orthodoxy, the principal conceptual mechanism for imposing the will of the dominant religious authority was in place. Etymologically, "heresy" represents the option for choice in one's belief and action; practically, though, it became both the sign and the seal of religious choices that are to be regarded as erroneous, inappropriate, or outright dangerous. From the sixth-century Isochrists, followers of Origen who believed in an eschatological universal salvation, to twentieth-century Oneness Pentecostals, charismatic modalists who challenge the traditional conception of the Trinity, the declaration of heresy has served as a significant means of denominational control and the imposition of authoritative religious identity.

Albert Truax and the Burnsite Heresy

In the late nineteenth century, dismayed by what they regarded as the decline in Methodist religiosity, a number of revivalist holiness movements emerged that were dedicated to returning Methodism to a camp-meeting style of emotional fervency and mass evangelism (cf., for example, Anderson 1979; Clark 1948; Dieter 1975, 1980; Semple 1996; Synan 1997). In Canada, this included the Canada Holiness Association, a group of clergymen gathered around the Reverend Nelson Burns, a Methodist minister whose poor health had precluded him from taking a pulpit, and who made his living as a teacher instead. Burns was convinced that something in his lifestyle had brought about his constant ill fortune, and, after a period of intense prayer, he pledged that he would obey the guidance of the Holy Spirit in any and all aspects of his life. Out of what he called his Georgetown experience, he wrote *Divine Guidance,* a small book that posited a radical personalism and proposed that anyone who accepted the guidance of the Holy Spirit as he had done would, in fact, be following the example of Jesus Christ. He taught that the guidance of the Spirit should determine one's actions, not the dictates of the Bible or the precepts of the church. For these views, which challenged both the scriptural basis of Christian practice and the Methodist Church's authority in mediating that practice, he was expelled in 1894 from both the American Holiness Association and the Methodist Church of Canada.

Burns's teachings, however, were having an impact on the church, and at least three Methodist circuits in Ontario had been affected by his particular brand of antinomian personalism. In an anonymous 1891 letter to *The Christian Guardian,* an "enquiring methodist" claimed that "those who adopt his views become infallible and absolutely perfect, and their experience is of such a high order that they cannot have fellowship with the members of the Church unless they come up to where they imagine themselves to be in the light (a new light they say)" (Enquiring Methodist 1891). Similar to some of the criticisms that would later be leveled at neo-Pentecostals, a holier-than-thou atmosphere pervaded those who followed what came to be known as the Burnsite heresy. The letter continued: "This thing has been cursing this circuit for about four years; the financial and spiritual interests of the circuit injured; Summerville church ruined; the work of God paralyzed; sinners scoffing, and all saying, Why do you leave Burns in the Conference or in the Church? Why is the Expositor [Burns's journal] published in the Guardian office? I know we are all on the side of mercy, but how long?" Arguably, Burns was ousted by the denomination less for his doctrinal deviance than for the effect his deviant teachings were having on the peace, good order, and economic condition of the Methodist circuits. However, among the more troublesome Burnsite teachings were the primacy of experience over Scripture, a neokenotic theology in which Jesus was seen as a fully human person emptied of all divine attributes, and a rudimentary form of universalism in which adherents denied the eternal punishment of the damned.

In June 1893, a year before Burns's expulsion, eight charges of heresy were brought by the Methodist Church against his lieutenant, the Reverend Albert Garnet Truax. Like Burns, Truax had been raised in a strict Methodist home. And, despite his early rejection of the faith in which he grew up, he became a Methodist minister in 1882. Attracted by Burns's zeal and the personalist spirituality he espoused, however, Truax joined the Canada Holiness Association. All told, 31 separate counts were brought by the church, alleging that Truax had either denied Methodist doctrine or failed to support sufficiently those doctrines he did affirm. Among other infractions, and true to his Burnsite beliefs, he was alleged to have "disparaged the authority of Holy Scripture"; he claimed "to know the will of God by direct revelation"; he denounced the historic creeds of the church "in nearly every sermon"; and he "made light of the duty of prayer" (*Niagara Conference v. Truax* 1893a, 1893b, 1893c).

The first charge laid by the tribunal was that "in his public teaching he has assailed the doctrine of the Divinity of Christ" (*Niagara Conference v. Truax* 1893b). In this, Truax participated in the various kenotic controversies that had circulated in the Church since the Reformation. These disputes revolved around differing interpretations of Phil. 2:5–8, in which Paul spoke of Jesus "emptying himself" in order to take on human form. Supporting the traditional view of a Christ who is fully and ontologically both human and divine, traditional theological thought has understood this passage to mean a limited kenosis; certain aspects of an infinite deity must be curtailed in hypostasis with a finite humanity. When Truax proclaimed a belief different than this—that is, that the kenotic Jesus stood as an exemplar of true humanity before God—the Niagara Conference concluded that he had "not positively taught the divinity of Christ" (*Niagara Conference v. Truax* 1893a, 1893b, 1893c).

Despite the explicit summons of the tribunal, Truax did not attend his trial, nor did he send anyone to speak on his behalf (*Niagara Conference v. Truax* 1893c). In a letter to the presiding minister, John Wakefield, Truax stated that he had preaching engagements on the evenings of both the trial day and the day following. As well, he had no interest in presenting himself to answer charges he regarded as patently absurd. In short, he believed that the conference had lost the right to try him. Recognizing, however, that the heresy trial was meant less to get him to recant his beliefs than to remove him from the Methodist ministry, Truax continued:

I see no good reason why I should resist efforts to put me out of the Methodist ministry when I no longer desire to remain in that ministry. If you are curious enough to ask why I no longer desire to remain a Methodist minister I will tell you. God has called me to preach a Gospel of righteousness and the Methodist Church has decided (if the Niagara Conference be representative) that it will not have such a Gospel. I am convinced of this since the last session of the Niagara Conference and hence since that time I have not accounted myself orthodox according to the interpretation of the standards by my Conference. The meaning of righteousness as understood by the Niagara Conference is certainly not what I would call *Christian* righteousness. (Truax 1893)

The important phrase here is "orthodox according to the interpretation of the standards of my Conference." According to Truax, it was not he who had departed the fold of Christian orthodoxy, but the Niagara Conference of the Methodist Church. He (and by implication Burns) represented the true orthodoxy passed on to the Church by Jesus Christ through the Holy Spirit. Truax ended his letter: "As far as I am concerned I have always offered the Niagara Conference what Methodists have always been seeking after (professedly at least), viz. the gospel of righteous living. The majority have distinctly rejected it and now I turn to the Gentiles" (Truax 1893).

Not surprisingly, when the Methodist Church called a commission to investigate the charges against Truax, the vast majority of them were found to be sustained. He was declared "out of harmony with the doctrines and teachings of the Methodist Church," and removed from its rolls as a minister (*Niagara Conference v. Truax* 1893a). The tribunal concluded that "this Conference would also regard and declare Mr. Truax to be unworthy of membership or any official position in the Methodist Church so long as he maintains the hostile spirit and unscriptural views manifested and expressed in his statements as given in the evidence and charges preferred." Truax's was only the first of several trials against the Burnsites—including the removal of Burns himself from the Methodist ministry a year later. Their attempts at a personalist reform of the church had invoked the administrative power of the institution to maintain denominational harmony and good order. In this case, the troublemakers were ousted; not all trials for heresy concluded so.

Walter Righter: The "HRETIC" of Newark

The license plate on his red Subaru station wagon reads "HRETIC." To many in the Protestant Episcopal Church, he is a hero; to at least as many others, his license plate says it all. In late September 1990, while acting as the assistant bishop of Newark, the Right Reverend Walter Righter ordained Barry Stopfel, a gay man living in a committed relationship, to the episcopal diaconate. As a result, a little more than four years later 10 Episcopal bishops, led by the bishop of Dallas, James Stanton, filed official charges, known as a presentment, and asked the church to convene a Court for the Trial of a Bishop, in Righter's case, for heresy. In a denomination that has existed for more than 200 years, this is only the second time such a trial has taken place. In 1923–24, the Reverend William Montgomery Brown, the retired bishop of Arkansas, was tried and convicted of teaching contrary to the doctrine of the Episcopal Church. He had declared that Christianity had been supplanted by communism. Righter notes that "with today's medical knowledge, we now know he was suffering from senile dementia" (1998, 59).

Filed in late January 1995, the substance of the presentment was a pastiche of statements Righter had signed or accounts of meetings he had attended during his episcopal career as the bishop of Iowa and the assistant bishop of Newark. These were interspersed with charges arising from two specific ordinations: Righter's ordination of Stopfel to the diaconate in 1990, and Bishop John Shelby Spong's ordination of another gay man, Robert Williams, to the Episcopal priesthood a year earlier. In the fabric of the presentment, the various church statements provide the warp, and Righter's alleged dissention from them the woof. The final rending of the episcopal garment, however, was Stopfel's ordination.

Three months after Spong's ordination of Williams, Edmond Browning, the presiding bishop of the Protestant Episcopal Church, and his Council of Advice issued a statement that affirmed the denomination's 1979 position on "the traditional teaching of the church on marriage, marital fidelity and sexual chastity as the standard of Christian morality" (*Stanton et al. v. Righter* 1995c). As is most often the case in mainline denominations, the issue of homosexuality becomes an overt problem of practical life only when gay men and lesbians refuse to remain either celibate or silent as the price of their ordination. While the 1979 statement admitted that sexual orientation, in and of itself, should not be a "barrier" to ordination, this admission was tempered by an injunction that candidates adhere to "behavior the church considers wholesome." Therein lay the rub. "Wholesome" sexual behavior was, by definition, that which occurred between a husband and a wife within the confines of their marriage. "Therefore," the statement concluded, "we believe it is not appropriate for this Church to ordain a practicing homosexual, or any person who is engaged in heterosexual relations outside marriage" (*Stanton et al. v. Righter* 1995c). Provided they met all the other criteria for ordination, gay men and lesbians could be ordained as long as they remained celibate—and presumably silent. Out of the closet in the world did not mean out of the closet in the church.

Referring specifically to Spong's action, however, Browning's statement concluded that "Bishops are called to safeguard the unity of the church. . . .

We believe that good order is not served when bishops, diocese, or parishes act unilaterally. We believe that good order is served by adherence to the actions of the General Convention" (*Stanton et al. v. Righter* 1995c). Which raises, of course, the issue of who controls denominational hierarchies such as the General Convention, and what penalties ensue when one contests the decisions of those hierarchies.

Following Browning's reaffirmation of the 1979 statement, in September 1990 the House of Bishops of the Episcopal Church added their own support to the traditionalist position in what became known as Resolution B-1a. Stanton's presentment charged Righter with dissenting from Resolution B-1a and voting against the affirmation of Browning's earlier declaration. Put simply, according to the logic of the presentment, which was fleshed out in a long discourse on the meaning and place of "doctrine" in the life of the church (see *Stanton et al. v. Righter* 1995a), dissent from the hierarchically mandated view of the church was tantamount to heresy. As Michael Rehill, the chancellor of the Diocese of Newark and Righter's counsel in the case, noted in his official response to the presentment, however, "to hold that voting in the minority in the House of Bishops constitutes a heretical dissent from the 'declarations of the House of Bishops' would be to create a very dangerous precedent indeed" (*Stanton et al. v. Righter* 1995b). Given that 75 other bishops also dissented from the statement, Rehill's is a masterful understatement, to be sure.

In the midst of these various documentary references, Stopfel's ordination goes almost unnoticed in the presentment. It states simply that "On September 30, 1990, Respondent (who was then Assistant Bishop of Newark) ordained to the diaconate one Barry L. Stopfel, in the Diocese of Newark" (*Stanton et al. v. Righter* 1995c). The defining aspect of this was Stopfel's committed relationship with his longtime partner, Will Leckie, and his intention to continue in that relationship. In the midst of the tumult created by the ordinations of Williams and Stopfel, the often controversial Bishop Spong brought to the 1994 General Convention what he called A Statement of Koinonia, the pertinent part of which declared: "But let there be no misunderstanding, our lives and our experience as bishops have convinced us that a wholesome example to the flock of Christ does not exclude a person of homosexual orientation nor does it exclude those homosexual persons who choose to live out their sexual orientation in a partnership that is marked by faithfulness and life-giving holiness" (*Stanton et al. v. Righter* 1995b, 1995c). In this statement, the denominational battle lines were drawn more clearly than ever before.

When Righter signed Spong's Koinonia Statement, Stanton and his copresenters concluded that he had once again heretically contested the will of the Episcopal hierarchy. However, like those who dissented from the Browning statement, since Righter was only one of 71 bishops who signed the Spong document, one is led to wonder why a number of other bishops have not been brought for presentment to trial. For all this, however, Stanton's presentment against Righter boiled down to two public actions and two counts of heresy.

The public action and public teaching of Respondent are therefore:

(a) A practicing homosexual can be properly ordained to the ministry of The Episcopal Church.

(b) Respondent will not be bound by teaching statements of The Episcopal Church declaring it is impermissible to ordain practicing homosexuals. (*Stanton et al. v. Righter* 1995c).

The specific charges of heresy derived from these. First, by dissenting from the Browning statement and by signing the Koinonia document, Righter was "teaching a doctrine contrary to that held by this Church" (*Stanton et al. v. Righter* 1995c). Second, by ordaining Barry Stopfel, Righter showed himself contemptuous of the canons of the church and in violation of his own ordination vows.

In determining how to approach the case, both parties were invited to submit papers on what the court understood as the central issue: the nature and place of doctrine in the faith and life of the church. Righter's position was contained in the official response to the presentment (*Stanton et al. v. Righter* 1995b); Stanton and his copresenters filed a separate statement, The Accusers' Position on Doctrine in the Heresy of Walter Righter (*Stanton et al. v. Righter* 1996a). While no opportunity would be given either side for specific rebuttal, in response to the accusers' paper Rehill immediately filed a Motion to Strike Improper, Immaterial and Scandalous Matters and to Limit the Argument of the Church Attorney (*Stanton et al. v. Righter* 1996b). Arguing that the presenters were employing bait-and-switch tactics, Rehill contended that Stanton et al.'s paper on doctrine was "not responsive to the question posed by the Court. On the contrary, it is a blatant attempt to rewrite the Presentment and thereby deny the Respondent the opportunity to prepare a proper defense, and it is replete with immaterial, scandalous and offensive material calculated to inflame the public and prejudice the Court" (*Stanton et al. v. Righter* 1996b). Specifically, Rehill argued that "in their 'Paper' the Presenters have engaged in an outrageous and vicious appeal to stereotypical homophobic prejudice through the continual use of misrepresentations, miscitations, misquotations and intentionally misleading and inflammatory language." Even a cursory comparison of the original presentment (*Stanton et al. v. Righter* 1995c) and the later paper submitted by the presenters (*Stanton et al. v. Righter* 1996a) reveals the validity of Rehill's concerns, and he responded:

For example, the Presenters have interchangeably used the terms "pederasty" (p. 2), "uncontrolled desire" and "sexual violations" (p. 3), and "pedophilia" (p. 6) to describe the Presenters' grotesque concept of "homosexual practice." Presenters then argue that such conduct is immoral. It is inconceivable that there is any Christian who would not join in condemning such conduct, but to accuse all non-celibate gay and lesbian persons within the Episcopal Church (and particularly its homosexual Candidates for Holy Orders) with such conduct is irresponsible and intellectually dishonest. (*Stanton et al. v. Righter* 1996b)

Eventually, the final statement of the court was read by the bishop of Delaware, Cabell Tennis, in Wilmington's cathedral church of St. Andrew. Based on the documents submitted by both parties, and the briefs presented at two pretrial hearings, all of which amounted to more than 1,300 pages of material, the actual issue before the court for the Trial of a Bishop was *whether* Walter Righter would be tried by the Episcopal Church as a heretic. As Righter notes somewhat wryly in his autobiography, this took place "even though it would have seemed to most observers that a trial had already taken place" (1998, 134). In a lengthy decision reprising the history and facts of the case (*Stanton et al. v. Righter* 1996d), and from which only one of the nine bishops on the panel dissented, the court entered two motions on its own behalf summarily dismissing each of the two counts brought against Righter. Though it appeared as though there had been a trial for heresy, there would be no trial for heresy after all.

Although the presenters filed an official Statement of Exceptions to the court's decisions (*Stanton et al. v. Righter* 1996e), and expressed their gratitude for Bishop Andrew Fairfield's dissenting opinion, they elected not to appeal those decisions (*Stanton et al. v. Righter* 1996c). In a final attempt to establish the validity of their claims, however, their notice concludes: "The only appeal of this case that will be taken is an appeal to those who accept the authority of the Holy Scriptures of the Old and New Testaments in the sense intended by the Author of 2 Timothy 3:16–17" (*Stanton et al. v. Righter* 1996c). That passage reads: "All scripture is inspired by God and useful for refuting error, for guiding people's lives and teaching them to be upright. This is how someone who is dedicated to God becomes fully equipped and ready for any good work."

THE CHURCH IN THE CIVIL DOCK

That the 1960s were a time of civil and ecclesiastical turmoil is something of an understatement. In *The Gathering Storm in the Churches*, his discussion of the growing tension between Protestant clergy and the laity they served during that period, Jeffrey Hadden described the struggles of that period as having "every evidence of being the most serious ferment in Christendom since the Reformation." Hadden continued that "the Protestant churches are involved in a deep and entangling crisis which in the years ahead may seriously disrupt or alter the very nature of the church"

(1969, 3, 5). As events unfolded, Hadden's analysis could scarcely have been more prescient, and, for a few years in the late 1960s, two Presbyterian churches in Savannah, Georgia, epitomized these crises as they fought to maintain their congregational integrity in the midst of what they perceived as serious denominational disruptions. Almost three decades later, virtually identical dynamics came to bear in a Methodist congregation in Hamilton, Bermuda. Rather than an ecclesiastical court, however, each of these situations brought the church to the civil dock.

"Can Two Walk Together?": Southern Presbyterians in Savannah, Georgia

When the Reverend Todd W. Allen stepped into the pulpit of Eastern Heights Presbyterian Church on April 17, 1966, he took as the text for his sermon a passage from Paul's second letter to the Corinthians: "Be ye not unequally yoked together with unbelievers, for what fellowship hath righteousness with unrighteousness?" (2 Cor. 6:14). For several years, it had been apparent to Allen and his flock—as well as to his colleague, the Reverend Dale Umbreit, pastor of the nearby Mary Elizabeth Blue Hull Memorial Presbyterian Church—that conservative congregations in the Presbyterian Church in the United States (PCUS) had been unequally yoked with their denomination, the "southern" Presbyterian Church. And today, he hoped, that yoke would be slipped.

That morning, Allen attacked a number of recent trends in the larger church, especially what he regarded as a creeping moral relativism, unbiblical support for civil disobedience, and reckless denominational participation in both the National and the World Councils of Churches. Allen told the congregation, for example, that two years earlier the Synod of Georgia had "put *Playboy* Magazine down beside the Bible and [said], 'Let us see what *Playboy* will say to the Bible and let's let the Bible speak to *Playboy*'" (1973, 3). While there are certainly a number of readings possible from a statement like that, Allen interpreted it to mean that denominational infatuation with neo-orthodoxy had erased any clear normative difference between the Holy Bible and the Gospel according to Hef. "The New Morality doesn't condemn pornography and smut," he continued, "it says, let us see what God is saying to us through pornography" (3). Similarly, Allen accused the denomination of teaching Presbyterian youth to disobey the law, quoting from a recent Board of Christian Education publication: " 'if the law says that you may not picket or gather peaceably for purposes of protest, then you **violate the law**, appealing to a higher law to justify your actions' " (4). Despite the fact that Allen had also quoted an earlier portion of the same Christian education article, a part that explicitly discouraged violent action and enjoined readers to "quiet protest" supported by "morally justifiable reasons," Allen chose to interpret the message as: "That's what they're teaching our young people in our literature today—violate the law" (4). That there were other interpretations possible is clear; that Allen was building a pulpit case for what would follow that morning is equally so.

As the closing chords of the final hymn drifted away, the members of Eastern Heights prepared for the real business of the morning: the decision to leave the PCUS and, though something of an ecclesiastical oxymoron, establish themselves as an "autonomous Presbyterian Church." Earlier that week, Allen and the session of the church had prepared a resolution for adoption by the congregation, charging that the PCUS had "violated its constitution and departed from the faith and practice as held by said Church at the time Eastern Heights Presbyterian Church became affiliated." Specifically, these precipitous moments in the life of the PCUS included the ordination of women; "making pronouncements and recommendations which concern civil, economic, social and political matters"; support for "the removal of Bible reading and prayers by children in the public schools"; the introduction and acceptance of neo-orthodox theology; and participation in the National Council of Churches, "which advocates such things as the subverting of parental authority, civil disobedience, and intermeddling in civil affairs" (Eastern Heights Presbyterian Church 1966).

The congregation was hardly unaware of these proceedings. More than two weeks prior, the session of the church had met and discussed current trends in the PCUS as well as the various responses congregations might make. Four days before the congregational meeting, Allen sent a pastoral letter to all members of the church outlining the situation and detailing the rather drastic response the elders of their congregation would propose. In that letter, he reiterated his position that the PCUS would not "withdraw from the National Council of Churches or that it will return to its conservative beginnings and heritage" (Allen 1966). That same evening (April 14), the Eastern Heights women's group had also scheduled an information meeting.

In the eyes of Allen and the ruling elders of the congregation, there was only one faithful course open to traditionalist members of the church: Eastern Heights would declare "itself to be an autonomous Presbyterian Church under the active leadership of Christ Jesus" and "sever all connections with and remove itself from all ecclesiastical control, jurisdiction and oversight of the Presbyterian Church in the United States" (Eastern Heights Presbyterian Church 1966). The congregation adopted the resolution by a unanimous vote, 122–0. Across town, while not unanimous, a similar motion was passed by majority vote at Mary Elizabeth Blue Hull Memorial.

Both churches made the same argument: in its acceptance of the positions detailed in the resolution, the Presbyterian Church in the United

States had broken the covenant under which member congregations had joined the denomination. Thus, it had invalidated any contractual obligation for those congregations to remain. The next day, Allen sent letters to the Stated Clerk of Savannah Presbytery, informing him of the congregation's decision, and, since he no longer considered himself under the authority of the denomination, asking that his own name be removed from the clerical roll of the presbytery. While one wonders how seriously the PCUS as a whole might view the defection of a few hundred disgruntled congregation members in a denomination that was fast approaching its peak membership of nearly a million (see Luidens 1990, 36–38), there were two far more serious issues at hand. By seceding from the PCUS, the Savannah traditionalists were both challenging the legitimacy of the denominational government to determine the direction of the church, and claiming sole ownership of two not insignificant church plants.

Within a few weeks, the Savannah Presbytery had appointed an Administrative Commission to respond to the actions taken by the two churches and to forestall any other congregations that might be thinking along similar lines. Well aware that few congregations would take such drastic action apart from the leadership of their pastors, especially given that Presbyterian polity at the time named the pastor as moderator of all official church meetings, the Administrative Commission's first action was to declare the two Savannah pulpits vacant and to remove their congregational sessions from office. Officially, these actions alleged that, in proposing the resolutions of April 17, Allen, Umbreit, and their congregational elders had exceeded their authority. For their part, fearful that denominational officials would seize physical control of the church property—in the words of the Administrative Committee's mandate (Eastern Heights Presbyterian Church n.d.: 4), "assume original jurisdiction"—the two congregations filed for injunctions preventing Savannah Presbytery from interfering in their church life. By implication, this granted clear ownership of the church property to Eastern Heights and Hull Memorial. Just before Christmas 1966, the Superior Court of Chatham County ruled that the PCUS had indeed substantially abandoned the doctrinal and constitutional standards in force when the two congregations had affiliated. And, in light of what was then regarded as a contractual breach, control of the property was awarded to the congregations (for a fuller description of these events, see F. Smith 1999: 184–207; for legal comment and discussion, see "Comments" 1969; Gerstenblith 1990; Peters 1969).

Savannah Presbytery appealed the decision to the Georgia Supreme Court, and a legal battle that was to last more than three years began. The stakes were high. Practically speaking, the denomination faced losing not only two substantial church properties, but potentially many others if the Eastern Heights and Hull Memorial congregations were permitted to withdraw with their church plants intact, and thus establish a denominational precedent. For their part, if the congregations lost, they would be required to relinquish church property that they and their families had built, and that the two congregations had occupied for nearly a century. In this fight, the denomination was confronted with a direct challenge to its authority and its right to decide the direction of Presbyterian identity; Eastern Heights and Hull Memorial risked losing their church homes and that part of their religious identity that resided in them.

Owen Page, a Savannah attorney, acted on behalf of the Eastern Heights congregation. In a 1967 "News and Events Report" to the congregation, Todd Allen asked Page to summarize what he considered the key aspects of the case. In Page's opinion, for the Georgia Supreme Court two issues stood out: "the status of the church corporation," and "the issue of the violations of the constitution of the Presbyterian Church by total involvement of the denomination in socio-political issues and programs" (Page 1967). According to Page, while the first aspect addresses issues of legal title to church property, who owns it and according to what legal principles, the second actually goes to the heart of the case. If a denomination departs from the doctrinal, moral, ethical, or social principles in place at the time affiliated congregations joined, does that departure constitute a breach of contract and remove any responsibility to the denomination on behalf of individual congregations? Page argued that it did, and that, once breached, individual congregations were under no further denominational obligation. It is not the case, he noted, that denominations cannot make changes in policy, position, and direction; they simply cannot make them in a unilateral manner, without due consultation with and the informed consent of constituent congregations. If those congregations agree to the changes, then there is a new contract in place. If not, a breach has occurred.

In January 1968, the Georgia Supreme Court upheld the decision of the lower court, and allowed Eastern Heights and Hull Memorial to keep their respective properties. Before that decision could be transmitted, however, the Savannah Presbytery was granted a Stay of Execution in order to appeal the Georgia decision to the United States Supreme Court. In a letter to Allen, Page pointed out that the U.S. Supreme Court challenge placed the two churches in a very different position. If the Writ of Certiorari was granted—that is, if the U.S. Supreme Court agreed to review the findings of the lower courts—then "we are in a new ball game" (Page 1968). If not, if the U.S. Supreme Court would not agree to hear the case—the position for which Page would argue—then "the long road of litigation is over," and the positions of Eastern Heights and Mary Elizabeth Blue Hull were secure (Page 1968). In 1970, two years after the first Georgia Supreme Court decision, and nearly four years after the battle began, the U.S. Supreme Court ruled that there were no constitutional issues to be decided in the cases; the PCUS had exhausted its legal recourse.

In the context of what he regards as authentic Presbyterianism, historian Frank Smith considers the decisions of the Eastern Heights and Hull Memorial churches "among the most dramatic and crucial events for the Continuing Church" (1999, 184). While there were setbacks in the years to come—despite the success of the two earlier congregations, some churches were not permitted to withdraw from the denomination and retain their property—"these two brave churches" did demonstrate that congregations need not accept what they viewed as fundamental violations of denominational doctrine, polity, and practice. More than a quarter of a century later, though, similar battles are still being waged.

"In Accordance with the Doctrine, Rules, and Usages": Wesleyan Methodists in Bermuda

Hamilton, Bermuda. Year-round, the temperature averages 75° Fahrenheit. For one small Methodist congregation, however, temperatures seemed to soar well beyond that in the years following The United Church of Canada's (UCCan's) 1988 decision that homosexual orientation would not automatically bar a person from seeking ordination or commissioning within the denomination. Five years later, the Methodist Synod of Bermuda, which operates as a presbytery of the UCCan's Maritime Conference, voted on whether to remain a part of the denomination in the face of increasing theological, doctrinal, and practical liberalization, or to secede. As a synod, the Bermuda Methodists chose to stay, but the vote was split along largely racial lines. Congregations whose membership was predominantly black wanted to disaffiliate from the United Church entirely; racially mixed or predominantly white congregations opted to remain.

In the months following the synod decision, two factions emerged and fought for control of Grace Methodist Church, a mostly black Wesleyan Methodist congregation on the north shore of the main island. While neither side in the dispute could be characterized as overjoyed at the General Council's decision, each saw that decision as affecting both the UCCan and their continued affiliation with it in radically different ways. For one group, led by lay preachers Gwynneth and Willard Lightbourne and comprising over 80 percent of the congregation, the decision on gay ordination was the final blow in a relationship that had grown increasingly strained over the past few decades. The Lightbournes and their followers wanted Grace Methodist to sever all ties with both the Methodist Synod of Bermuda and The United Church of Canada. If the Methodist Synod would not leave the UCCan, then Grace would leave the synod, establishing itself as an autonomous Methodist congregation. Although the minority faction, led by church members Richard Pulley and LaNeane Henry, did not approve of the General Council's decision any more than the Lightbournes, they believed neither that gay men or lesbians would actually be ordained by the church, nor that they should separate from the synod or the denomination on the basis of the 1988 decision.

In June 1995, however, what had to that point been a low-intensity church conflict erupted as both parties asserted their claims to the Grace Methodist property and control of its church life. That month, 48 members of the congregation signed a letter to the secretary of the Methodist Synod of Bermuda stating that, since more than 80 percent of the congregation had voted "to relinquish affiliation with the United Church of Canada" (*Wesleyan Methodist Trustees et al. v. Lightbourne and Lightbourne* 1996), they were tendering a one-year notice of disaffiliation from both the local synod and the parent denomination.

Perhaps hoping tensions would ease with the passage of time, the synod took seven months to reply to the Grace Methodist letter. And, when they finally did reply, rather than deal directly with property issues, synod officials referred the dissenters to sections in the United Church *Manual* that dealt with the dissolution of a congregation and the transfer of members from the United Church to other denominations. Any claim that the Lightbourne faction felt they had to the Grace Methodist property was simply ignored by the synod, a fact that did not escape those who were later called upon to decide the issue. Indeed, in her decision regarding the case, Madame Justice Norma Wade-Miller wrote, "I pause here to interject that this is not a case of the congregation disbanding. They are protesting the [UCCan's] decision" to ordain or commission gay men and lesbians (*Wesleyan Methodist Trustees et al. v. Lightbourne and Lightbourne* 1996).

Acrimony between the two parties increased until the synod informed the congregation that, as of July 1, 1996 (the date the original Lightbourne disaffiliation was to have taken effect), the synod would assume responsibility both for the conduct of worship at Grace Methodist and for the day-to-day oversight of the pastoral charge. The synod appointed the Reverend Victor McLeod, a minister from a Methodist congregation in St. George, to conduct worship and celebrate the sacraments on July 7. After that, a supply minister from Montréal would continue the ministry at Grace on the synod's behalf. The synod's decision resulted in a bitter confrontation between the two factions. Consider the Reverend McLeod's testimony, taken from Justice Wade-Miller's decision.

The organ was locked, the piano was tampered with. So we proceeded to put the piano in order. Mrs. Thomas who had been the organist up until this time and whom I had called to ask if she will play for the service told me that she would be playing the organ, but not for the Synod. We proceeded to secure someone to play the music of the worship and when the piano was in readiness she (Mrs. Ileen Vanzort) proceeded to play the piano. In the meantime Mrs. Thomas showed up and she took the place at the organ. I had noted that Mr. Lightbourne was present and meeting with the choir and so I proceeded to indicate to him and the choir that Synod had notified them I was to conduct the service. I proceeded to attempt to conduct the service with disruptions from Mr. Lightbourne. We proceeded to carry the service out. We announced one hymn Mr. Lightbourne called another and the organist being the louder was disruptive. We gave communion but it was a disruptive service. (*Wesleyan Methodist Trustees et al. v. Lightbourne and Lightbourne* 1996)

Picture the scene that hot July day. As the minister rises to announce a hymn, a lay leader shouts him down, demanding that the congregation sing a different hymn. As the piano strikes the opening chords for "How Great Thou Art," the organ answers back with "Guide Me, O Thou Great Jehovah." One can only imagine the disruptions that took place during the sermon and the celebration of the Eucharist.

Out of that final confrontation, however, two cross-claimant lawsuits were filed. Attendant motions and interlocutory applications notwithstanding, since both writs ultimately sought the same result—officially sanctioned control over the Grace Methodist property—the Supreme Court of Bermuda consolidated the actions and considered them as a single case (*Wesleyan Methodist Trustees et al. v. Lightbourne and Lightbourne* 1996). In strictly legal terms, the case revolved around who were the rightful owners of the property, and it was on this basis that lawyers for the United Church argued. The resolution, however, hinged on very different issues.

Ian Outerbridge, a conservative United Church member, lawyer, and veteran of numerous civil litigations with theological or doctrinal disputes at their core, argued that, like the Savannah cases nearly three decades before, this case was essentially doctrinal. Three deeds (1885, 1899, 1971) conveyed the trusteeship of the disputed property for the purpose of building a "suitable church to be used for the celebration therein of the worship of Almighty God . . . *in accordance with the doctrine, rules and usages of the Methodist Church and no other uses, intents or purposes whatsoever*" (*Wesleyan Methodist Trustees et al. v. Lightbourne and Lightbourne* 1996; emphasis in the original). As did attorney Owen Page, Outerbridge maintained that recent doctrinal and practical decisions by the parent denomination had effectively breached the terms of this trusteeship. Compelled by Outerbridge's argument, it was this underlined portion that Justice Wade-Miller deemed the crux of the case.

"The fundamental issue for the court to determine," she wrote, "is what is comprised within the ambit of the limiting words, 'in accordance with the doctrine, rules and usages of the Methodist Church and for no other uses, intents or purposes whatsoever' " (*Wesleyan Methodist Trustees et al. v. Lightbourne and Lightbourne* 1996). With this, the organizing principle of the case shifted from the often sterile domain of property law to the more volatile arena of theology and church doctrine.

Outerbridge called as an expert witness the Reverend Dr. Victor Shepherd, another conservative United Church member, a Wesley scholar, and a vocal opponent of liberal decisions the UCCan has made in recent decades. In addition to appearing on the stand during the weeklong trial, Shepherd prepared a detailed brief comparing "the theology and doctrine of The United Church of Canada today" with "the theology and doctrine of the Methodist Church as exemplified by the Twenty-five Articles of Religion of John Wesley and the doctrinal beliefs and practices of the Methodist Church in 1925" (Shepherd 1998). Not surprisingly, Shepherd's testimony was a thoroughgoing condemnation of recent United Church decision making. In his lengthy written opinion, Shepherd analyzed recent UCCan documents and doctrinal statements on human sexuality, same-gender covenanting, the authority and interpretation of Scripture, the person and work of Christ, the place of Christianity in the context of world religions, and the new United Church hymnal, *Voices United*. Comparing them with the founding doctrinal statements of Methodism (The Twenty-Five Articles of Religion), Shepherd opined that each of the recent decisions made by the United Church would have been rejected totally by John Wesley and, thus, constituted a substantial breach with the Wesleyan foundation on which Grace Methodist came into being.

While synod lawyers argued that Shepherd's statements were "just an opinion," they produced neither countervailing testimony nor evidence to refute Shepherd. Indeed, Justice Wade-Miller noted in her decision that she was surprised that the synod called no expert witnesses of its own. Rather, counsel for the synod conducted the case on the grounds that it was a fairly straightforward property dispute and ignored the doctrinal foundation on which that dispute rested. Citing legal scholar Margaret Ogilvie, who has written extensively on church-related litigation (see Ogilvie 1992, 1996), Wade-Miller noted that "the eruption of disputes about the ownership of church property from Church courts into the civil courts is almost invariably the final result of an irreparable rift within a church about a fundamental doctrinal matter" (cf. Ogilvie 1992, 377). Further, "in situations where congregational schisms have occurred on doctrinal lines, property has been found to inhere in those who subscribed to the original doctrinal position on which the congregation was established" (Ogilvie 1992, 389).

In her decision, Justice Wade-Miller found that the Pulley faction, those who wanted to retain ownership of the Grace Methodist property and remain within the Methodist Synod and the United Church of Canada had acted *ultra vires* to the trust by which the congregation had been established. She dismissed their case and found in favor of the Lightbourne faction. United Church officials appealed the decision to the Appellate Court of the Bermuda, and in June 2001, Wade-Miller's decision was overturned on appeal. Control of the Grace Methodist church property was

returned to Richard Pulley and LaNeane Henry. The case, and its attendant controversy, continues.

EXPERIENTIAL CHARISMATA AND RENEWAL:
THE EXPERIENTIAL RESPONSE

While its twentieth-century origins go back to such well-known Pentecostals as William Branham (1909–1965), David Du Plessis (1905–1987),
and Oral Roberts (b. 1918), the official beginnings of the charismatic movement in mainline Protestantism are generally located in a Passion Sunday
sermon preached in Van Nuys, California, on April 3, 1960 (cf. Bennett
1970; Bennett and Bennett 1971; Hocken 1988; Quebedeaux 1976; Synan
1997). That day, Father Dennis Bennett, the priest at St. Mark's Episcopal
Church, rose to explain to his congregation that for a number of months
he and other members of St. Mark's parish had been manifesting Pentecostal gifts of the Holy Spirit, most notably speaking in tongues. At the
time, St. Mark's was a rapidly growing congregation. In the seven years
of Bennett's leadership, membership had increased fivefold and Bennett
was assisted in his duties by three curates (Quebedeaux 1976, 54). Though
Bennett admits that the group actively opposed to neo-Pentecostalism at
St. Mark's was not large, it was very vocal, and as awareness of the change
that had taken place in their pastor gradually filtered through the congregation, rumors of religious fanaticism—including "secret conclaves in
the dead of night" (Bennett 1970, 50)—increased. While charismatic manifestations was not unknown in mainline circles, they were more often
than not associated with the "holy roller" crowd, behavior regarded as
decidedly inappropriate for a dignified Episcopal congregation like St.
Mark's. In the face of the rumors, Bennett chose to depart from the traditional Passion Sunday preaching schedule and address directly the issue
of the charismatic elephant in the St. Mark's sanctuary.

According to Bennett, it was not until the second of three morning services that serious problems occurred. At its conclusion, one of his curates
"snatched off his vestments, threw them on the altar, and stalked out of
the church, crying: 'I can no longer work with this man!' " (Bennett 1970,
61). Another congregation member opposed to the emotionalism of charismatic manifestations in a church whose members quite self-consciously
refer to themselves as "God's chosen frozen" was outside the building
trying to convince congregants arriving for the third service to "throw out
the damn tongue-speakers!" During that third Passion Sunday service,
Bennett resigned from St. Mark's. A few days later, in the midst of Holy
Week, he sent a letter to all members of the parish, reiterating his position,
assuring them that he was not resigning from the Episcopal priesthood,
and urging them not to withhold their financial pledges from St. Mark's.
Despite Bennett's actions, his bishop, Francis Bloy, was no more sympa-

thetic to his situation than many in his parish. Not only did Bloy not support his priest, he installed a temporary rector at St. Mark's and issued an episcopal edict forbidding neo-Pentecostal activities on diocesan property.

Suddenly persona non grata in the Episcopal Diocese of Los Angeles, Bennett found himself without a parish and branded locally as a religious fanatic—a curious situation for a professional clergyperson. A few months later, though, he was invited to accept a call as rector of St. Luke's, a small inner-city church in Seattle, Washington. For years, St. Luke's had been in decline, and hovered regularly on the brink of closure. Thus, the presiding bishop of the Diocese of Olympia, William Fisher Lewis, saw little danger in Bennett continuing his neo-Pentecostal ministry in what was a dying parish anyway. St. Luke's, however, did not die. Under Bennett's leadership—although Bennett would say the leadership of the Holy Spirit—it grew to become one of the largest and most vibrant congregations in the diocese (Bennett 1970; Quebedeaux 1976, 56; Synan 1997, 230).

Known variously as Neo-Pentecostalism, Charismatic Renewal, and the Charismatic Movement, the experience of charismatics at St. Mark's differs from classic Pentecostalism in three important ways. First, obviously, manifestations of the Spirit take place in mainline churches—among others, Episcopal, Lutheran, Methodist, Presbyterian, and Roman Catholic—and outside the denominational domain of classic Pentecostalism. Second, glossolalia is not required as evidence of salvation, and does not serve as an indicator of one's faith status. While such requirements are not universal in classic Pentecostalism, manifest evidence of spiritual gifts, particularly glossolalia, is a much more regularized component of congregational life and worship. Third, those who do manifest gifts of the Holy Spirit in the context of Charismatic Renewal tend to stay within their own denominations rather than move to one that is more intentionally Pentecostal; that is, they believe their calling is to remain where they are as a force for renewal. Synan suggests that by the morning of Passion Sunday 1960, "practically every denomination already had many 'closet Pentecostals,' who had received the experience but had remained quiet for fear of displeasing church officials" (1997, 230). Given Bennett's experience in the Episcopal Church, such circumspection was hardly unwarranted.

Since the late 1960s, social scientists have sought to explain the rise of the charismatic movement in a number of ways. In this search, for example, various forms of deprivation theory have been deployed—charismata fill the void when other needs or wants go unfulfilled. Considering mainline neo-Pentecostalism in the context of Charles Glock's classic restatement of deprivation theory, Cecil Bradfield (1979) contends that the various domains of deprivation include not only economic, but also social, ethical, psychic, and "organismic" factors (cf. Glock 1964). In the face of a culture stripped of any traditional sense of the sacred, he argues that "neo-Pentecostals are seeking a type of existence that gives security, personhood, and community and which makes all of life sacred" (Bradfield 1979, 65). While Kilian McDonnell also considers deprivation theory as it applies to charismatic renewal, he more fully addresses the "persistent and widespread suspicion that glossolalics are psychologically deprived. This suspicion is to be found not only at the level of folk psychiatry but among persons trained professionally in the behavioral sciences" (1976, 152). Indeed, investigations into psychotic or altered states of consciousness as possible explanatory mechanisms for charismatic experience are not uncommon (cf., for example, Copestake and Maloney 1993; Francis and Jones 1997; Francis and Thomas 1997; Young 1998). Like Bradfield, Margaret Poloma (1982) addresses the issue from within the context of secularization theory—that is, that charismatic manifestation is an experience of spiritual renewal in the face of a culture that increasingly devalues the spiritual (cf. Bruce 1998; Reed 1991). Admitting that "no major scholar studying American religions during this century was able to predict the rise of the charismatic movement," she contends that the charismatic renewal is not a retreat from the secular, but a dialectic phenomenon in which the secular experiences a resacralization through charismatic manifestation (Poloma 1982, 238). Discussing Protestant evangelicalism and charismatic renewal in Latin America, however, David Stoll paints a much darker picture. In his analysis, the explosive growth of neo-Pentecostalism in Central and South America has at least as much to do with advancing the interests of U.S. foreign policy and helping to prosecute a number of "covert and immoral 'dirty wars'," as it does encouraging people to accept a new and more vibrant mode of faith expression (Stoll 1990, 327).

In keeping with the theoretical perspective I am suggesting for this book, however, I would contend that mainline charismatics are simply responding to similar precipitous moments as other reform groups and movements. Not only has *society* lost much of its sense of the sacred, charismatics argue that the same is true for the *church*. The introduction of what was perceived as a rather sterile neo-orthodoxy, institutional participation in social action and civil disobedience, and the devaluation of the soteriological centrality of Jesus challenged charismatics just as they did noncharismatics. While many noncharismatics chose more open confrontation with denominational authorities over these issues, those who experienced neo-Pentecostal charismata sought denominational renewal through prayer and celebratory witness. That experience became a core element in the charismatic renewal movement's cognitive praxis. As just one example, consider neo-Pentecostalism in the United Methodist Church (UMC).

Since its beginnings in the mid-1970s, Aldersgate Renewal Ministries

(ARM), the charismatic renewal movement within the UMC, has been known variously as United Methodist Renewal Services Fellowship, the Renewal Fellowship, or by its rather unwieldy acronym, UMRSF. Whatever the name, though, its stated purpose has always been clear: the spiritual renewal of the UMC through regular and faithful exercise of the gifts of the Holy Spirit. In addition to annual Aldersgate Conferences, which attract charismatic Methodists from across the country, ARM encourages the creation of regional affiliate groups and sponsors charismatically oriented Life in the Spirit seminars. Unlike more confrontational groups such as the Good News Movement, which has deliberately avoided any institutional ties, ARM functions as an agency of the UMC's General Board of Discipleship.

Although there was some initial resistance to the formation of an official charismatic organization, two main reasons account for the ARM's willingness to work within the institutional structure of the United Methodist Church. First, despite the fact that they share similar concerns about the state of the church and operate from similar theological positions as noncharismatic, evangelical reform movements, United Methodist charismatics worked very hard to avoid being seen as a source of division in the denomination—a characterization that has haunted many groups like Good News since their inception. Second, in 1976, the UMC adopted specific guidelines for interacting with the charismatic renewal movement that recognized, first and foremost, that "like other new movements in church history, the charismatic renewal has a valid contribution to make to the ecumenical church" (Discipleship Resources 1996, 698). Similar acknowledgment of the legitimate roles played within denominational life by more confrontational reform groups has been less forthcoming. These also highlight the two major constituencies within the UMC with whom the charismatic renewal is called to interact—the denomination proper, and the noncharismatic, evangelical reform movement.

That the UMC felt it necessary to address the charismatic renewal in some official way is hardly surprising. Wesleyan holiness movements have been a part of Methodist history since the early nineteenth century (cf., for example, Dieter 1975, 1980; Tuttle n.d.). Similar to the reaction of the Good News Movement, the 1976 UMC statement, "Guidelines: The United Methodist Church and the Charismatic Movement" (Discipleship Resources 1996), recognized that all Christians are charismatic in that it is the Holy Spirit who quickens their hearts to the truth of the faith, encourages them in their own faith journey, and equips them for ministry in the world. That said, however, "as a concession to popular usage" (a convention I am following here), the "Guidelines" reserved the term for those whose religious experience is marked by glossolalia, ecstatic prophecy and interpretation, and manifestations of supernatural healing. In addition to some historical and theological context provided by Robert

Tuttle's essay "The Charismatic Movement: Its Historical Base and Wesleyan Framework," lest noncharismatic Methodists ignore their own holiness roots, the statement provides standards of conduct for all constituent groups: how pastors, both charismatic and not, ought to interact with each other and with the laity, and how charismatic and noncharismatic laity ought to express themselves and their faith experiences in the context of a church marked by theological pluralism and ecumenical consideration. Finally, to forestall situations like Dennis Bennett's treatment by Bishop Bloy, a closing section discusses the responsibilities denominational officials bear those clergy who manifest charismatic gifts. As an organizing principle for understanding and incorporating the charismatic renewal into the life of the church, the document states: "If the consequence and quality of a reported encounter with the Holy Spirit be manifestly conducive to division, self-righteousness, hostility, and exaggerated claims of knowledge and power, then the experience is subject to serious question. However, when the experience clearly results in new dimensions of faith, joy, and blessings to others, we must conclude that this is 'what the Lord hath done' and offer him our praise" (Discipleship Resources 1996, 698).

From the beginning, while the UMC charismatic renewal has shared both theological orientation and, in many cases, membership with evangelical reform movements like Good News, the relationship has not always been an easy one. While hardly limited to the United Methodist Church, in the early years of the charismatic renewal, neo-Pentecostals were accused by their evangelical peers of splitting churches, of being so obnoxious in the expression of their new-found spiritual joy that they alienated those around them, and of making glossolalia the benchmark for authentic Christian experience, thus taking the focus off more traditional evangelical norms. In some cases, these charges were warranted, but not all. Yet, for all that, noncharismatics realized very early that charismatics were concerned about the same issues in the church as they, that they were no happier about denominational direction and decline, and that they believed God was calling the UMC to renewal *and reform* in a manner not dissimilar to that advocated by evangelicals.

In a 1973 issue of *Good News Magazine,* Charles Keysor, one of the founders of the Good News Movement, addressed the issue of neo-Pentecostalism in an article titled, bluntly, "Tongues-Speaking: Good or Bad?" (Keysor 1973). At the annual Good News convocation the year before, a charismatic layperson had been invited to share her experience in dialogue with a noncharismatic member of Good News. "Apparently," wrote Keysor, this "has caused some of our friends to think that the Good News Movement now promotes glossolalia (tongues-speaking)." Before his analysis of the situation, though, Keysor stated simply, "this conclusion is not justified," and urged his evangelical colleagues to seek a middle way between the indiscriminate acceptance of charismata on the one hand and its wholesale rejection on the other. If the reform and renewal movements found themselves split over tangential issues—for example, "Do you speak in tongues?"—Keysor asked, "Could Satan win a greater victory?" He concluded with a word of advice to each side in the dispute. To charismatic Methodists he wrote, "Tongues-speakers need to face these facts. They should realize that they sometimes put a serious strain on the evangelical community. At the very time when unity is desperately needed among believers so they can confront the secular world with the Good News of Jesus, the tongues-speaking controversy divides us into two warring camps!" To noncharismatic evangelicals, he opined that "non tongues-speakers need to examine their own close-mindedness. They need to ponder whether or not they are too dogmatic in denying the Holy Spirit a right to work in ways strange and unusual. Those who do not speak in tongues also need to remember that if the reality of Christ is evident in people's lives, then tongues-speaking (or non tongues-speaking) means little."

The controversy did not disappear right away. Indeed, four years later, Keysor felt compelled to address it again (1977). While he would not condemn the charismatic renewal, as had many liberals in the church, neither would he fully embrace it if it meant diminishing the reform movement's fundamental evangelical commitment. "The central place belongs, after all, to Jesus Christ only!" he wrote. "When anything usurps His rightful place, that is, at best, a serious mistake; at worst it is heresy. Good News desires Christian unity centered upon Jesus Christ as we meet Him through Scripture quickened by the Holy Spirit. No other common ground is possible or adequate for authentic Christian unity." Any reformation predicated on experience or understanding different from this was unacceptable to the evangelical Methodists of the Good News Movement.

THEOLOGY AND POLITICS: THE EVANGELICAL-FUNDAMENTALIST RESPONSE

The most basic component of the conservative reform and renewal movement in mainline North American Protestantism has been those groups who advocate evangelical theology as the foundation of denominational reform. *Ecclesia semper reformanda est*, as the saying goes. "The church always needs to be reformed." Of course, the central questions in this are: What shape will reform take in any given instance? Who gets to decide that shape? And, in whose interests will that shape be decided? For some, reform means precisely such denominational actions as the extension of the rites and sacraments of the church to those not traditionally permitted to receive them—for example, communion offered to divorced church members, baptism of nonmembers, the ordination of women, and of gay men and lesbians. For these, the process of reform is a release from the strictures of the past and the embrace of a future the path of which may be influenced but not known (see Stark and Bainbridge 1987, 27). For others, reform means just the opposite: the return to a well-known past and the security of clearly defined doctrinal and ecclesiastical boundaries. For these, theological debates, inappropriate involvement in social issues, conformity to secular culture in a misguided attempt to be "relevant" have all pulled the church away from its traditional and confessional moorings, and every effort must be made to resecure the faith. While I will discuss more fully the conservative theological response in four mainline Protestant denominations in Parts 2 and 3, a brief consideration of one other will serve to introduce the topic here.

In 1957, the Evangelical and Reformed Church and the Congregational Christian Churches, each denomination itself barely a quarter of a century old, merged to create the United Church of Christ (UCC; cf. Gunnemann 1999; Horton 1962). Wide divergences in ecclesiastical style, social and theological positioning, and historical background have produced in the UCC a fertile medium for the advancement of new traditions. Among the distinctions claimed by forerunners of the constituent denominations is the first black person ordained into ministry (Lemuel Haynes, 1785) and the first woman (Antoinette Brown, 1853); the United Church of Christ also claims the first openly gay man called into ordained ministry, William Johnson (1972). In 1975, the 10th UCC General Synod passed a resolution that "deplored the use of scripture to generate hatred, and the violation of civil rights of gay and bisexual persons," and in 1977, Anne Holmes became the first openly lesbian woman ordained in the denomination.

Denominational decisions regarding human sexuality and the presence of gay men and lesbians in the church were hardly greeted with unanimous approval. With the liberal drift of the denomination becoming clearer with each passing year, the United Church People for Biblical Witness (UCPBW) was formed shortly after Holmes's ordination to call members of the denomination back to what it regarded as biblical faith. In 1983, with the help of systematic theologian Donald Bloesch (see Bloesch 1982, 1984, 1985), the UCPBW produced The Dubuque Declaration. Essentially an abridgment of many of the classic creeds upon which the UCC had drawn for its original doctrinal platform, The Dubuque Declaration is similar to many such confessional statements and movement manifestos devised by conservative reform groups. In part, the statement declares the group's faith in the triune God, belief in the ontologically divine-human nature of Jesus Christ, and the need for regeneration based on Christ's substitutionary atonement. As we will see in many cases, an emphasis on both the historic creeds of the Church and the biblical witness anchors the group's confession.

A year later, the United Church People for Biblical Witness changed its name to the Biblical Witness Fellowship (BWF) and expanded its mission to include congregational reform as well as reformation of the UCC along more "traditional" lines (cf. Cimino 2001, 39–62). For nearly a decade, the group was recognized as an official interest group within the UCC; in 1995, however, that designation was dropped by the denomination. Since its beginnings as a group opposed to particular denominational directions and policies, BWF has grown to become part of the larger parachurch association of reform-minded groups within mainline Protestantism. It operates a referral service on behalf of UCC congregations seeking theologically conservative pastors (read: "pastors of biblical integrity"), as well as for pastors seeking congregations opposed to current denominational direction and policy. In fact, at the back of their booklet, *Seeking a Godly Pastor* [(Biblical Witness Fellowship n.d.)], a guide for pulpit search committees, the BWF provides a list of seminaries and Bible colleges from which "interim or permanent pastoral placement" might be sought. Among others, these include such evangelical and fundamentalist educational strongholds as Denver Seminary, Dallas Theological Seminary, Fuller Theological Seminary, and Regent University Seminary. BWF maintains an active presence at denominational conferences and publishes occasional papers on such issues as human sexuality, changes in liturgical materials, and the introduction of "feminist Neo-paganism" into the church through the highly controversial Re-Imagining Conferences—all subjects to which we will return.

SUMMARY

In any number of mainline churches and over any number of issues, people leave, vowing never to return. Closed Communion; requirements for membership or adherence prior to the celebration of baptism or weddings; doctrinal disputes over women's ordination, the authority and interpretation of Scripture, or lay participation in the celebration of worship. Most of these—indeed, all of these—have at times led members out of the church. While the presenting issues are most often framed in terms of one or another of the concerns above, I would argue that at their core these disputes are about identity and truth. More precisely, who has the power to name authentic identity, and the authority to delineate the boundaries of truth by which that identity is informed. Former PC(USA) moderator Robert Bohl regards the growth of conservative reform movements in his church as part of "the struggle for the very soul of the Presbyterian Church" (Daly 2000b, iii). Put differently, who decides what constitutes a faithful, authentic Presbyterian, or Episcopalian, or Methodist? Alan Schooley's charges that former UCCan moderator William Phipps's comments to the *Ottawa Citizen* were heretical and rendered Phipps an apostate assert the ability to divine between truth and error. To Bohl and Daly, the problem with the such conservative reform groups as the Presbyterian Lay Committee is plain; to Schooley and other UCCan conservatives, the danger represented by liberals such as Phipps equally so. The problem, of course, is that things are not so clear at all.

Whether the presenting problem is an Episcopal presentment for the trial of a bishop, the rightful allocation and distribution of church property, or the alleged breach of contract that occurs when a church changes in some way the doctrinal standards under which clergy pledged to serve, at some point each of the cases discussed in this chapter is about identity, and the presumed right to challenge when that identity is threatened. Walter Righter's opponents did not argue the ordination of Stopfel. They accepted it as a fait accompli, and argued instead that in conducting the ordination Righter had contested the legitimate doctrine of the Episcopal Church, and voided both his ordination vows and his right to be a bishop. In both the Savannah Presbyterian and the Bermuda Methodist cases, lawyers for the conservative side of the debate argued that the parent denominations had so changed the parameters under which these churches came into being that they had lost the right to decide who is and who is not an authentic church member.

On each side of the debate, there are issues of power at work. By highlighting the power that is often wielded by denominational hierarchies, conservative reform and renewal movements challenge what have come to be regarded as the dominant meaning structures within their denominations. In doing so, they create a new societal space, a space in which a new understanding of denominational polity and process develops. And it is to these movements that I would like now to turn.

PART II

Confronting the Precipice

There are two religions competing for the hearts and minds of men in the pew: Christianity and liberalism. They are diametrically opposed to one another. In their understanding of God, man, the Bible, Christ and salvation, they are polar opposites.

—Paul Howden, Reformed Episcopal Church

In an extreme form this new religion calls paganism Christianity and declares that immorality is morality. It is basically a form of pantheism or monism using a Christian vocabulary to cover a rejection of the basic dogmas and moral teachings of orthodox Christianity.

—Peter Toon, Episcopal Church (USA)

Should women theologians be encouraged to study, teach, and lead in the church? Clearly! Are the theological insights of women needed? Of course! Should women be silenced merely because they are women? Never! But, to say that is a long way from endorsing something called feminist theology— a quest for spiritual and mystical insight that begins not with revelation, but with very limited and incomplete human experience, and that too often ends in neo-paganism.

—Sylvia Dooling, Presbyterian Church (USA)

CHAPTER 4

Irreconcilable Differences: Presbyterian Church (USA)

INTRODUCTION

For many Presbyterians, C67 was the straw that broke the camel's back. In the late-1960s, at the alleged apex of mainline Protestantism in North America, the United Presbyterian Church in the United States of America (UPCUSA), the northern church in American Presbyterianism, approved a new statement of Presbyterian faith known as the Confession of 1967. Intended to update the centuries-old language of the Westminster Confession, C67 actually galvanized latent dissatisfaction within the denomination and set the stage for conservative reform movements that continue to this day. While its preamble was meant to ameliorate concerns by arguing that C67 was neither a system of doctrine nor an exhaustive treatment of Christian theology, there was sufficient liberal language in the document to cause more traditional Presbyterians grave concern. The section on "The Grace of Our Lord Jesus Christ," for example, begins: "In Jesus of Nazareth true humanity was realized once for all." Nothing was said about the ontological hypostasis of divine and human, and the concept of a substitutionary atonement was rendered as one of many "expressions of a truth which remains beyond the reach of all theory in the depths of God's love for man." Similarly, in the section on "Revelation and Religion," C67 states that the "Christian finds parallels between other religions and his own and must approach all religions with openness and respect. Repeatedly God has used the insight of non-Christians to challenge the church to renewal. But the reconciling word of the gospel is God's judgment upon all forms of religion, including the Christian." In

the new confession, the authors recognized that they had articulated neither a systematic theology nor a complete doctrinal framework for the
church. Rather, the purpose of the statement was "to call the church to
that unity in confession and mission which is required of disciples today."
In the proclamation of that call, "reconciliation" was to be the dominant
theological leitmotif, and the church's mission to facilitate this reconciliation—which, among other things, meant the recognition of humanity as
"one universal family," "peace, justice, and freedom among nations," and
the abolition of poverty as an "intolerable violation of God's good creation" (see Presbyterian Church [USA] 1999).

However artfully stated, though, Ronald Nash, a Reformed theologian
and philosopher, argued that the new confession's "real purpose" was to
render the clear orthodoxy of the Westminster Confession sufficiently ambiguous as to "give theological liberals within the U.S.A. church more
room to maneuver" (Nash 1987, 89; cf. Fry 1975; Hillis 1991). While some
liberals saw the new confessional statement as "the most important missionary event in our church in the twentieth century" (Smart 1968, 1),
more conservative members interpreted its reliance on reconciliation as a
credal foundation for the trivialization of the UPCUSA. John Fry, former
pastor of First Presbyterian Church in Chicago and director of the news
department at *Presbyterian Life*, insisted that reconciliation as an organizing principle diminished the church's ability to distinguish between competing interpretations of denominational doctrine (Fry 1975). Since few
church members would contest the need for reconciliation, Fry argued,
especially when reconciliation is understood as the functional equivalent
of the gospel, "Presbyterians can't really fight over the confession, or fight
over fighting, and anyone win. There are no sure ways to determine the
validity of the differences" (1975: 7). Indeed, denouncing the confession's
support for an increased denominational role in secular issues, he maintained that the "most influential person in the UPCUSA since 1971 has
been Angela Yvonne Davis" (Fry 1975: 38). Something of a cause célèbre
in the 1960s, the UPCUSA donated $10,000 to Davis's defense fund when
she made the FBI's Ten Most Wanted list as an accomplice in a deadly
1970 escape attempt from the Marin County courthouse. "She broke the
church wide open without trying," concluded Fry (1975: 38; although, cf.
Hoge 1976; Hoge, Johnson, and Luidens 1994, 177).

The online history of the Presbyterians for Renewal group (www.
pfrenewal.org; cf. Nash 1987) put the tensions that developed within the
denomination as a result of C67 a bit more diplomatically, contending that
emergent reform movements in both the northern and the southern Presbyterian churches "gave emphasis to biblically-based stances on a variety
of issues in an ecclesiastical climate in which sociological or political dynamics were stressed." Put differently, traditionalist members of both
communions were incensed by what they perceived as unwarranted and,

worse, unpopular intrusions by the church into secular politics, especially highly charged situations like the Davis affair. As well, the civil rights movement, protests against the escalating war in Vietnam, and criticism of government economic policy were all considered matters of the world, and consequently unfit for church participation. In this regard, the gap between clergy and laity, as well as between laity and denomination, increased. Though both clergy and laity believed they understood the mission of the church very clearly, both defined that mission very differently.

In his groundbreaking study of the split between clergy and laity in the 1960s, Jeffrey Hadden noted that at that time 83 percent of Presbyterian clergy believed that Christians misunderstood "the implications of Christianity for the race issue" (1969, 106–7). A large majority of laity, on the other hand, "rejected the position that Martin Luther King, Jr., was making Christianity relevant" (Hadden 1969: 137–38). Further, while laymen and -women were "divided on whether clergy should speak out on social, economic, and political issues," they did believe that clergy who participate in demonstrations do more harm than good and most would be upset if their clergyperson participated in a such a demonstration (Hadden 1969: 134–36).

For traditionalist groups, these events plainly illustrated a movement away from the primacy of the Bible in the church's life (however symbolic and tenuous that primacy had actually been), and the relinquishing of the church's fundamental—that is, spiritual—mission in favor of social and cultural interventionism. For many who had been uneasy about denominational direction for some years, the advent of the 1967 Confession confirmed their worst fears. In their view, C67 did not address the concerns of traditional church members, and Presbyterians United for Biblical Concerns was organized to influence the wording of the new confessional document. A number of similar groups formed in the northern church as well as the southern, among them the Covenant Fellowship of Presbyterians. In 1983, when the northern and southern churches united to create the Presbyterian Church (USA), these various groups gained an ecclesiastical structure more conducive to joint action.

THE PRESBYTERIAN LAY COMMITTEE (PLC)

While the Confession of 1967 acknowledges that the Scriptures were "given under the guidance of the Holy Spirit," that was qualified by the admission that they "are nevertheless the words of men" and were conditioned by the times and places in which they were written. If C67 proved a watershed in the life of the UPCUSA, this qualifier epitomized the problem facing the denomination as far as the founders of the Presbyterian Lay Committee (PLC) were concerned. Formed in response to the confessional draft that became C67, the PLC is the oldest continuing reform movement in the PC(USA), and among the oldest in postwar mainline Protestantism. Its most visible presence is *The Layman,* a bimonthly broadsheet that contains reform-oriented denominational news items, editorials, and information. Currently, *The Layman* is mailed free to more than half a million PC(USA) households, and is the largest circulation Presbyterian publication in the world (Daly 2000b, 20).

According to the official history of the PLC, the original committee members were "people of means and action," "leaders in their churches" and "leaders in corporate America" (Presbyterian Lay Committee 1997). While accurate, this understates somewhat the corporate status of the early PLC, whose members included among others: J. Howard Pew, chairman of Sun Oil, now Sunoco, and cofounder of the Pew Charitable Trusts; George Champion, chairman of the Chase Manhattan Bank and member of the influential Council on Foreign Relations; Roger Hull, president of the Mutual Life Insurance Company; Hugh MacMillan, a senior Coca-Cola executive; and Paul Cupp, chairman of the American Stores Company. That is, all were senior members of America's corporate elite; many had the ears, not only of business, but of the executive and legislative branches of government; and all were known for their conservative political, economic, and social views. In his analysis of the early PLC, Daly (2000b) details other prominent business and governmental figures involved in the Presbyterian Lay Committee, as well as the web of conservative commercial and political interrelations these men (and a few women) shared. Daly, however, essentially rejects (or at least minimizes) the notion that theology played any more than a nominal role in the PLC's formation. Rather, for the early PLC, theology was simply the ecclesiastical language in which the committee's drive to preserve or entrench a national platform of free-market capitalism had to be couched in order to make it palatable for a mainline church. Denominational agitation for racial justice, civil rights, an end to the war in Vietnam, and support for the World Council of Churches (which, in turn, was perceived to be supporting various communist regimes around the world), threatened that platform, and the PLC sought to frustrate denominational initiatives by framing the decisions in terms of an improper entry by the church into the social sphere and a crude abandonment of traditional Presbyterian values.

Today, Daly is one of the PLC's most trenchant critics, and claims the Lay Committee "is among the best-funded and most politically oriented right-wing organizations in mainline Protestantism" (2000b, 11). Further, "operating as a standing inquisition," Daly declares that "the PLC's role has been to target, attack, and neutralize key leadership sectors and initiatives within the national structure of the church." Indeed, the PLC's "political inquisition against church leadership is the foundation of the renewal movement's bid for institutional power."

On the other hand, it could be as well stated that the PLC, and conservative reform movements like it, are indeed doing their best to frustrate denominational policies and initiatives; they are indeed seeking to exercise some measure of institutional control within their denomination. But they are doing so because they sincerely believe the PC(USA) is on the wrong course; they genuinely accept the proposition that the church's role has little to do with the construction and reconstruction of human society and think it ought to remain solely within the domain of private piety and personal morality. Without ever really saying why, however, Daly's analysis assumes that this distinction is a bad thing. What he does not consider is the possibility that these really are Presbyterians who see their church slipping away, and who really do want to arrest the slide. According to its own statement of purpose, the organization under whose auspices Daly's research was carried out, the Institute for Democracy Studies, is "devoted to the study of anti-democratic religious and political movements and organizations in the U.S. and internationally" (Daly 2000b: 170). The underpinning assumption, of course, is that the organizations such as the PLC are antidemocratic.

Again, another way of understanding the situation is that these groups are acting in a profoundly democratic way. That is, they are seeking to influence the outcome of denominational processes through the various democratic avenues available to them: rallying together in support of their cause, caucusing and lobbying at denominational synods and conferences, and publishing the views of movement intellectuals in an effort to persuade potential stakeholders of the righteousness of their beliefs. To date, they do not appear to have broken any laws, planted listening devices in denominational headquarters, hired personnel to burgle synodical offices, or attempted to bribe church officials. Granted, they present a perception of the denominational situation that is vastly different from the official, more liberal view, but this is hardly a crime. Where this official view asserts a denominational unity in diversity, conservative reform movements such as the PLC suggest the situation is more accurately one of irreconcilable differences. Where the denomination backs positions that challenge the hegemony of free-market capitalism, reform movements see this as an unacceptable incursion of the church into the natural pattern of social and economic processes. Using the tools available to them—the liberals those of denominational command and control, the conservatives those of publicity and protest—each group seeks to convince the Presbyterian constituency of the validity of its position. Whether one agrees with the positions taken by either side, to suggest as Daly does that one side or the other is acting in an antidemocratic fashion stretches the analysis a bit too thin.

However, that the PLC does perceive drastic problems in the PC(USA), and that this perception constitutes the sine qua non of its cognitive praxis, is clear from even the most cursory review of their published material. Consider, for example, *The Layman*'s coverage of recent PC(USA) General Assemblies. In 1998, one correspondent criticized the worship service that opened the 210th General Assembly, citing liturgy performed in languages that went untranslated for much of the congregation, a lengthy sermon that derided corporate culture in the United States, and, preceding the celebration of communion, a liturgical dance "the meaning of which went unexplained" (Jensen 1998). Another wrote to applaud the decision by the church to discontinue funding for a controversial women's group, the National Network of Presbyterian College Women, on grounds that the group had become doctrinally unsound (Adams 1998). Two days after that motion, though, *The Layman* reported that following "a carefully orchestrated, tearfully executed late-night demonstration, a move to restore funding to the National Network of Presbyterian College Women for one year was approved" (Mills 1998). Numerous delegates, reported the PLC, felt betrayed by the reversal, and by what they regarded as a blatant abuse of process that had been not merely allowed at the General Assembly but facilitated by members of the denominational hierarchy.

A year later, at the 211th General Assembly in Fort Worth, Texas, one of the most contentious issues for the PLC was an overture that the denomination mandate the use of inclusive language (including that used by the controversial Re-Imagining Movement) for all PC(USA) congregations (Mills 1999b; cf. Berneking and Joern 1995; Biblical Witness Fellowship 1999; Hailson and Gerber 1998; Kjos 1997). Since the overture included a requirement that all congregations report to the denomination how the use of inclusive language was being enacted, the PLC correspondent concluded: "It would only take one more small step to require such statistical reports of every congregation every year and penalize those that failed to meet statistical standards for using inclusive God-language" (Mills 1999b). Despite the PLC's fears, including "the specter of witchhunts, so beloved of pro-gay-ordination activists" (Mills 1999a), the overture was rejected by the General Assembly by a wide margin.

In at least two areas, the political agenda of the PLC is abundantly clear: the place of the United States in the landscape of global geopolitics, and its criticism of those movements that challenge the alleged (and natural) hegemony of free-market capitalism as it is embodied in the United States. In its January–February 1998 issue, for example, *The Layman* ran an article criticizing members of the Presbyterian Peace Fellowship who had been arrested the previous November for trespassing onto and protesting the U.S. Army School of the Americas (USARSA) at Fort Benning, Georgia (which was renamed in 2001 the "Western Hemisphere Institute for Security Cooperation," or WHISC). Called by its opponents the "School of the Assassins," the USARSA is the major training depot for government military, paramilitary, and police forces in Latin America (cf. Danner 1994;

LeoGrande 2000; Nelson-Pallmeyer 1997; Schirmer 2000). In the *Layman* article, editor-in-chief Parker Williamson characterized those arrested as "part of a coalition of leftist religious groups" who had "failed to win support for Latin America's Marxist guerrilla movements" (1998c). Quoting Dianne Knippers, president of the Institute on Religion and Democracy, a conservative umbrella organization that regards the reform of society as inextricably linked to Christian evangelicalism within that society, Williamson concludes that " 'instead of accepting socialism's defeat and the victory of free-market democracies, critics of the school are bent upon vengeance against the U.S. military' " (Knippers, in Williamson 1998c).

Two years later, *The Layman* published an abridged version of "U.S. Army School of the Americas: Paradigm or Pariah," an open letter to the PC(USA) written by an Army Reserve chaplain who had visited the USARSA briefly. "The truth is," wrote Jim DeCamp, who in civilian life is a Presbyterian pastor, "that USARSA is a top-notch institution, exerting a positive influence throughout Latin America." Responding to both political and religious criticism of the USARSA, including annual calls that it be closed and regular protests outside its gates, DeCamp argued that the school "promotes the democratic values of freedom of religion and press"; it "preserves peace in the region"; and introduces "Latin Americans to our nation's good will" (DeCamp 2000).

In his article, DeCamp seeks to answer some of the major criticisms of the USARSA, including that graduates of the school have been responsible for gross violations of human rights in their home countries. DeCamp does not deny this; rather, he answers with the argument that a few bad apples should not prejudice the entire harvest, contending that "fewer than 1 percent" of USARSA graduates have been linked to human rights violations. "Since a disturbing number of our seminary graduates have committed adultery, should our seminaries therefore be closed? Who in our denomination holds a school accountable for the moral failures of its graduates?" (DeCamp 2000). What DeCamp does not say is that USARSA (now WHISC) graduates "have been linked to nearly every major human rights violation that has occurred in Latin America since the school's inception 50 years ago" (School of the Americas Watch 2001). As well, the difference between the U.S. Army School of the Americas and, say, Princeton Theological Seminary is that seminaries do not regularly train graduates to commit adultery, nor does the training provided regularly encourage the commission of adultery. On the other hand, at the USARSA, it is precisely the skills learned by students—for example, counterinsurgency ("Democratic Sustainment" and "Peace Operations" courses) and interrogation—that are used to suppress democratic freedoms and violate human rights in graduates' home countries. This somewhat important distinction is ignored by DeCamp, but exemplifies the manner in which conservative political positions are often rhetoricized by denominational reform movements.

Since the late 1980s, *Layman* editor-in-chief Parker Williamson has been one of the most prominent voices in the PLC, and among its leading movement intellectuals. In the 1970s, while serving as a hunger activist on the General Assembly Mission Board of the Presbyterian Church of the United States (that is, prior to union, the southern Presbyterians), Williamson recalls that the defining moment in his relationship with the denomination came when he learned that money raised by the church was being used through the World Council of Churches (WCC) to aid what he considered Marxist revolutionaries and guerrillas, including the Patriotic Front of Robert Mugabe and Joseph Nkomo in what was then Rhodesia. In August 1978, Patriotic Front guerrillas shot down an Air Rhodesia passenger plane and massacred survivors on the ground. According to Williamson, the Patriotic Front had been among the groups that had received Presbyterian mission funding. " 'When I found out, I went ballistic.' Williamson said, 'I felt I had betrayed Presbyterians by my participation in that program' " (Presbyterian Lay Committee 1998; cf. Williamson 1999). Williamson began speaking out against political movements that gained financing and credibility through organizations like the WCC. He opposed liberation theology and what he regarded as the inappropriate politicization of the Christian faith. Intensely critical of the World Council of Churches, he inveighed against "church funding for radical groups that preach and practice violence," of which the Patriotic Front of Robert Mugabe was the principal offender (Presbyterian Lay Committee 1998; cf. Williamson 1999).

It would be easy to pigeonhole people like Williamson and his colleagues as nothing more than conservative reactionaries who care only for the faith and nothing for the people who embody that faith, or who simply mask conservative geopolitical agendas in pious rhetoric. While such a characterization is often made by both theological and political liberals, it is by no means accurate. Williamson's faith is embodied in his work; it is simply work done differently than much of the denominational mainstream. Williamson, for example, was "one of three students from Union Theological Seminary to join Martin Luther King on his march to Selma" (Presbyterian Lay Committee 1998). He has led racially integrated congregations and has been active in such areas as low-income housing and hospice programs, as well as denominational antihunger coalitions.

What is clear from an examination of the PLC and of its critics, however, is that neither understands (or is inclined to admit) the implications of their claims for the other. Put differently, those, like Daly, who maintain that the Lay Committee is nothing more than a "political inquisition" designed to arrest or curtail the social mission of the PC(USA) miss the theological structure that has developed around the committee's opposition to denominational policies. On the other hand, in its condemnation of alleged PC(USA) intrusion into the political arena, and its constant call for Presbyterians to place "faithfulness to Scripture and denominational standards ahead of personal political agendas" ("Commissioning History" 1998), the PLC either misses or ignores the political dimensions inherent in its own policy statements. Speaking out in favor of an organization like the U.S. Army School of the Americas is no less a political statement, and makes no less claim to a particular political vision, than do calls by liberal Christians for its closure; implicit in conservative criticism of the World Council of Churches on the grounds that it uses theology to promote socialism is a political statement invoking free-market capitalism as a world norm. More often than not, both sides in the debate simply talk past one another.

THE PRESBYTERIAN FORUM (PF)

Like almost all religious organizations, many reform and renewal movements have taken advantage of the Internet and wider access to computers and Web authoring tools as necessary implements for both the publication of their message and the ongoing construction of their cognitive praxis (cf. Hadden and Cowan 2000a). Among these efforts is the Presbyterian Forum (PF). Begun in 1997 by Bob Davis and Robert Dooling, the forum (and its online information service, the *Presbyterian Review*) is "committed to sounding the clarion call" for reform and renewal in the PC(USA) (Presbyterian Forum n.d.). Through its Web site and such print publications as the *General Assembly Gazette,* a four-page broadsheet produced each day for commissioners to the denomination's General Assemblies, the Presbyterian Forum comments on hot-button issues in the church and advises conservative members of the denomination on the implications of these issues, as well as potential responses to them. Like most other conservative groups, the forum recognizes that the process of denominational reform is a long, often arduous one. In the face of this, Davis's plan for change has three components: "Connection, Engagement, and Bearing Witness." Each, he contends, will assist the PC(USA) in returning to the faithful witness he believes his church has abandoned.

First, "Connection" addresses a common concern among reform and renewal groups: the perceived alienation of denominational hierarchies from local congregations. Decisions that affect church members at the grassroots level are made with little or no input from those members; when proposals for change are advanced, local congregations feel their voices are patently ignored by church authorities and officials. In Davis's words (2000a), there are "a vast number of Presbyterians who feel separated from the decision-making processes at every level." In 1997, Davis, a graduate of Fuller Theological Seminary, started contacting local con-

gregations and pastors, searching for a way to bring these disaffected local
congregants and clergy together. Through the *Presbyterian Review* Web site
and occasional print mailings, the PF maintains contact with this widely
dispersed audience. For those who resonate with PF material, Davis's
group helps provide a conceptual framework for the cognitive praxis to
which PC(USA) reform groups are dedicated. That is, it not only names
the current problems, but provides authoritatively regarded explanations
for those problems, as well as potential responses in which participants
could engage.

He readily acknowledges, however, that information alone will not
bring about the reform he and his colleagues desire; there must be proactive engagement for change to take place. Four mechanisms embody this
second component and advance the PF's conservative reform agenda.
First is shepherding. While controversial in its connection with the International Churches of Christ and other shepherding movement churches
(cf. Giambalvo and Rosedale 1996), for Davis and the PF, shepherds are
loosely analogous to Roman Catholic *periti*, the theological advisers who
served delegates to the Second Vatican Council. In the context of PC(USA)
General Assemblies, pastors and elders associated with the Presbyterian
Forum promise to pray for delegates to the General Assembly, try to advise them on the different issues they will encounter, and encourage them
during the demanding days of a General Assembly schedule.

Next, in The Rock, the Presbyterian Forum seems to have paid attention
to what many sociologists have concluded (and what many evangelical
denominations have known for a long time) is a key factor in the renewal
and health of any church: the retention and empowerment of church
youth. Begun in 1999 as a PF ministry, "The Rock" stands for "Together
Helping to Evangelize and Renew Our Community." The youth wing of
the PC(USA) reform movement, The Rock "is designed to inform young
people about the issues they are likely to inherit" in the church, and open
up a social space within the PC(USA) for those youth and young adults
who "are not ashamed to proclaim, 'The Bible is God's Word! Jesus Christ
IS Lord!' " Similar to the shepherds, The Rock is dedicated to grassroots
organizing, starting Rock Groups in local congregations and presbyteries,
and in increasing conservative youth and young adult participation in
denominational government.

Working in partnership with other reform and renewal groups is the
third mode of engagement with the church. With the Presbyterian Renewal Network (PRN), an umbrella coalition of reform and renewal
groups within the PC(USA), the Presbyterian Forum established an infor-
mational caucus at the 212th General Assembly called the Pre-Assembly
Forum. Meeting for two days prior to the assembly, the event was intended to brief commissioners on issues the PRN felt were particularly
important at that assembly. Well-known leaders from various Presbyterian

reform and renewal movements were on hand to speak to delegates, including Sylvia Dooling (Voices of Orthodox Women, and wife of Presbyterian Forum cofounder Robert Dooling), Terry Schlossberg (Presbyterians Pro-Life), William Giles (Presbyterian Coalition), and Parker Williamson (Presbyterian Lay Committee). While not well attended in 2000—only 14 commissioners out of a possible 558 came to the event—Daly (2000a) notes that "it is this kind of effort that can potentially weld together a conservative bloc strong enough to 'win' a General Assembly." Despite the disappointing attendance at the Pre-Assembly Forum, Davis still maintains that those commissioners who did take part "played a major role" in the General Assembly's business.

Finally, the Presbyterian Forum acts as a clearinghouse for conservative reform information in the PC(USA). According to Davis, questions from conservative members of the church range from parliamentary procedure to Presbyterian history, and from church liturgy and hymnody to evangelism and mission strategy. He answers these queries as he is able, always framing his replies, though, in the context of a denomination in dire need of change.

The third component in the PF plan—the need for a proactive witness—most clearly articulates both why the PF believes change is required and why groups such as the Presbyterian Forum are necessary. In decisions and postures stretching back more than two decades, the PC(USA) has strayed from the scriptural and confessional standards upon which the church was founded. In calling for a reformation of the church, it is these standards that must be reinvested with meaning. For Davis and other members of conservative reform groups, events at the denomination's 212th General Assembly could not illustrate that need more clearly.

For eight days in June 2000, Long Beach, California, hosted the PC(USA)'s nearly 600 General Assembly delegates. Less than a mile from the Pacific Ocean, they debated commissioners' resolutions ranging from support for a peace process in the Middle East to concern for women in the Southern Baptist Convention who have been denied ordination; they voted on a wide variety of presbytery and synod overtures, including a request for clarification of the conditions under which ministers from other denominations would be accepted into the PC(USA), and an amendment to the church's rules of procedure that would prohibit either spontaneous or planned demonstrations within the confines of the court.

For groups like the Presbyterian Forum, a number of these overtures directly impacted the conservative reform agenda. For example, two presbyteries brought overtures (Ovt 00–12 and 00–26) asking the General Assembly to explicitly prohibit same-sex unions, as contentious an issue in the PC(USA) as in other mainline denominations. Another overture proposed an amendment to the constitution of the church affirming the preeminent role of Scripture in the life of the church (Ovt 00–21). A third,

Overture 00–37, followed close aboard and asked that a church task force be established "to conduct a study of abortion focused solely on explicating the biblical witness in a manner faithful to the scriptures and consistent with the confessional standard" (Overture 00–37 2000).

While both overtures forbidding same-sex unions were approved by the General Assembly, a victory for the conservatives, both the affirmation of biblical preeminence in the PC(USA) and the request for a biblical study on abortion received nonconcurrence. In each of the rejected cases, the committees responsible for considering the overtures decided that the proposed actions and amendments added nothing new to the way in which the PC(USA) already deals with those issues. A number of other overtures treating various aspects of the discussion around homosexuality were referred to the 213th General Assembly (2001) in Louisville, Kentucky, at which the most hotly contested topics involved the proposed deletion of the so-called fidelity and chastity provision of the PC(USA) *Book of Order* and the proposed repeal of a long standing "authoritative interpretation of church law prohibiting the ordination of gay men and lesbians.

At the Long Beach General Assembly, though, one of the most contentious issues was what conservatives regarded as the blatant hypocrisy between the stated theme of the conference and the way in which particular docket items were discussed and dismissed by the gathering. "Unity in Diversity" was the unofficial theme of the conference, and the assembly logo, three persons woven into a stylized water drop and gathered together under a descending dove, bore the words: "For All Are One in Christ." As Bob Davis wrote in the first of nine *General Assembly Gazettes,* "unity . . . unity . . . unity" had become a mantra even before delegates had arrived in southern California. Citing a *Presbyterian Outlook* editorial, Davis continued that "there is an overwhelming tendency at the General Assembly level to celebrate diversity while denying any division within the Presbyterian Church (U.S.A.)" (Davis 2000b). An overture brought by Beaver-Butler Presbytery, located just north of Pittsburgh, however, was determined to place recognition of that division squarely onto the assembly's agenda.

Overture 00–5's purpose was stated bluntly: "On Declaring That There Exists in the PC(USA) an Irreconcilable Impasse Regarding Biblical Authority, Biblical Interpretation, Jesus Christ, Salvation, Ethics, Leadership, Sanctification, and the Church" (Overture 00–5 2000). Essentially, it argued, there were in reality two churches in the PC(USA): one for which these aspects of Christian faith and practice were important, another which had for many years effectively abandoned any real commitment to them. The overture, which, while approved, was also contested at the presbytery level, arose from the decades-long dispute over homosexuality in the church, and the attendant theological, ethical, moral, and biblical debates that constellate around it (Small 1999). In the accompanying rationale, the overture's authors contended that the loss of "common ground on core theological issues creates division" in the church, and that "church members and officers are increasingly disconnected from and even hostile to the denomination because it spends so much time and energy disputing these issues without resolving them" (Overture 00–5 2000). Even denominational officials, stated the overture, recognized the recent emergence of diametrically opposed and mutually exclusive theological camps within the church. As a first step toward healing, Ovt 00–5 asked that the divide at least be recognized by the denomination in some intentional manner. Building on the logic of an "irreconcilable impasse," Beaver-Butler also brought Ovt 00–6, which asked that a task force be appointed to determine how those congregations that disagree with denominational decisions might disaffiliate from the PC(USA) while retaining their real and financial property.

Like so many other overtures that had implications for the 2001 General Assembly's discussions around homosexuality in the church, 00–6 was finally referred to the following year's meeting (at which the church's Advisory Committee on the Constitution recommended the assembly disapprove the overture). Not so 00–5. While supporters argued that it was time theology became a central issue in the church once again, opponents of the overture, such as Richard Leon, the moderator of the Committee on Theological Issues, which brought a motion to disapprove 00–5 to the floor of the court, and directed the Stated Clerk of the Assembly to forward to the church a brief pastoral letter on the issue. Expressing appreciation for Beaver-Butler's "devotion to theological issues," even though they disagreed that an "irreconcilable impasse" exists, the letter continued, "We choose rather to see differences positively and believe that differences in fact have the potential to make our unity in Christ even stronger" (Assembly Committee on Theological Issues 2000). A motion from the assembly floor to append to the letter a list of the eight areas in which the overture believed the impasse existed was also defeated.

The debate over Overture 00–5 and the question of an irreconcilable impasse is an excellent example of the struggle to name authoritatively the situation in which the church finds itself. Each side in the debate "chooses to see" the problem in fundamentally different ways; each seeks to mobilize support for its naming of denominational reality. For the conservative reform movements, the denominational hierarchy view the crisis in the church through rose-colored glasses that seem all but permanently attached; denominational officials, on the other hand, suggest that any intimation of irreconcilable differences is tantamount to giving up on God.

For its part, the Presbyterian Forum responded to these events with a number of articles in the *General Assembly Gazette*. Doug Brandt opined that the committee's unanimous rejection of the overture actually proved its "basic thesis" (2000, 1). Bob Davis (2000) interpreted the committee's response as fear: "Clearly the differences [described in the overture] are too threatening to talk about." In a *Gazette* editorial the day the overture was defeated, he mused that, even in committee and table group discussion, the split between the fantasy of unity and the reality of division was evident. Observers reported that it was as though the two groups were speaking "contradictory languages," and simply talking past one another. For Davis, a common metaphor for the division within the PC(USA) was "an elephant in the living room." And, "if that's the case," he continued, "the discussion at this Assembly has been about how well behaved the family pet is while refusing to consider whether a living room is an appropriate place for an elephant."

PRESBYTERIAN COALITION (PC)

The question of irreconcilable differences and the manner in which these ought to be resolved was not new to the church. In responding to a 2001 overture (Overture 01–9 2001) from the Presbytery of South Kansas, for example, which asked for a "process of churchwide spiritual discernment considering the current division within our denomination," the Office of the General Assembly commented that the current disputes resembled other moments of decision in American Presbyterian history—notably, the 1837 General Assembly split into "Old School" and "New School" Presbyterianisms, and "fundamentalist/modernist controversy" of the 1920s. The General Assembly noted that the Presbyterian situation at the end of the twentieth century bore "an uncanny resemblance" to that at the beginning. The denomination was in danger of splitting, and concerns were high over who would "win."

In September 1999, members of the Presbyterian Coalition, an umbrella organization aimed at coordinating efforts among the various reform groups in the PC(USA), gathered at the Dallas-Fort Worth Hyatt for their third annual convention to consider these very questions. While 1,000 people had come to the meeting in 1997, and 500 in 1998, a core group of just over 200 met in 1999 to continue discussions on the future of their church. At that meeting, though, a key agenda item was whether or not the time had come for evangelical Presbyterians to admit that the denomination had moved so far beyond the pale of orthodoxy that they could no longer remain within the church. Until that point, in traditionalist Presbyterian conversation the prospect of schism was considered impolite at best, anathema at worst. In a session devoted to that precise question, however, two leaders in the PC(USA)'s conservative wing argued the relative merits of either remaining within the denomination or effecting a "gracious separation" from it. While both admitted that there were serious theological and practical differences extant in the church, they disagreed on whether those differences warranted a denominational split.

The Reverend Jerry Andrews, comoderator of the Presbyterian Coalition and pastor of the 1,200-member First Presbyterian Church of Glen Ellyn, Illinois, argued against separation, contending that the only faithful path amounted to a "line-by-line, paragraph-by-paragraph" dialogue on the *Book of Confessions* between the liberal and conservative wings of the church. Only through that process could the two sides in the dispute stop talking past one another and begin to lay the groundwork for a PC(USA) that remained united. The Reverend Mark Toone, on the other hand, pastor of Gig Harbor's Chapel Hill Presbyterian, one of the fastest growing congregations in the denomination, maintained that the church had reached a "Paul and Barnabas moment." In Toone's view (A. Smith 1999), the problem was tragically simple: irreconcilable differences did exist in the church and must be faced honestly and openly. Citing the half-million members the PC(USA) had lost in the preceding decade, Toone asked whether any authentic kind of reconciliation was possible. Entrenched in beliefs both factions consider faithful and prophetic, would the two sides in the struggle ever be able to live in peace? And, if not, which was clearly Toone's conclusion, has this impasse so reduced the ability of the PC(USA) to be an effective witness for Christ that the only faithful course was one of gracious separation?

For Andrews, the issues on which the various factions in the church agree still outweigh those on which they are separated; for Toone, they do not. Supporting both positions, the Presbyterian Coalition (Presbyterian Coalition 1999b) remains committed to the work of denominational reform and renewal "in and through the existing structure of the PC(USA) whenever possible," but recognizes also that there may come a time when such work is no longer tenable.

"A movement of Presbyterians committed to exalting Jesus Christ, energizing congregations, and upholding historic Biblical leadership standards," the Presbyterian Coalition also emerged in reaction to the possibility that the PC(USA) would not explicitly prohibit the ordination of gay men and lesbians. As for so many other traditionalist denominational members, this issue catalyzed a sense of frustration that had been building for a number of years. Decades of membership decline, a church bureaucracy that seemed ever further removed from the congregational laity, and a theological liberalism that many perceived was driven by a small but vocal minority within the denomination brought those thousand Presbyterians to Dallas in September 1997. Over the course of their conference, different reform strategies were raised, discussed, and debated. As they would two years later, some favored disengagement or outright separation; others believed that only a renewed confessionalism could heal the rifts within the church.

Diagnosis of the problem was the first order of business for the 1997 meeting. And, as most mainline Protestantisms have discovered, the crux of the issue was that a broad denominational rubric known as "Presbyterian" served merely to mask a wide, at times oxymoronic spectrum of theological opinion. Biblical inerrantists shared the same denominational home as participants and organizers of the well-known Re-Imagining Conference, which brought Goddess spirituality into the mainline in a way never seen before. Presbyterians who believe in all sincerity that homosexuality is a perversion, "an abomination before God," claim the same denominational identity as Presbyterians who, again in all sincerity, believe that the various modes of sexuality are gifts of God equally and thus to be equally celebrated.

At the heart of the various individual controversies, however, traditionalist Presbyterians believe that many of the changes in denominational policy and structure disparage the core confessions of Christian life: the Bible as the Word of God, and the affirmation of Jesus as Lord. Recognizing that these confessions are held to be incompatible with the changes taking place in the denomination, the preamble to each of the strategy papers introduced at that 1997 meeting stated concisely: "We cannot call ourselves a confessional church and ignore even the most rudimentary theological themes which weave themselves through every one of our confessional statements" (Presbyterian Coalition 1999a).

At the 1998 Presbyterian Coalition Gathering, again held in Dallas, two important documents were adopted that mapped out both the percipient reality of life in the PC(USA) and the reform deemed necessary to correct what the coalition regarded as the denominational aberration. Union in Christ: A Declaration for the Church is the theological statement underpinning the PC's cognitive praxis, while "Turning Toward the Mission of God" is a six-part strategy paper outlining the manner in which reform and renewal efforts should be implemented.

Written in liturgical style, as though for antiphonal reading, "Union in Christ" is a series of opposing statements that construct a dialectic between the call for union in Christ and a list of cultural and ecclesiastical practices that must be rejected before that union can be faithfully realized. Substitutionary atonement, a uniquely efficacious Christian soteriology, an authoritative revelation vested solely in Christian Scripture, and a clearly defined morality are the boundaries around which this opposition is organized. Structured thus, the PC's statement is far more revealing for what it rejects than for what it embraces. Few Presbyterians, for example, of whatever theological persuasion, would dissent from such broad proclamations as "Jesus Christ is the gracious mission of God to the world," or "As the body of Christ the Church has her life in Christ"—both affirmations from the PC's Union in Christ statement (Presbyterian Coalition 1998). It is the manner of faithful living demanded by the oppositional rejections derived from these affirmations, however, that separate the Presbyterian Coalition from, say, the Covenant Network of Presbyterians, a group devoted to affirming the place of gay men and lesbians in the life and work of the PC(USA).

These rejections (Presbyterian Coalition 1998) include "We turn away from forms of church life that seek unity in theological pluralism, relativism or syncretism," a clear criticism of the PC(USA)'s perceived surrender to non-Christian theologies and agendas, such as the Re-Imagining Conferences and aspects of the World Council of Churches (cf. Williamson 1999). "We turn away from forms of church life that discount the authority of Scripture or claim knowledge of God that is contrary to the full testimony of Scripture as interpreted by the Holy Spirit working in and through the community of faith across time." As is so often the case when the Bible is invoked in the course of a church dispute, implicit in this rejection is the notion that those against whom the PC fight are the ones who "discount the authority of Scripture" and "claim knowledge of God" that differs from that which has served the church traditionally. That, historically, Scripture has had neither a monolithic reading nor a universal interpretation, let alone a standard translation or an agreed-upon canon, is ignored. Finally, the rejection, "We turn away from forms of church life that fail to pray for and strive after a rightly ordered sexuality as the gracious gift of a loving God" brings the Presbyterian Coalition full circle, back home to the dispute over the place of gay men and lesbians in the Christian Church. The preamble to the Union in Christ document establishes the framework within which these rejections are located, a PC(USA) that is committed to "reaffirming its Christ-centeredness, reclaiming its biblical faith, and remobilizing its missionary service." All of which implies that the denomination as it is currently constituted and directed has abandoned these standards.

Building on the principles established by the Union in Christ statement, the Presbyterian Coalition's "Strategy for the Transformation of the PC(USA)" (Presbyterian Coalition 1999b) is a six-part plan that encompasses virtually all aspects of denominational life. The renewals proposed for mission and theological education are representative of much the document has to offer. In order to renew its sense of mission, the church must rediscover its "zeal for the unreached and a desire to see persons and cultures transformed to the glory of God," that is, the evangelistic conversion to Christianity of "unreached peoples." "Obstacles" to this goal include "an incipient universalism," a rejection of the foundational principle from "Union in Christ" that Jesus' "incarnation discloses the only path to God." For traditionalist Presbyterians, as for many other conservative Protestants and Catholics, one of the main abandonments of the last century has been the Christian principle of *extra ecclesiam nulla salus*— "outside the church, there is no salvation." In this case, the "church" means the larger body of believers who adhere to an exclusivist Christology and soteriology. Put differently, if Buddhists are no less beloved of

God *as Buddhists;* if Muslims *as Muslims* can expect salvation no less for their worship of Allah, and Jews no less for their rejection of Jesus as the Messiah; if Mormons, Jehovah's Witnesses, Wiccans, Santerians, and Druids can all grasp an equal measure of divine favor, then what compelling reason exists to follow the Christian, let alone the Presbyterian path (cf. Cowan 2000; Williamson 1998a)?

To counter this, the PC strategy paper (Presbyterian Coalition 1999b) proposes a number of initiatives by which the PC(USA) can contribute to missions projects intended to evangelize and convert the unchurched. Rather than withholding funds when congregations are unhappy with denominational decisions or policies, the PC strategy encourages church boards "to designate mission giving to acceptable projects within the denomination." In this, though, they are not averse to looking beyond denominational borders. Cultivating "strategic partnerships for Trinitarian Christian mission with renewal movements" within the PC(USA) is only one avenue; like-minded missions organizations in other denominations, as well as fundamentalist parachurch missions such as Youth with a Mission and Campus Crusade for Christ, are possibilities as well.

For the Presbyterian Coalition, theological education in the PC(USA) is in as critical a condition as missions (cf. Leith 1997; Williamson 1998c). According to the strategy paper (Presbyterian Coalition 1999b), "ideological currents alien to the faith of the church" now hold the theological education within the PC(USA) "captive." No longer are the colleges and seminaries of the church the guardians of the faith and the centers of preparation for those who will provide congregational leadership. Rather, they have become "primarily responsive to the interests and agendas of the academic guilds," and produce graduates "who are ill-equipped for pastoral ministry."

The response of the PC to these problems is more direct than for missions, and for obvious reasons. For the majority of Presbyterians whose commitment to the church may extend no further than weekly attendance at worship, missions work is considerably less tangible than issues of ministry preparation. If they ever meet a missionary, it may come as part of a missions awareness service or as a guest speaker in the pulpit. However, because anyone who does attend worship is affected by the worship leadership in one way or another, the issue of education for congregational ministry is one that hits much closer to home.

Consider the case of a newly ordained graduate from an institution like McCormick Theological Seminary in Chicago. During the course of her education, in addition to the core course work in biblical exegesis, preaching, worship leadership, and pastoral care, a student might also have taken classes on the history of the civil rights movement and the church's participation in it, the place of homosexuality in the church, or process theology. While these are hardly negative in and of themselves, they are often far removed from the concerns and experiences of congregations that student might be called upon to serve. Problems can ensue, for example, when the new ordinand finally arrives at her first pastoral charge, likely a smaller congregation, perhaps a multipoint rural charge. Replete with what she believes to be cutting-edge learning, she seeks to bring that learning into a congregation that is neither prepared nor willing to accept such teachings. The tension between the preparation for ministry received by students and the expectations congregations have of ordinands placed in their midst is often exacerbated by perceived (and actual) differences in theology, missiology, and liturgical understanding. There is a gap between the seminaries and the congregations that, in the minds of traditionalist Presbyterians, is only growing wider.

Or, consider a chapel service at Columbia Seminary, 1 of 10 PC(USA)-related institutions. Held in late 1998, it celebrated National Coming Out Day, an international event that offers gay, lesbian, and bisexual persons a socially supportive venue to "come out" to others about their sexuality. While seminary officials denied that the service was explicitly sanctioned by the institution, and while the content of individual chapel services remains the provenance of students and faculty, for traditionalist Presbyterians services such as this represent a clear and present danger to the health of the denomination. As well, according to *The Layman,* evangelical students who refused to attend once the purpose of the service became clear would only speak anonymously for "fear of reprisals from seminary professors and the presbyteries in which they are under care" (Kincaid 1998).

Similarly, earlier that year, noted theologian Rosemary Radford Ruether, whom traditionalists regard as a "radical feminist" (Sykes 1998) and a heretic, delivered the annual Sprunt Lectures at Union Theological Seminary (Virginia). In a RealVideo presentation archived on the *Layman* Web site (www.layman.org), *Layman* editor-in-chief Parker Williamson opines that the "fascinating gargoyles" sculpted into the exterior of the seminary buildings "are not doing their job" (1998e). Designed originally to ward off "rain or demons or both," Ruether apparently "slipped in right past the gargoyles" to deliver the lectures. In an "interesting sidebar," Williamson noted that Union was then under pressure to meet requirements mandated by two major accrediting organizations. He continued that "for many, it seems reasonable to suggest that Union Seminary should be more attentive to its scholarly and theological purposes than to ear-tickling heresies." While Union claims accreditation from both bodies in question, Williamson and conservative Presbyterians clearly link the question of accreditation with the decline in traditionalist theological education.

In light of these perceived problems, the Presbyterian Coalition strategy paper (Presbyterian Coalition 1999b) proposes a number of concrete actions. First, seminaries "that promote Trinitarian faith, uphold the constitutional standards of the church, and equip candidates for the mission of the local congregation" must be clearly identified. That is, following the rejections stated in the Union in Christ document, candidates for ministry in the PC(USA) ought to be directed to those theological schools that resist or reject the importation of nontraditional God-language, that deny homosexuality any normative place in the life of the family or the church, and that promote an evangelistic over a socially active missiology. Additionally, the coalition proposes that congregational financial support for these institutions be based on similar principles. Those seminaries that support the traditionalist agenda receive support; those which do not, receive nothing. Congregations are encouraged to "aggressively identify, recruit, and support faithful and gifted individuals for service in the ministry of our church"; that is, find and assist conservative students. Since students are not the only, or even the most influential participants in the seminary experience, however, the coalition also recommends that "promising candidates for advanced training toward service in seminary teaching positions" also be identified and supported. As theologian John Leith noted in his lament for theological education in the Presbyterian Church, "seminary faculties were increasingly appointed out of Ph.D. applicants and without any relationship to the constituency of the seminary" (1997, 89; cf. Oden 1995; Reeves 1996). Seminary faculty, while well trained theologically, had little or no pastoral experience, and so could relate neither to the lay constituency served by the seminary nor to the practical needs of students who would be called to serve that constituency.

VOICES OF ORTHODOX WOMEN (VOW)

While all reform and renewal movements are open to both men and women, the organizational majority of these groups is clearly male. The Voices of Orthodox Women (VOW), however, is one of the few reform and renewal groups established by women and, although their statement of purpose does welcome the involvement of men, exists primarily for women. The VOW message is unequivocal: "In submission to the Scriptures, we believe the intrusions of culture into the life of the church must be exposed and resisted; *most particularly,* that radical feminism is irreconcilable with biblical orthodoxy: an idolatry—in both church and culture—to be unmasked" (Voices of Orthodox Women n.d. [a]). Some conservative reform groups are dedicated to fighting policy changes around ordination or theological education; others take as their point of contention the introduction of nontraditional worship resources, such as prayers or hymns written in inclusive language; and, as we have seen, still others come into being explicitly to argue for the exclusion of homosexuals from ministry in the church. Asserting the primacy of conservative theology at precipitous moments in the church and adherence to what they define as the essential tenets of the Christian faith, VOW is committed to the reform of women's ministry in the PC(USA).

Citing "a contemporary culture that is in moral and intellectual free-fall"—a phrase that has come into greater and greater currency in reform rhetoric—they include among the problems confronting and distorting Presbyterianism "radical feminism" (with all of its attendant doctrines and ideological commitments), "sexual anarchy" (basically, any sexual activity outside of a religiously sanctioned heterosexual marriage), and "fundamentally defective understandings of Christian mission" (that is, the singular truth of Christianity taking precedence over any "dialogue" in which relative truths are recognized). VOW does not have an established membership; instead, the VOW Web site operates as an information network, clearinghouse, and feedback loop for the traditionalist opinions of its founders, a source of reprints of media articles and church presentations it considers relevant to its mandate, and a public forum for like-minded PC(USA) women to air their concerns about the state of the denomination. Like the Presbyterian Forum, cofounded by Sylvia Dooling's husband, Robert, VOW functions primarily as a venue for the opinions of emergent movement intellectuals.

The term orthodoxy has been appropriated by a number of conservative groups in their work to reform their particular denominations and will be discussed in more detail below (see also chapter 9). Recognizing that its use could be problematic, however, causing more confusion than it clears away, one of the initial questions that VOW answers is its own choice of the term. According to VOW (Voices of Orthodox Women n.d. [b]), in orthodoxy some will envision "bearded men in black robes presiding over mysterious, smoky rites"—an obvious, if somewhat dubious reference to the liturgical tradition and priesthood of the various Eastern Orthodox Churches. Others will think of closed-minded, often arrogantly self-righteous fundamentalists, "bereft of humility and love." VOW, on the other hand, distinguishes what it regards as the etymology of the word as it developed from "correct belief" as opposed to "incorrect belief" (that is, heterodoxy and heresy), to the meaning deployed since the great ecumenical councils of the fourth and fifth centuries C.E. (that which conforms to the credal statements developed at those councils). VOW understands its use of the term orthodox as locating it firmly in the midst of the apostolic theological stream that descended from those councils. This location occurs in two parallel ways.

First, by affirming the universal truth and atemporal nature of the conciliar creeds, VOW's faith is bounded by the theological limitations of those creeds. That these limits, these boundaries, however, are socially constructed and demand a measure of defense in the face of challenge to their authenticity and veracity is clear: "We believe it is absolutely essential for faithful men and women to defend this historic faith against the arrogant intrusions of contemporary culture" (Voices of Orthodox Women n.d. [b]). Essentially, these "arrogant intrusions" are interpreted as anything that has taken the church beyond the legitimate boundaries of denominational theology, doctrine, and practice as they are interpreted by conservative reform groups. The construction of boundary legitimacy, then, is intimately and inextricably tied to the co-construction of arrogant intrusion—the "Othering" process that is central to the emergence of social movements such as VOW. VOW believes that, at the very minimum, legitimate Christian theology is circumscribed by a fully hypostatic trinitarianism and the Protestant tenets of *sola Scriptura, sola fide.* Further doctrinal boundaries, those set by the Presbyterian *Book of Order,* for example, constitute the second margin by which VOW's orthodoxy is bounded and maintained. Here, three common evangelical themes are evident: belief in a God who is wholly other than creation, but who acts providentially within that creation; belief in a temporally linear *Heilsgeschichte* that moves ultimately and inexorably according to God's plan; and belief in the complete historicity and uniquely salvific nature of the Christ event as it is recorded in the gospels and interpreted evangelically.

Second, VOW recognizes that there will be those who oppose its claim to orthodoxy, who denounce its attempts to reform the church, and who will try to portray it as heartless fundamentalists bent on returning the PC(USA) to a social, cultural, and religious severity rivaled only by that of Calvin's Geneva. Sylvia Dooling (Voices of Orthodox Women n.d. [b]) contends, though, that "if such indictments do, in fact, come, we know ourselves well enough to know that they are not true—that they will merely be the rhetorical contrivances of 'voices' who hope to silence our voice without exposing themselves to the rigors of the much-needed debate." Rather than dissuade VOW, these other, more critical voices actually strengthen the group's resolve. In fact, like many other conservative reform groups, it is precisely in these countervailing voices that the very identity of groups like the Voices of Orthodox Women inheres.

Numerous issues attract VOW's attention, from homosexuality to the portrayal of women in PC(USA) culture, from church resources deemed inappropriate to church conferences it believes cross the line into outright heresy. Until 2000, for example, VOW had endorsed congregational use of a Bible study prepared annually by the staff and writers of *Horizons,* the PC(USA)'s bimonthly magazine for women. *Esther's Feast,* however, the study for 2001–02, was unanimously rejected by VOW's board of directors. According to VOW evaluators (Voices of Orthodox Women 2001), the study was eisegetic as opposed to exegetic, and the "consistent tenor and method of the study undercuts the biblical text it purports to illumine. . . . The Word is interpreted through the experience of women," they declared, "rather than submitting one's experience to the Word." Marginal glosses and study questions addressed to women's feelings were "insulting" and reinforced "the stereotype of women as those who are unthinking and overly emotional creatures." Because it portrays men in a consistently negative light, VOW alleged *Esther's Feast* "encourages division rather than reconciliation between men and women." This problem is exacerbated by the resources recommended for further study, most of which are "by professors and authors known to embrace radical feminist philosophy, and who are not concerned to uphold the essential tenets of the Reformed faith."

Arguably one of the most controversial of the many precipitous moments in recent PC(USA) women's history has been the Re-Imagining Conferences that began in 1993 and have continued in 1998 and 2000. Planned originally to celebrate the midpoint in the World Council of Churches Ecumenical Decade of Churches in Solidarity with Women, the first Re-Imagining Conference was held in Minneapolis and drew more than 2,000 people from around the world. An ecumenical congress with organizational participation from most mainline denominations, the conference was designed as a forum to re-imagine what traditionalist denominational members regard as incontestable kerygmatic statements and beliefs: the person of God, the person of Christ, and the nature of the relationship between God and humanity (cf. Berneking and Joern 1995). In addition to organizational personnel, the PC(USA) contributed more than $80,000 to the event. Advocating "thealogy" from a feminist-womanist-*mujerista* perspective, conference participants used various alternative names and images for God in ritual and liturgy, including perhaps the most controversial, Sophia, an aspect of the divine feminine. The Reverend Hilda Kuester, a Disciples of Christ pastor who wrote what became a very controversial milk-and-honey ritual dedicated to Sophia, and which was interpreted by many Re-Imagining opponents as a replacement for the traditional Eucharist, reflected later that she had been "waiting all my life to have a public opportunity to thank the Creator for sexuality, sensuality, and physicality" (Kuester, in Berneking and Joern 1995, 18).

Outraged by this and similar sentiments, many denominational members reacted in horror to media reports emerging from the conference. Conference organizers and participants were denounced as heretics and blasphemers, and accused of importing paganism into the church. Thousands of letters protesting the conference were received by various church officials, with hundreds of congregations threatening to withhold denominational funding. Mary Ann Lundy, a conference planner and associate director of churchwide planning for the PC(USA) was a frequent target of traditionalist criticism; indeed, she left her position in the wake of the Re-Imagining controversy (cf. Berneking and Joern 1995, 121–23). In an effort to clarify issues and ameliorate tensions, the executive director of the church's General Assembly, James Brown, sent a pastoral letter to all

Presbyterian congregations in January 1994. Reminding the church that this was not primarily a Presbyterian event, and that those who gathered did so as a diverse people of faith, Brown sought to defuse traditionalist criticism through assurances that many of the issues had been either interpreted incorrectly or taken out of context. With respect to some of the feminine imagery for God that was used at the conference, Brown reminded the church that, as it searches for a more inclusive language about God, any language it chooses cannot ultimately exhaust the mystery of the divine (Berneking and Joern 1995).

Neither action appeased conservative reform groups, which quickly realized that they had on their hands an issue that, if it would not so much galvanize support for *their* cause, would almost certainly reduce support for the more liberal wing of the church. For one thing, a bedrock principle of conservative reform and renewal movements is that the traditionally masculine language for God has been (and ought to be) interpreted as the only authentically biblical (and by extension liturgical) language. Unfortunately, in his attempt to mollify the concerns of Presbyterians, Brown simply affirmed what traditionalist members of the PC(USA) believed was wrong with the conference and its denominational supporters in the first place.

In response to the Re-Imagining Conferences as well as problems VOW perceived in areas such as the PC(USA) Women's Ministry Programs, the annual "Women of Faith" awards, and the National Network of Presbyterian College Women (NNPCW), VOW surveyed its own constituents in an effort to gather information on the level of knowledge about and support for designated women's ministries in the church. The survey instrument was designed in cooperation with the Presbyterian Renewal Network and was distributed to the VOW mailing list. Of the 1,100 surveys distributed, 315 were eventually returned. While VOW (Voices of Orthodox Women 1999) recognized the almost completely tainted nature of the survey sample and made "no claim to external validity beyond the people actually polled," they nonetheless believe that the "findings are an accurate representation of the opinions of a large population of Presbyterians whose judgments deserve to be considered carefully by those who direct the Women's Ministry Program Area" of the PC(USA).

Given the target sample, results of the survey were predictable. The Women's Ministry Program Areas were considered "too left-wing and divisive," "self-serving and abiblical," and "a disaster for years." Use of "Sophia" as language for the Divine, as well as the Re-Imagining Conferences ought to be abolished; the focus of women's ministry ought to be "on Jesus, not women." Current denominational leadership in women's ministries was not representative of PC(USA) women as a whole. And, because it is not seen as upholding the creeds and traditions of the church, support for the NNPCW ought to be discontinued.

While Sylvia Dooling admits the obvious methodological problems with the survey, she also writes in a VOW editorial (Dooling n.d.) that "VOW did not attempt to discover the objective truth by taking an opinion poll." In terms of the evolving cognitive praxis of the conservative reform movement, and the work of movement intellectuals, the VOW survey— and Dooling's statement about it—is a useful window into the nature of worldview construction and maintenance. That is, where they disagree with the cognitive praxis of conservative reform movements, the opinions of denominational Others, social facts which may contradict conservative interpretation of events, and the array of larger contextual issues that in- form and influence denominational processes simply do not matter. As a tactical excursus, while such exercises as these may serve to reinforce the validity of their own interpretations, if conservative reform and renewal movements ever hope to mount a serious intellectual challenge to denom- inational direction and decision making, attempts such as these to solidify data support for their cause will need to be seriously rethought.

THE CONFESSING CHURCH MOVEMENT WITHIN THE PRESBYTERIAN CHURCH (USA)

In many ways the Confessing Church Movement within the Presbyte- rian Church (USA) has brought the denominational children of John Cal- vin and John Knox full circle. Just as the reformers felt the need to stand for the truths of Christianity as they understood them against the per- ceived heterodoxies of Roman Catholicism (and later Anabaptism), many latter-day heirs of Presbyterianism believe they have arrived at a similar moment in the life of their church. What began with the Confession of 1967 as a prime example of theological slippage, but has continued with the growth of increasingly uncritical interreligious dialogue, poorly conceived mission strategies that are no longer centered on evangelism, and what many regard as the patent heresy of the Re-Imagining Conferences, now requires for many PC(USA) members a reaffirmation of the central theo- logical tenets to which they believe God calls all Christians. Tenets that they consider the PC(USA) as a denomination to have abandoned. And, just as the Presbyterian Lay Committee was one of the first active reform and renewal movements within what is now the PC(USA), it is also in the van- guard of the denomination's nascent confessing movement, providing Web site services, organizational support, and speakers for reform and renewal events that focus on a new Presbyterian confessionalism.

As a grassroots evangelical movement, the Confessing Church Move- ment (CCM) began on March 13, 2001, with a sessional resolution from the official board of Summit Presbyterian Church in Butler, Pennsylvania, a congregation in the same presbytery that brought Overture 00–5 to the 212th General Assembly. In no uncertain terms, the resolution laid out what the board believed were the kerygmatic elements of the Christian faith: an exclusive soteriology, grounded in the atoning sacrifice of an ontologically divine Christ; a reaffirmation of the Bible as the sole written revelation of God to humanity; and, a clear and explicit condemnation of any sexual activity outside of the confines of heterosexual marriage.

In conservative confessionalism such as this, confessionalism that arises as a result of denominational liberalism, theological subtleties do not well serve the cause of church reform. Rather, with varying degrees of success, attempts at clarity, precision, and statements void of ambiguity become the order of the day. Thus, the first clause in Summit Presbyterian's confessional statement (Summit Presbyterian Church 2001) begins: "We confess that Jesus is the only way to salvation and a relationship with God." Lest this still be considered vague or indistinct, the statement continues: "We profess and believe that Jesus and God are one!" and "We profess and believe that one cannot have a relationship with God outside of Jesus." Second, "We believe the Bible is the unique and authoritative witness for the church's life." Another example of how issues of manuscript redaction and transmission, translation, and contextualized hermeneutics do not well serve the conservative agenda, the statement continues: "We profess and believe that as the ages pass, there are no new revelations that show the Bible to be wrong or outdated." Despite the surface clarity of the statement, what it means at a deeper level remains unclear. Is the Confessing Church Movement arguing for biblical infallibility insofar as its account of the relationship between humanity and God is concerned, or does it intend a scriptural inerrancy that extends, for example, to the historicity of a six-day creation, of a literal Adam and Eve, or of a historical Jonah? Finally, citing 1 Corinthians 6:9–11, the statement returns to its precipitating issue—sexuality in the church: "We profess and believe that the Bible and Jesus Christ are clear that any sexual expression outside of a man and woman within the confines of marriage is a sin."

To this point, in the context of debates around these issues conservative reform movements had been satisfied merely to state their opposition to various denominational policies and initiatives, support them with appeals to Scripture and the creeds of the church, and lobby for their defeat or rescission. In the statement brought by Summit Presbyterian, however, an important shift occurred: a confessional theology was wedded to a confessional piety. The cognitive praxis that had been implicit in PC(USA) conservative movements was made explicit in what amounted to a reform manifesto. Both a profession of faith and the rejection of particularized behavior believed to contravene that profession were now tied together in the body of the confession itself.

In each of the three major sections of the statement (Summit Presbyterian Church 2001), following the doctrinal profession, a message is sent to the church regarding the practical implications of that section. That is, in the PC(USA) no person is to be ordained as minister, elder, or deacon who believes "that there are other ways to God, other ways to salvation, outside of Jesus"; or who will "officiate in any same sex unions, blessing services, marriages, or any other ceremony which invokes the blessing of God on sinful relationships"; or "who are involved in any un-repented sinful behavior, sexual or otherwise, from which Scripture calls us away."

By invoking the language of confession, the lines of debate are drawn in very different ways than was heretofore the case. Prior, there were issues of disagreement and dispute; and, however rancorous the argument, however bitter the words that passed between contending parties, both sides proceeded from ostensibly similar confessional ground. Now, though, in claiming for its own the language of confession, and particularly that of a confessing church, the playing field has shifted. What had been implicit and in many cases subtextual was suddenly rendered explicit and categorical. It had the potential to polarize the church further, pushing to opposite sides those who held the confessional high ground (that is, the traditionalists) versus those who had abandoned the confessions of the church (that is, the liberals). As will be discussed more fully in chapter 8, statements such as the Summit Presbyterian resolution are important landmarks in the evolution of conservative reform movements. As movement manifestos they contribute to the development and credibility of movement intellectuals, and they provide for the crystallization and externalization of the movement's cognitive praxis, an important component in the transmission of movement goals and values to succeeding generations.

In mid-March 2001, the Summit Presbyterian Church confessional statement was unanimously approved by the congregation. Nearly two weeks later, congregational representatives brought it to a meeting of the Beaver-Butler Presbytery for approval. If passed, the Summit statement would be adopted as the confessional statement of the entire presbytery. During the ensuing discussion, however, the statement did not receive nearly the ringing endorsement it had at the congregational level. Questions and answers about the orthodoxy of the statement, its implications for the denomination, and the basic legitimacy of Summit's position flew across the room. Finally, the debate was closed and the question called. 46 voted to adopt the confession; 42 voted to reject it. The motion passed—barely.

Within a few days, though, the Summit Presbyterian confession was posted on the Presbyterian Lay Committee Web site, and within weeks published in *The Layman*. Articles began to appear in both secular and denominational media about a confessing movement that had sprung up in the PC(USA). Within just a few months, numerous other congregations had joined the movement, offering up similar confessional statements. According to CCM statistics, less than three months after the Beaver-Butler decision more than 220 PC(USA) congregations, representing more that 83,000 members, had joined the movement. Not a huge number, considering the size of the PC(USA)—2.5 million members, in 11,200 congregations—but indicative of the seriousness with which many Presbyterians regard the situation nonetheless.

What the membership figure does not distinguish, however, is the number of people within those congregations who either opposed or were reluctant to join the confessing movement. No information was made available about the congregational processes used to arrive at the decision to support the confessing movement. In many instances, congregation members are no more in support of a decision to join something like the confessing movement than they are in support of the denominational policies that provoked the movement in the first place. Indeed, very often, congregations are microcosmic reflections of the denomination as a whole, encompassing as wide a theological spectrum within one church as the denomination does within all. There are a number of reasons why members might be reluctant to join, ranging from the perception that such a movement is one more wedge destined to split the denomination, to outright disagreement with the theological and pietistic principles contained in the confessional statement itself.

Confessing Church Movement spokespeople, however, are adamant that the movement is not a wedge to split the denomination; they have no desire to leave the PC(USA). Further, the central issue is denominational abandonment of those confessional principles embraced by the movement. "The main crisis in the PCUSA today is not about ethics or morality," wrote one pastor, whose North Carolina congregation joined the Confessing Church Movement just weeks after its inception. "Ethics and morality are what many people tend to talk about today when they don't want to talk about God. The main crisis is about revelation" (Burnett 2001). Like most conservative reform movements, the CCM perceives itself as a prophetic undertaking, calling the church back from apostasy to faithfulness, from heresy to orthodoxy, and from immorality to righteousness.

CHAPTER 5

A Voice for Repentance:
The United Methodist Church

EARLY CALLS FOR REFORM: THE GOOD NEWS MOVEMENT

Unlike the Presbyterian Lay Committee, it was not church involvement in the civil rights movement or America's escalating war in Vietnam that brought about the first of United Methodism's conservative reform movements. The drastic decline in mainline Methodist adherence, which would drop membership in the church by more than a million in a single decade, would not become readily apparent for several more years. Likewise, issues around homosexuality had not yet come to the fore. Instead, what generated the first reform movement in postwar mainline Methodism, at that point the largest mainline Protestant denomination in North America, was an issue that, on the surface, might appear almost mundane by comparison with later denominational conflicts. This controversy would not take place so much on the floor of General Conference meetings or in front of U.S. embassies, but in the basements of any number of Methodist churches, in the Sunday School rooms between flock-art posters of Noah and the Ark and papier-mâché models of the crèche.

Like its cousin to the north, The United Church of Canada, in the mid-1960s the Methodist Church introduced a new church school curriculum, replacing the one that had been in service for many decades. Departing from the path cut by less academically rigorous curricula, curricula that simply accepted and transmitted the classical interpretations of the Christian faith with little or no critical comment, this new material incorporated information and insights from more liberal biblical scholarship, a more open stance toward ecumenism, and a much diminished emphasis on traditional soteriology. This was to be the fledgling reform movement's first battle.

In the face of developments like the new curriculum, acute dissatisfaction that so few evangelical voices were making themselves heard in the Methodist Church prompted Charles Keysor, an Elgin, Illinois, pastor, to write "Methodism's Silent Minority" (1966), the first popular plea for orthodoxy in the face of advancing theological liberalism. Originally published in the *New Christian Advocate*, a magazine for ministers in the Methodist Church, Keysor's article outlined what he believed to be the "major evangelical convictions" that ought to be at the heart of the denomination, but were slipping rapidly to the margins" (Heidinger n.d., 13). While Keysor used "evangelical," "conservative," and "fundamentalist" interchangeably, he maintained that a more accurate term for all of these was "orthodox." Further, this orthodoxy had "developed a theological epicenter known as 'the five fundamentals' " (Keysor 1966, 10), the same five fundamentals that evolved from the Niagara Bible Conferences in the late nineteenth century and the fundamentalist-modernist controversies of the early twentieth: the inspiration of Scripture; the Virgin Birth of Christ; his substitutionary atonement; his physical resurrection; and especially his soon Return.

While Keysor characterized the last of these fundamentals as orthodoxy's "vibrant sense of eschatological expectancy" (1966, 12), he was considerably less sanguine about the future of orthodoxy within the evolving Methodist Church. Even then, the gap between the ecclesiastical hierarchy and both laity and frontline clergy—especially those who adhered to an evangelical perspective—was evident. "Persecution is not impossible," he wrote, citing a "high official in Nashville" who had vowed to " 'stamp out the last vestiges of fundamentalism from The Methodist Church!' " and a bishop who had "threatened to drive from his conference any man who affirmed from the pulpit Christ's Second Coming."

Presaging John Leith's (1997) reflections on mainline Protestant preparations for ministry, Keysor predicted quite correctly the "continuing eclipse of orthodox influence" in Methodist seminaries. Both evangelicalism and neo-orthodoxy, however, would gradually pale before the rise of a fully orbed liberalism in the church. For Keysor, the evangelical perspective seemed "destined to remain as Methodism's silent minority" (1966, 12). As a result, he declared: "Here lies the challenge: We who are orthodox must become the un-silent minority! Orthodoxy must shed its 'poor cousin' inferiority complex and enter forthrightly into the current theological debate." Directly challenging the popular notion that theological conservatism was all but exclusively the province of the uneducated and the unenlightened, Keysor insisted that "orthodoxy is more complex and more profound than its many critics seem to realize. Intellectual honesty—let alone Christian charity—demands more objectivity than the church now accords its silent minority."

After the article's publication, Keysor and those who began the Good News Movement (GNM) soon after were amazed not by what the Elgin pastor had written, but by the response it generated from the church at large. Reflecting on the earliest moments of the GNM, James Heidinger, for more than two decades the publisher and editor of *Good News Magazine*, noted that Keysor received more than 200 responses to the article, "most of them coming from Methodist pastors!" (Heidinger n.d., 13). Two major themes emerged from that correspondence, neither of which is uncommon in the social experience of marginalization: correspondents felt that they were the only orthodox believers left in the Methodist Church, and, because of that, frontline clergy (and laity) who were evangelical felt increasingly isolated from the denominational hierarchy and from their more liberal peers.

Those letters and telephone calls gave Keysor a clear mandate. In response, he helped organize the Good News Movement and launched *Good News Magazine*, the longest-running voice for evangelicals in the mainline Methodist Church. As I indicated, while the first controversy in which the GNM participated was not so obviously volatile as such later conflicts as the Re-Imagining Conferences and the place of gay men and lesbians in the official life of the church, it did mobilize the nascent movement and provide an initial reference point for its activities.

A year after the new curriculum arrived, Keysor's *Good News Magazine* ran a three-part series roundly condemning it for its lack of "a strong Biblical base" as well as its departure "from the historic Methodist doctrines" (Heidinger 1987, 22). The following year, a group of Good News members met with the denominational curriculum committee to discuss their concerns. According to Heidinger (n.d., 14), the evangelicals were treated "with obvious impatience and condescension." "One bishop," Heidinger recalled, "informed the Good News delegation that they must realize that all contemporary scholars support the Bultmannian notion that much of the Bible is myth." In the years since that initial battle, Good News has continued to monitor educational materials produced by the UMC, "evaluating both doctrinal content and the possible introduction of new God-language which would be unacceptable to most United Methodist evangelicals" (Heidinger 1987, 24). While the GNM has been highly critical of numerous positions taken by the church over the years, and often scathing in its criticisms, Heidinger and other members are clear that their primary concerns have always been theological and doctrinal, and that most of problems in the UMC find their roots in the departure from traditional Methodist beliefs.

Since 1970, the movement has convoked gatherings of evangelical Methodists for strategy and support in their shared struggle to reform the church. For them, as for all evangelicals, Christianity is defined by certain ineluctable beliefs, a kerygma that no amount of theological experimentation can breach and remain authentically Christian. Early in the struggle, and to offer a countervailing voice in the face of the UMC's increasing embrace of theological pluralism, the Good News board of directors appointed its own Theology and Doctrine Task Force, and directed it to write a statement of Christian essentials for the movement.

At the 1975 GNM convocation, held at Lake Junaluska, North Carolina, An Affirmation of Scriptural Christianity for United Methodists was presented for discussion, and later endorsed by those gathered there. Rather than a credal statement that declares "We believe," the Junaluska Affirmation is a doctrinal proclamation that echoes very closely the content of the historic creeds, as well as the Wesleyan Confession of Faith and Articles of Religion. Each article, however, begins "Scriptural Christianity affirms . . . ," clearly implying, of course, that those theological or doctrinal formulations that differ ought not be considered scriptural Christianity. Like the term orthodox (which implies, indeed requires the oppositive heterodox), scriptural Christianity as represented by the evangelical wing of the United Methodist Church is consciously contrasted with the unscriptural Christianity embodied in its more liberal wing.

Without doubt, the most visible component of the Good News Movement, and the major vehicle for its cognitive praxis, is *Good News Magazine*, begun by Keysor as a small digest and now a bimonthly magazine whose production quality matches that of any major evangelical publication. Feature articles, new clippings and commentary, announcements and advertisements, and correspondence from readers keep the reform and renewal agenda prominently before the church. Serving as the main venue for reform leaders, in the last decade feature articles have appeared on the nature of holiness in the Christian life (Gyertson 1997); the question of confessionalism within the UMC (Abraham 1996; Harper 1995; Kinghorn 1994); Celtic Christianity (Cagney 2000; Hunter 2000; Price 2000); spiritual revival (Davids 1995; Gabel 2000; Gyertson 1995; Perkins 2000; Robb 1998); and, of course, the often acrimonious debate over homosexuality in the church (Pannenberg 1997; Rutledge 2000; Seamands 1998; Socarides 1994).

Like the Presbyterian Lay Committee, wider denominational reaction to the Good News Movement has been mixed, to say the least. Early in its career, while it was vilified by critics as "JUNK!" (Heidinger n.d., 13), it was hailed by others, notably evangelical theologian Carl F. H. Henry, then editor of *Christianity Today*, as " 'a mighty fine beginning—congratulations' " (Henry, in Heidinger n.d., 13). Since that time, letters to the editor offering both brickbats and bouquets have arrived with predictable regularity. A sample of these reveals both the esteem and the opprobrium with which the Good News Movement is regarded.

"I am most favorably impressed by your keenness in ferreting the heresy in the UMC," writes one reader, a veteran of both overseas mission and the UM Board of Global Missions (Smith 1994). Another clergyperson is not so impressed. "Please do not send you [sic] judgmental magazine to the church I serve or to myself," she writes, contending that it is not the conservative theology of the GNM she finds offensive, but the "mean-spirited and self-serving" manner in which the Good News vision is so often presented (Schrader 1994). In that same issue, while one reader commends *Good News* for "exposing the 'Re-Imagining' Conference," another declares, rather unequivocally: "I write to protest in the strongest and most strident tone possible your vicious, heartless, un-Christian attacks on those who differ from your right-wing, exclusivist, fundamentalist position. I think it unconscionable that you look upon yourselves as representing 'typical' United Methodists" (Morgan 1994, 3). In another issue, one reader encouraged the *Good News* staff to "Keep up the good work, it sure is a breath of clean, unbiased air" (Frozene 1994). In the same issue, however, another complained that "Your uncomplimentary gift of the *Good News* magazine just arrived." This reader was "particularly disturbed by the negativism and destructivity" in articles by executive editor, Steve Beard, suggesting that "orthodoxy to him seems to be the radical right politically, then religiously" (Wolf 1994).

In addition to theological disputes over the norms of Christian faith and practice, claims to the separation of church and state, and the need to *keep* the two domains separate notwithstanding, in the battle for the soul of the church politics and religion are inextricably mixed. Indeed, one often becomes the *semeion* of the other. Mark Tooley, a frequent contributor to *Good News* and the director of United Methodist Action (UMAction), is a good example of this dynamic. Tooley has been critical of the UMC's General Board of Church and Society (GBCS) for a wide variety of offenses, including "opposition to the death penalty," "hostility to welfare reform," and "its aid to Cuba's repressive communist regime" (Tooley 1997). In one contribution to *Good News Magazine*, he was especially critical of Thom White Wolf Fassett, the general secretary of the GBCS, for his remarks in defense of these various church positions. Fassett responded the following month, affirming the role of the Good News Movement within the spectrum of the United Methodist Church while acknowledging at the same time its "selective reporting" and "particular editorial view." Distressed by Tooley's article, however, he continued: "When you employ a writer, representing a non-Christian, anti-United Methodist organization to produce a re-written and misleading fabrication of a speech by a general secretary of the United Methodist Church, the value of your advocacy and the integrity of your witness can no longer be taken seriously" (Fassett 1997). He continued that the "first step in restoring integrity is to publish the truth," and offered *Good News Magazine* the complete text of his remarks to the GBCS.

The letters to the editor, articles such as Tooley's, and the interchange between Fassett and the *Good News* editorial staff, are all instructive in the character of discourse that often takes place between liberals and conservatives both in United Methodism, and in much of mainline Protestantism. More often than not speaking past one another, neither appears interested in really hearing what the other side has to say. That Tooley (1997) represented Fassett's remarks selectively, for example, is clear. He castigated Fassett and the GBCS for "its hostility to welfare reform," but pointedly failed to mention that the GBCS's opposition to the proposed welfare reform bill (portions of which President Bill Clinton also opposed, even as he signed it into law) was based on its punitive nature. Imposing term limits on welfare without consideration of individual cases, rejecting education as valid work, and the bill's intention to punish those perceived as lazy at the expense of those truly in need, were all seen by the GBCS as unhelpful and immoral. None of this was included in Tooley's critique.

Fassett (1997), on the other hand, characterized the Institute on Religion and Democracy, the parent group of UMAction, as "a non-Christian, anti-United Methodist organization," when it is, rather, a parachurch political lobby operating from precisely the same religious dynamics (albeit from a very different theological standpoint) as the GBCS. For their part, rather than attend to Fassett's criticism, the editors of *Good News* defended Tooley and pointed out that Fassett had provided no specifics to support his allegation that Tooley's piece was a "misleading fabrication." "We remain unclear of what exactly Rev. Fassett is disputing," the editors (*Good News* 1997, 3) concluded, "unless, of course, he believes that differences of opinion are equivalent to 'misleading fabrications.' " A few months later, *Good News* published a letter from a reader (Salvidar 1997) who was grateful for the exchange, experiencing it as a "wake-up call." "After having read Reverend Fassett's letter," he wrote, "I now wish to join and encourage others to support Mr. Tooley's organization in its efforts to free the UM Church from the ultra-liberal influence of certain national leaders."

Rather than simply ask who won the argument—a fruitless pursuit at best—it is more important to note how both sides in the debate seek to control the symbolic terrain of the battleground. Who is misleading or misrepresenting whom becomes much more than simply a point of argument; it becomes a tactic in the unfolding struggle for legitimacy and authority within the denomination. For any social movement, cognitive praxis evolves in debates like this. While it may take the form of letters to the editor, essays by emerging movement intellectuals, arguments and counterarguments made between opposing constituencies, all contribute to the development and consolidation of movement positions.

ED ROBB EVANGELISTIC ASSOCIATION

One of the most prominent evangelical leaders in United Methodist circles is Edmund W. Robb, for nearly three decades the executive secretary and lead evangelist of the Ed Robb Evangelistic Association (EREA). In 1964, after pastoring large Methodist congregations in Texas for nearly 20 years, Robb met with a group of laypeople to discuss the increasing abandonment of orthodoxy by the Methodist Church. Unlike Keysor, who regarded the problem as the importation of neo-orthodoxy into the church, for Robb the problem was the replacement of evangelistic preaching with a social action gospel. Appalled by this development, Robb felt called to expand his ministry, to preach to a larger parish than simply his congregation in west Texas. And, two years after the organization of the EREA, Robb's bishop released him from a traditional pastoral relationship and appointed him a full-time evangelist. As he traveled across the country preaching, his concern over the future of the denomination grew and, as a result, he was responsible—either in whole or in part—for many of the reform and renewal movements that exist in United Methodism and wider mainline Protestantism. Besides the EREA, Robb participated with Keysor in beginning the Good News Movement in 1967; a decade later, he started A Foundation for Theological Education (AFTE); and, four years after that, with Michael Novak and Richard John Neuhaus, he cofounded the Institute on Religion and Democracy (IRD).

While rooted in similar concerns for the health of the church, each addresses the problem in a different way. Whereas the Ed Robb Evangelistic Association is devoted to renewing the preaching mission of the United Methodist Church, the IRD (which will be discussed more fully below) is dedicated to revising its ethical and social positions, and AFTE is aimed at reforming both the direction and substance of theological education in the UMC. Like many other mainline conservatives (for example, Knippers 1989; Leith 1997; Wainwright 1992), Robb considers the erosion of sound theological education directly responsible for much of the decline in the church. "If we have a sick church," he declared in a keynote address to the 1975 Good News Convocation at Lake Junaluska, "it is largely because we have sick seminaries" (Robb 1989, 1). To help cure the disease that had infected these institutions, AFTE's primary function has been to disburse the John Wesley Fellowships, which provide significant financial support to evangelical doctoral candidates. Ideally, upon graduation these new scholars would go on to teach in UM seminaries, thereby reforming the denominational education system from within (Kinghorn 1989). In addition, AFTE sponsors conferences and colloquies to further support evangelical students in the seminary process and provides an evangelically oriented academic journal, *Catalyst*, free to every Methodist seminarian.

As a full-time evangelist for more than three decades, Robb took his message of evangelical reform and renewal around the world, preaching across the United States, as well as from Russia to the Philippines, from Singapore to Peru, and from Latin America to the Middle East. Evangelism, however, and the evangelistic imperative, does not exist in a vacuum; it is, by nature, oppositional, and reacts to the perceived inadequacies of local religion and culture in an effort to effect a particular measure of repentance and conversion. When Paul went to Athens and preached on the Areopagus (Acts 17), he did not approach the Greeks as though they lived in a religious void. While the text says that he was revolted at the idolatry to which the city was given over, he used the Athenians' unabashed religious pluralism as an opportunity to confront them with their sin and convert them to the new faith he had brought with him from Palestine. Because it seeks to effect a change in personal (and thereby societal) orientation, evangelism is always based on confrontation with whatever are perceived as the dominant social or religious ills of the day. Though Robb's primary motivation in his preaching may be evangelistic, such confrontation is no different for the EREA.

Like many American evangelicals and fundamentalists, Robb associates the establishment of Christianity, especially Protestantism, with the flourishing of what is regarded as American-style democracy, freedom, and prosperity. At a 1990 conference on world mission and evangelism, organized by a number of Methodist reform and renewal groups, he opined that a "civilization is the incarnation of its religion" (Robb 1991, 119). He continued:

Some time ago I went to South America. I noticed that the continent had great natural resources, but nevertheless poverty abounds. I also observed that revolution, dictatorships and instability are characteristic of Latin America; but in North America freedom, prosperity and stability prevail. Why? I remember my history. The conquistadors came to South America in search of gold, while the Pilgrim fathers came to North America in search of God. (Robb 1991, 119–120)

He proclaims similarly in a *Challenge to Evangelism Today* editorial: "Wherever the Christian faith has gone, especially in its Protestant expression, political freedom has followed" (Robb 1990). While many of his denominational critics regard statements like this as a hyperbolic mix of evangelistic rhetoric, historical-geopolitical naïveté, and incipient racism, the equation of conservative Christianity with an almost dogmatic pro-Americanism is a note that Robb and a number of his conservative coreligionists sound with some regularity.

In 1982, for example, Robb participated in a debate sponsored by the National Council of Churches (NCC), a favorite target of mainline evangelicals, on "The Relationship of Christianity and Democracy" (cf. Institute on Religion and Democracy 1982). Billed as a dialogue between church leaders who had resolved the issue of whether the churches ought to be involved in political and social issues, but differed significantly on the manner of that involvement, the event was organized "to discuss directly the criticisms you may have concerning the approaches of the National Council and the mainline denominations" (Neuhaus 1982, 1). While Robb and Richard John Neuhaus castigated the NCC both for its perceived irrelevance and for its responsibility for the current "theological obscenity"—by which Neuhaus meant the division of the church along the lines of one's political positioning (Neuhaus 1982, 3)—NCC staffers James Armstrong and Arie Brouwer criticized the IRD for its narrowness of political and theological vision, and the "mendacious posturing" (Brouwer 1982, 20) of its founding document, "Christianity and Democracy" (which was authored by Neuhaus). Once again, while not all the discussion was captured, the published proceedings illustrate the tenor common to liberal-conservative conversation: dogmatic positions that affirm the values of engagement and dialogue, but maintain the realities of entrenchment and monologue.

"Christianity and Democracy," the founding document of the IRD and the initial statement of its cognitive praxis, declares that "anti-communism," while not "a sufficient political philosophy, . . . has been, and remains, an indispensable component in discerning the signs of these times. Those who did not understand this failed to recognize the bloody face of our age and, however benign their intentions, contributed little toward the establishment of a more humane world" (Neuhaus 1981). According to Neuhaus, unless one looks at the world through an anticommunist lens, one is both deceived as to the reality of the problems facing the world, and contributes little or nothing to their solution. Rather, according to Robb and the IRD, groups such as the NCC and the World Council of Churches (WCC) only exacerbate world problems by refusing to support the extension of American politics and economics abroad.

For many conservative members of mainline churches, one word summarizes the way they feel about the decisions their denominations have made and the directions they have taken: betrayal. Ed Robb is no exception, and his magnum opus on the topic, written with his daughter, Julia, is *The Betrayal of the Church: Apostasy and Renewal in the Mainline Denominations* (Robb and Robb 1986). *Betrayal* is not a theological treatise, but a jeremiad aimed at the religious left, and the Robbs reserve some of their harshest criticism for the various theologies of social and political liberation. In a *Challenge to Evangelism Today* article, Julia Robb charges that "missionaries all over the world," as well as "many denominational hierarchies and agencies" have accepted liberation theology uncritically and without opposition from "American Christians" (1987, 3). "Liberation Theology is taught by the radicals," declares her father, in "An Open Letter to My Moderate Friends." "This perversion of the gospel is supportive of violent revolution and has definite Marxist sympathies. We see this dramatically illustrated in their support of the Sandinista Marxist dictatorship and in their opposition to the democratic government in El Salvador" (Robb 1986, 4). In *The Betrayal of the Church,* the Robbs devote more than three chapters to liberation theology, especially as it has evolved in Latin America, a case worth examining closely more for what it does not say than for what it does.

Theologies of liberation are "extremely dangerous," contend the Robbs, both because they strip believers of their focus on the Divine and replace it with the human, and because the "idea of violence is inextricably woven into liberation theology" (1986, 118). According to the Robbs, liberation theologians argue that the only way in which the Kingdom of God will be established is through revolution, an overthrowing of all that keeps the people enslaved to poverty. "This is often explained as a type of self-defense, economic repression being the original aggressive action." This is a very curious argument, since elsewhere in the book, the Robbs spend a good deal of time castigating groups that advocate pacifism or support for disarmament and include a number of them in an appendix of "radical" and "unsuitable" organizations—for example, Clergy and Laity Concerned (a nuclear-freeze group); the American Friends Service Committee (a pacifist organization rooted in Quakerism); Fellowship of Reconciliation (an ecumenical pacifist group); and Witness for Peace (a nonviolent, high-risk accompaniment program).

What is most clear about the Robbs' own political theology is their polarization of Christianity and Marxism-Leninism, a floating concept that serves as a code phrase for all things anti-Christian, and by extension anti-American. Any group that seeks disarmament, that advocates for diminished American (now multinational and transnational) corporate involvement in the two-thirds world, or that suggests that free-market capitalism might not be the global boon both political and religious conservatives declare it to be, is by definition anti-American. Because of its inherent and often trenchant critique of free-market capitalism and the deleterious effects it has on society, this condemnation includes, of course, liberation theology (on various aspects of liberation theology, cf., for example, Berghoef and DeKoster 1984; R. Brown 1988, 1993; Gutiérrez 1973, 1984; Miranda 1974, 1982; Novak 1991).

In their arguments against liberation theology, the Robbs explain (1986, 130–31) what they regard as the real reasons for the grinding poverty in Latin America. Citing at third-hand, for example, a Venezuelan journalist (from an article in *Catholicism in Crisis,* a conservative Catholic magazine produced by Michael Novak, a well-known conservative intellectual and IRD board member), the Robbs blame the poverty in Latin America on "Hispanic culture," particularly its inability "to evolve into 'harmonious and cohesive nations' capable of improving the lot of their people." His-panic culture, according to the Robbs, is "impotent" in its geopolitical relations, unable to sustain a stable government other than a dictatorship, has made no " 'noteworthy' contributions to the sciences and arts," and suffers from "its own feelings of inferiority" (131). This being the case, "it is extremely difficult . . . to persuade Latin America to be objective about itself as it has a long intellectual history of blaming everything but its own nature." Its fundamental racism notwithstanding, what is conspicuously absent from the Robbs' construction of Latin American reality, and their consideration of liberation theology in general, is the long history of American interventionism and exploitation that has kept the various countries there poor and destabilized—all the better for capitalist invest-ment and control (cf., for example, Chomsky 1988, 1993, 2000; Chomsky and Herman 1979).

Closer to home, the religious left, of which the Robbs so vigorously disapprove, which they regard as entirely in control of mainline Protestant denominations, and whose influence Ed Robb's evangelism is dedicated to curtailing, is characterized by "an irrational faith in disarmament, sus-picion of American intentions and culture, disapproval of the free enter-prise system, and a belief in the goodness of many Marxist-Leninist governments" (Robb and Robb 1986, 192). As an explanation for these beliefs, which are clearly baffling to them, the Robbs propose a number of possible motivations, including "the search for meaning, insecurity, alienation from American culture, the secularization of American society, personal instability, self-destructiveness, anger, a tendency for Americans to embark on idealistic crusades, and simple [elsewhere he notes, "hy-pocritical"] self-interest" (Robb and Robb 1986, 193).

As other traditionalists have noted, though, for Ed and Julia Robb the problem clearly begins in the seminaries. Rather than being taught the various components of Christian truth, seminarians are encouraged to question those components, "to find out what they believe for themselves" (Robb and Robb 1986, 193). Because of this, as they quite correctly point out, there is often a significant gap between the belief structures of newly ordained clergy and those of parish constituencies they are called upon to serve. In addition to the strain this gap places on lay commitment to the church, they argue that it prevents many clergy from functioning effectively in the parish, and a number of these turn to work in the denominational bureaucracy (Robb and Robb 1986, 194). While they do acknowledge that not "all denominational bureaucrats are dropout liberal clergy, not even a great percentage," the Robbs contend nevertheless that such clergy are the ones who have gained denominational control, and "have set the tone and intellectual atmosphere for their bureaucracies" (1986, 194). They con-clude, not unreasonably, that since "bureaucracies tend to hire people with like ideas," the entrenchment of liberal Christianity within denominational hierarchies is assured (Robb and Robb 1986, 194).

For all this, what is clear for Ed and Julia Robb is the solution to the
problem. "Unfortunately," they write, "it is . . . rare for someone who has
worked for mistaken causes and believed false concepts to recant. Such
courage is unusual. Therefore, argument and presentation of facts will not
change a majority of the Religious Left. The only way on which its influence on the church can be lessened is to stop its funding or remove its
leadership from position within the denomination" (Robb and Robb 1986,
208). That is, reform must come more and more to resemble revolution.

UNITED METHODIST ACTION

If the Good News Movement is the doctrinal watchdog for the United
Methodist right, and the EREA its evangelical activism, the political lobby
of conservative Methodism is United Methodist Action (UMAction), the
UMC committee of the Institute on Religion and Democracy. Cofounded
by Ed Robb in 1981, the IRD is "an ecumenical alliance of U.S. Christians
working to reform their churches' social witness, in accord with biblical
and historic Christian teachings, thereby contributing to the renewal of
democratic society at home and abroad" (Institute on Religion and Democracy n.d.). While other conservative reform movements often claim
that their motives are other than political, that they are concerned merely
with the doctrinal reform of their church and want the church out of
politics altogether, UMAction makes no such claim. Working for "reform
in the mainline churches," IRD (in this case UMAction) seeks explicitly to
"focus on the political activities" of those churches (UMAction n.d.).
Rather than see churches cease political action and involvement, in reality
"reform in accordance with biblical and historic Christian teachings"
means to replace what participants regard as a liberal (read: "radical")
social agenda with one more congenial to conservative mores. In the eyes
of UMAction, however, this is a daunting, nigh unto impossible, task.
"Although you pay their salaries," quotes an UMAction information pamphlet, "United Methodist bureaucrats do not care whether you agree with
their extremist policies" (UMAction n.d.). In an effort to provide a countervailing pressure to this liberal hegemony, UMAction attends UMC
events and meetings, reviews UMC publications, and interviews UMC
officials. From these, it produces UMAction Briefing, a quarterly newsletter
containing short articles on items of concern to denominational traditionalists, specific "Action Items" that detail steps conservative Methodists
can take to affect the situation, and news commentaries posted regularly
to the UMAction Web site (www.ird-renew.org). Most of these are written
by UMAction's director and most visible movement intellectual, Mark
Tooley.

Usually framed in the context of opposition to positions taken by leaders in the UMC, UM*Action*'s political statements are an encomium of conservative social and political concerns, including continued support for a strong U.S. military (for example, Tooley 1999b, 2000c, 2000h, 2000l, 2001a), and for Israel against the Palestinians in the Middle East (for example, Tooley 2000f, 2000k, 2000m, 2001d); an anticommunism reminiscent of the Cold War (for example, Tooley 1999a, 2000a), including criticism of the UMC and the NCC for the nature of their participation in the case of Elian Gonzalez (for example, Tooley 2000b, 2000d, 2000i, 2000j); antihomosexuality; opposition to abortion; and criticism of nontraditional theologies and spiritualities (for example, Tooley 2000e, 2000g).

Since a number of other reform and renewal organizations concentrate their efforts on opposition to homosexuality, abortion, nontraditional families, and the perceived doctrinal decay in the mainline churches to which these are attributed, and because UMAction's mission is to focus explicitly on political issues, as examples I would like to discuss briefly their consideration of two issues, UMAction's support for the development and expansion of the U.S. military, and its advocacy for the continued operation of the U.S. Navy bombing range at Vieques, Puerto Rico; and the continued development and deployment of both nuclear weapons and the Star Wars antiballistic missile defense system. Both of these offer a useful window into the way in which UMAction's faith stance is inextricably related to its political opinions.

Whether as a projection of U.S. political or economic interests, or in real or putative defense of democratic freedoms abroad, a strong military has always been a cornerstone of postwar U.S. domestic and foreign policy. Many individuals and groups within mainline and evangelical Christianity, however, see this principle as detrimental both to the stability of nations and to the establishment of just societies at home and abroad. To take just one obvious aspect of this, money that is used to fund the research, development, and manufacture of increasingly sophisticated weapons systems is money that is, consequently, unavailable for social programs at home or legitimate aid programs abroad. The combat deployment of these forces, as seen, for example, in the Vietnam War and its aftermath, ongoing U.S. support for the Indonesian occupation of East Timor, various operations in Latin America, the 1989 invasion of Panama, the 1991 and 2003 Persian Gulf Wars, the 1999 NATO (though U.S.-led) bombing of the Federal Republic of Yugoslavia, the 2001–02 bombing of Afghanistan has, without exception, resulted in increased poverty and hardship in affected regions—a situation of which mainline denominations have been increasingly critical. Additionally, training facilities such as the U.S. Navy bombing range at Vieques, Puerto Rico, have come under severe criticism by church activists, as has the Western Hemisphere Institute for Security Cooperation (the recently renamed School of the Americas).

Consider Vieques, a small island off the east coast of Puerto Rico, with just under 10,000 residents. For decades it has served as a live-fire training area for U.S. Navy heavy weapons. In recent years, however, increasing numbers of protesters have entered or otherwise protested the range in an effort to halt Navy activity there. Citing environmental damage, noise pollution, the danger of unexploded munitions, and the immediate hazard to nearby populations from stray rounds, mainline church leaders and laity in the United States have joined with Puerto Rican advocates to seek the closure of the Vieques range. In news releases for UMAction and the IRD, Tooley, however, argues that these protesters are little more than "left-wing church leaders"—most prominently the UMC Council of Bishops and the General Board of Global Missions (GBGM)—"who support Puerto Rican separatism" (2000l, 2001a). According to Tooley, these "left-wing church leaders" are "anxious for a new hemispheric cause ever since the demise of Nicaragua's Sandinistas and other Latin American liberationist movements" (2000l). Though he acknowledges that few people would want a bombing range in their backyard, but that "they have to be located somewhere," Tooley marries the Vieques protests to a reduction in the U.S. Navy's ability to achieve force projection around the world.

"The Navy facility at Vieques provides the only arena on the East Coast for U.S. naval vessels, planes, and marines to test live-fire ammunition," he declares. "Without it, U.S. seamen and marines will be sent into combat situations without any live-fire training" (Tooley 2000l). While the one does not necessarily follow from the other, according to Tooley (who is citing media coverage of official Navy reports) this circumstance occurred in late 1999 when the USS *Eisenhower* and its accompanying battle group were forced "to leave for the Persian Gulf without adequate preparation" (Tooley 2000l; cf., for example, Bowman 1999; Bowman and Weisman 1999). In Tooley's view, the United Methodist Church's participation in and support for the protests at Vieques, what he terms the "illegal occupation of the facility" by demonstrators, subverts not only the ability but the right of the United States to effect its force projection around the world.

However, in criticizing the UMC's participation in protest movements, Tooley alleges that the GBGM "has even channeled funding to anti-Navy demonstrators at Vieques," granting "$5,000 in support of the illegal demonstrations" on the island (Tooley 2000l). In the article, he says no more than this and invokes the worst possible interpretation of events: The United Methodist Church is actively subverting the U.S. Navy, and by extension the U.S. government, by funding anti-Vieques demonstrators with money donated by decent, God-fearing Methodists across the United States.

When asked, however, exactly how much of that $5,000 was used in this way, and to whom the money was given, Tooley is much less clear. He claims that, while no specific group was mentioned, the amount "would have come" from GBGM budgetary documents. "The money likely paid for GBGM staff who participated in the demonstrations" (Tooley 2001c). In point of fact, Tooley has no proof where any or all of the money went. In reality, the money was sent to the Methodist Church of Puerto Rico, at the request of the bishop of Puerto Rico, Juan Vera-Mendez. According to Eliezer Valentin-Castagnon, a program director at the UMC's General Board of Church and Society, at no time was any money given directly to protesters at the Vieques range (Valentin-Castagnon 2001). In whatever capacity, however, in the cognitive praxis of the IRD, opposition to Navy activity at Vieques is, by definition, anti-American, antidemocratic, and, in the final analysis, antireligious. For Tooley and his conservative compeers, these relationships are simply self-evident.

Similarly self-evident is the ongoing need for robust U.S. nuclear and antinuclear weapons programs. When religious leaders opposed both the deployment of medium-range tactical nuclear weapons in Europe and funding for Ronald Reagan's Strategic Defense Initiative (SDI, or Star Wars) in the 1980s, Tooley maintains that their advice was "fortunately" ignored (2000c). However, he says, "some U.S. religious leaders are anxious to repeat their mistakes." Citing the nuclear disarmament initiatives sponsored by the leadership of mainline denominations, which "could lay claim to representing, however indirectly, over 100 million Americans," Tooley again appeals to popular geopolitical rhetoric in the service of a polarization between support for "democracy" (that is, U.S. hegemony) and "anti-Americanism" (that is, denominational positions challenging that hegemony).

According to Tooley (2000c), the initiative "fails to acknowledge how the Cold War nuclear confrontation ended—i.e., that U.S. strength and deterrence prevailed over Soviet weakness." This simplification of very complex social and political processes serves well the conservative agenda Tooley and his organization promote. The U.S. "won" the Cold War because the system it purports to represent (that is, democratic capitalism and a free-market economy) is inherently superior to the Soviet system (that is, despotic communism). He entrenches this polarization by critiquing the disarmament initiative's failure "to admit that nuclear weapons did play an incalculable role in the defense of human freedom, against both fascism and communism" (Tooley 2000c). Tooley himself, however, fails to suggest how these weapons of mass destruction helped the "defense of human freedom" in such places as Vietnam and Southeast Asia, Afghanistan, Chechnya, Bosnia and the rest of the former Yugoslavia and the Baltic states, the Middle East, South Africa, Rwanda, Somalia, Ethiopia, Tibet, and a large portion of Latin America—to name just a few. At the same time he accuses the framers of the initiative of treating "nuclear weapons as an abstract evil," he himself renders them abstract—or, more precisely, irrelevant—by avoiding these larger dimensions of the discussion. However, since they do not serve the purpose for which he writes, and for which organizations such as UMAction exist, these issues need not really concern him. That becomes abundantly clear toward the end of one article, "Church Leaders Repeat Mistakes over Nuclear Weapons" (Tooley 2000c). "Permeating this document and its supporting documents is a not very vague anti-Americanism," he writes, referring to the Interfaith Committee on Nuclear Disarmament's statement opposing renewed funding for SDI research, "These religious leaders are distressed that the U.S. might have missile defenses while others do not. The world would be at the mercy of hegemonic America!"

Which is, of course, precisely the Interfaith Committee's point.

While UMAction claims to oppose what it calls the UMC's "controversial political lobbying" (Tooley 2000h), it is not so much the *fact* of political lobbying that irks UMAction as it is the *nature* of the political stands taken. In a UM*Action Briefing* article on the antinuclear weapons initiative, Tooley (2000h) includes an "Action Item" asking supporters to contact the General Secretary of the GBGM and "urge him to exercise restraint in the Board's political statements. Ask him to focus on issues that unite rather than divide Methodists, such as alcohol and drug abuse, gambling, and programs to strengthen families." In a commentary on the IRD's opposition to the same initiative (Institute on Religion and Democracy 2001), "Tooley noted that IRD takes no position on the complex question of the best defense against missiles carrying weapons of mass destruction."

Of course, what Tooley and his colleagues fail to note is that both UMAction and the IRD *do* take positions. By critiquing the actions of mainline denominational leaders in terms of "anti-Americanism," alleged support for socialism and "left-leaning radicals," and opposition to nuclear weapons, they implicitly (and explicitly) take up the polar position. Attempts to indicate otherwise, their protestations of neutrality notwithstanding, often appear quite simply disingenuous.

UMAction's platform for renewal in the UMC is articulated in its Reform Agenda for United Methodists. Each of the agenda's 12 provisions details what the IRD believes denominational agencies must do in order to "reject all kinds of idolatry and reject worship of false gods and goddesses" (United Methodist *Action* n.d.). To reform the political agenda of the church, the document demands the immediate abolition of the General Council on Ministries (which is responsible for coordination between the various conferences, agencies, and program units of the UMC); the Board of Church and Society (whose portfolio includes most of the political and social positions opposed by the IRD), and the Commission on the Status and Role of Women (which the IRD holds particularly responsible for UM participation in the Re-Imagining Conferences). Once those units of the church that appear to deviate from appropriate social positioning have been eliminated, the IRD agenda, which reflects little more than the most conservative mores of government and business, can proceed unimpeded.

THE CONFESSING MOVEMENT WITHIN THE
UNITED METHODIST CHURCH

While the Web site for the Confessing Movement within the United Methodist Church (CM-UMC) does not say so explicitly, both the concerns the movement raises and the timing of its arrival in the church suggest that its precipitous moment was the 1993 Re-Imagining Conference held in Minneapolis. Less than a year after the 2,000 conference delegates re-imagined God as Sophia and shared what many members in participating denominations interpreted as a blasphemous communion of milk and honey, nearly 100 Methodist religious met to share their concerns over the future of the church. They agreed that there was now incontrovertible evidence that beliefs existed in the UMC that were incompatible with Scripture, as well as with both the Methodist Articles of Religion and the Confession of Faith. A year later, in 1995, over 800 United Methodists gathered in Atlanta to draft a statement in which those concerns could find confessional form. In the face of a theological diversity in the United Methodist Church that ranged from self-consciously fundamentalist to functionally neopagan, the nascent CM-UMC set before the denomination the limited alternative of an evangelical statement of faith and belief or a continued slide into heterodoxy and apostasy.

Like many reform and renewal manifestos discussed in this book, the statement drafted by the UMC's Confessing Movement is an exercise in what might be called contra theology, that is, a theological countervalence forged in specific opposition to prevailing trends within the church. In the CM-UMC's Confessional Statement, three affirmations of Christian belief precede three explicit repudiations of alternative theological interpreta-tion. The preamble reads in part: "The United Methodist Church is now incapable of confessing with one voice the orthodox Trinitarian faith, par-ticularly Jesus Christ as the Son of God, the Savior of the world, and the Lord of history and the Church" (Confessing Movement 1995). "Our Church suffers from private versions of the faith that do not find their root in Scripture," it continues. In response to what it regards as this tacit apostasy, the nascent Confessing Movement developed a statement de-signed to call the church back to theological, social, and ethical positions it had abandoned. Unlike many of the other conservative confessions, however, the CM-UMC statement limits itself to Christology, implying rather than explicating broader, derivative theological and ecclesiological claims and assertions.

Christologically, the statement is organized around the confession of Jesus Christ as the Son, the Savior, and the Lord. First, it declares unequivocally that confession of Jesus as "the one and only Son of God" is not merely one Christological option among many; it is open neither to personal interpretation nor individual opinion (Confessing Movement 1995). Rather, as "a matter of revelation," it is the fundamental marker of an authentic Christian belief. Consequently, adherents to the CM-UMC confession "repudiate teachings that claim the person of Jesus Christ is not adequate to reveal the fullness of God." In specific response to alternative gender images for the Divine, inclusive language, and the claim of some feminist theologians that the masculine Christ cannot incarnate a soteriology for women, the CM-UMC "[rejects] the claim that the maleness of Jesus disqualifies him as the true revelation of God." Finally, looking toward the next section in the confession, adherents "reject the claim that God can be fully known apart from Jesus Christ." That is, while any number of other religious communions can and do exist apart from an explicit confession of Jesus as the unique Son of God, including some which claim an explicit kinship with Christianity, none of these can make an authentic claim to full knowledge of God.

Deriving from the first confessional section, the second part of the statement emphasizes the soteriologically unique character of Jesus as "the one and only Savior of the world" (Confessing Movement 1995). Put differently, an authentic understanding of the atonement is rooted in the ontology of Christ, rather than, for example, an ethicomoral exemplar. In the face of alternative interpretations of the atonement—for example, in which Jesus functions in a manner similar to other soteriologic figures, or as a model in which our own true humanity may be found—the CM-UMC calls the church back to what it perceives has *always* been the orthodox position.

In addition to contra theology, the articulation of a confessional statement like this is also an exercise in boundary definition and maintenance—both essential components of a viable cognitive praxis. There is little danger inherent in Hindu, Buddhist, or even Wiccan constructions of reality, provided those constructions stay within the boundaries of their respective religious domains and, more importantly, stay *outside* the religious domain defined by allegiance to Christ. In their own domains they are either easily ignored, or easily rendered as the evangelistic Other, the so-called unreached people whose existence gives meaning to the Christian's own. Indeed, as the object of evangelistic concern, in their own domains their constructions of theological reality create the conditions for a meaningful construction of Christian reality. As the unreached other, they continually (re)constitute the evangelical raison d'être of the Christian Church. All of this suffers a significant shift, however, when these relative domains merge, when adherents claim membership in both domains and maintain the essential compatibility of both religious constructions of reality (cf., for example Reverend B 1996). Where there was once safety in clearly defined boundaries, there is now danger as those boundaries grow less distinct and more permeable. No more need prospective Christian adherents leave their foreign gods in the dust at the doorway of the church. Now they may bring them into the sanctuary itself, claiming pride of place for alternative, indeed, irreconcilable understandings of the Christian faith.

In the admission of these false gods to the Christian sanctuary—for this is how conservative reform movements regard such theological actions as the Re-Imagining Conferences—the Christian faith has quite simply ceased to be Christian. Thus, the crucial parts of the second CM-UMC repudiation read: "We oppose any redefinition of the Christian faith that diminishes or eliminates the saving work of Jesus Christ in order to make dialogue with others more agreeable. We reject any claim that regards the incarnation, crucifixion, and resurrection as merely one salvation among others" (Confessing Movement 1995). Though they are hardly alone in this, for the Confessing Movement there is only one possible mode of atonement. Accusing the denomination of both passively and actively diminishing one of the kerygmatic constitutives of Christianity in order to more palatably dialogue with other traditions, the CM-UMC alleges the essential abandonment of the Christian faith. Salvation through Christ is not one option among many; it is the only option, whether one acknowledges that or not.

Finally, the statement confesses "that Jesus Christ is the one and only Lord of creation and history." In and of itself, and however much they might debate the specific content of the claim, this is hardly a statement with which the majority of Christians would disagree. At this point, the particular theological content brought to the confessional statement by the CM-UMC is only implicit, referring obliquely to "those teachings and practices [that] arise [and] undermine or deny [Christ's] Lordship." What is implicit and oblique in the confession, however, is rendered explicit and direct in the repudiation. "We repudiate teachings and practices that misuse principles of inclusiveness and tolerance to distort the doctrine and discipline of the Church. We deny the claim that the individual is free to decide what is true and what is false, what is good and what is evil. We reject widespread and often unchallenged practices in and by the Church that rebel against the Lordship of Jesus Christ" (Confessing Movement 1995).

Lest one wonder too long what precisely the CM-UMC means by this, the first example it provides alludes specifically to the Re-Imagining Conferences, that is, "experimenting with pagan ritual and practice" (Confessing Movement 1995). Hinting as well at current debates within the United Methodist Church around various aspects of human sexuality, they also renounce "prevailing patterns of sexual promiscuity," "condoning homosexual practices," and "ignoring the Church's long-standing protection of the unborn and the mother." While these are entirely consistent with the conservative moral agenda as it is developed in almost all of American evangelicalism, these are two repudiations that could conceivably confuse the issue. And, lest they be accused of promoting only this agenda, however, the CM-UMC also rejects "consuming the world's goods without regard for the poor" and "resigning ourselves to the injustices of racial and gender prejudice"—values that, once again, few Methodists (or any mainline Christians) would have difficulty supporting.

Although the CM-UMC statement (1995) denies that individuals have the right "to decide what is true and what is false," its framers do not disclose precisely how *they* arrived at that very determination. Each confessional article begins with the phrase "in accordance with Holy Scripture and with the Holy Spirit's help." Yet, this is also precisely what many of those with whom they contend claim—the inspiration of the Holy Spirit and the recovery of biblical images for God that have been long suppressed by the Church. Once again, the interpreted, constructed nature of theology is hidden beneath the rhetoric of a named, objective certainty. While the individual may not be "free to decide what is true and what is false," it is clear that the Confessing Movement believes that it stands in the place of truth's arbiter.

Ultimately, the Confessing Movement within the United Methodist Church would like to see this confessional statement adopted by all "congregations, boards, divisions, agencies, seminaries, and conferences" in the denomination (Confessing Movement 1995). However, while the UMC has never had an "institutional guarantee of [doctrinal] diversity," neither has it had a similar guarantee of doctrinal homogeneity, a set of protocols by which significant deviance from a given denominational standard may be measured. If the CM-UMC's confessional statement were to be adopted, then such a standard might conceivably be realized, and the ability of the CM-UMC and groups like it to monitor doctrinal compliance enhanced. Although this is an unlikely scenario, the Confessional Charge declares "we will vigorously challenge and hold accountable those that undermine this confession."

EXCURSUS: E-SPACE IN THE SERVICE OF CONSERVATIVE REFORM

Prior to the advent of the Internet, only a few prominent individuals were able to function as movement intellectuals and play more than a passive role in the construction of mainline reform and renewal's cognitive praxis. Others could sign petitions, attend rallies, purchase literature, and interact with each other in support of their common perceptions and objectives. While all these are important aspects of the "ongoing conversation" Berger and Luckmann deem key to the maintenance of any particular worldview (1966), by and large, they could not participate in the *production* of the materials on which that worldview was based. They lacked access to the mechanisms of reform and renewal authority, to the creation of its cognitive praxis. Limited by the market constraints of commercial publishing, or the often prohibitive expense of self-publishing, they could participate primarily only as consumers of the reform and renewal's cognitive praxis; participation as contributors eluded them.

In 1993, that changed somewhat with the arrival of HTML (Hypertext Markup Language, the fundamental medium of the Internet). Over the next few years, Internet service providers began to appear with greater and greater regularity; home computers became more common, as did public access to computers through educational institutions and libraries; telephone companies began to include Internet service as a regular option in their standard connection packages. As Jeffrey Hadden and I have noted elsewhere, with WYSIWYG ("what you see is what you get") page editors, such as Dreamweaver or Microsoft FrontPage, "publishing on the Web became a domain no longer restricted to those conversant in the arcana of HTML or Java script . . . And, publication itself, long the Holy Grail for many a coffee table typist, is available to anyone with Internet access, server bandwidth, and thirty or forty dollars for the WYSIWYG software" (2000b, 4–5).

Such is the case with the "Unofficial Confessing Movement Page" (www.ucmpage.org), the Internet project of John Warrener, until 2001 the pastor at Palmyra Road United Methodist Church in Albany, Georgia (and now the pastor of Holy Hands Christian Fellowship, a congregation with no specific denominational affiliation). Appearing at the top of the site, the Unofficial Confessing Movement Page announces that "this Web site is 'unofficial' and in no way represents the views or opinions of 'official movements.' Its purpose is to provide timely information regarding movements of spiritual, biblical, and traditional Wesleyan Methodist renewal and concern in the Churches called Methodist." This disclaimer is important because Warrener is one of those traditionalists who believes the same alienation that exists between the denominational hierarchy and the laity also exists between what he calls the "elitist" reform movements—those that have some measure of institutionalization, like Good News and the IRD—and the grassroots clergy and laity who also oppose denominational decisions, but who lack access to the larger reform and renewal agenda. Warrener maintains that the true "remnant faithful" within the UMC have already left the denomination; those who remain and declare themselves members of organized reform and renewal movements are simply protecting their own measures of institutional investment—power, prestige, and, not insignificantly, pension funds.

His own departure from the UMC notwithstanding, for several months Warrener continued to operate the Unofficial Confessing Movement Page as a clearinghouse for what he considered the true grass roots of conservative reform in the church. It was the host site for a number of entries into the field, including e-zines such as *Josiah*, *Jude*, and *Michael's Sword*. Each of these electronic magazines is a mechanism by which the contributors can both express their outrage at the directions in which their church is going and contribute to the ongoing evolution of reform and renewal's cognitive praxis. Because those with access to the Web are likely to go there first for information, the Internet has opened up additional venues in the knowledge space created by these reform and renewal movement. Those who might not otherwise contribute suddenly find themselves with a potential audience as large as any claimed by institutional reform groups.

In addition to hosting these e-zines, Warrener's page also included an electronic bulletin board on which participants could post messages related to reform and renewal issues, a long list of reform-related articles acquired from a variety of sources, a link to the accountability watch of the Coalition for United Methodist Accountability, and the complete text of four books related to Methodist decline and renewal efforts (Morris n.d.; Robb and Robb 1986; Willimon and Wilson 1987; Wilson n.d.).

One of the e-zines Warrener hosted is *Josiah*, the product of a young UMC pastor named James Gibson. A graduate of Asbury Theological Seminary and ordained in 1993, Gibson has a flair for the dramatic in his writing and is active in both the Confessing Movement and the UMC anti-abortion campaign, serving on the advisory board of Lifewatch, the Taskforce of United Methodists on Abortion and Sexuality. Between 1994 and 1999, he was also the editor-in-chief of *Josiah*. While two issues of *Josiah* were mailed out in print form, its basic format was the electronic magazine, which Gibson distributed to a closed email list whenever he felt the situation in the church demanded it.

In the early part of his ministry, he regarded much of what passed around him for Methodism as a "monster which is raging out of control" (Gibson 1994a). Like Warrener, though, Gibson has grown disillusioned with organizations such as the Confessing and Good News movements, seeing little difference between them and the denominational hierarchy they oppose. Both, he believes, are desperately out of touch with the frontline clergy and the laity of the church. Among other things, he cites different strategies of recruitment to the Confessing Movement. In his own conference, South Georgia, reform supporters petitioned to have the entire conference join the Confessing Movement as a single jurisdictional unit. According to Gibson, though, this ran counter to the recruitment strategy favored by the institutionalized Confessing Movement, which wanted to populate the reform and renewal movement from the top down with large membership churches and "big steeple pastors."

At this point, Gibson and many of his younger colleagues see the reform of the UMC through the reassertion of doctrine as a dead end. The contending parties are simply too far apart. In their opinion, liturgical renewal centered in the set form of the Methodist Service of Worship is now the order of the day. A conservative reform of the United Methodist Church is still the agenda; it is now the manner in which that agenda will be carried out that divides the movement.

"The very term 'United Methodist' is an oxymoron," Gibson wrote in 1999, "and the denomination has largely become an embarrassment to Christianity in general and Protestantism in particular." Of what use, he asked, not unreasonably, are evangelical overtures, petitions, and resolutions made to the denominational hierarchy in hopes of either changing or entrenching the disciplines and statutes of the church when congregations, clergy, and bishops openly defy such statutes as already exist? Referring to several highly publicized holy union ceremonies performed by UMC clergy for gay and lesbian couples, Gibson declared that "widespread disobedience by rebel clergy hell-bent on forcing the church's blessing on deviant sexual relationships is a painful illustration of the folly of tired old evangelical strategies that focus on General Conference as the main battleground. It should be clear by now," he continued, "that evangelical priorities are misdirected." In this, Gibson is part of a younger generation of clergy who are unwilling to seek reform from within a denominational structure that it has deemed unresponsive to that generation's needs and vision. Not insignificantly, this includes the elder generation of conservative reform movements, and new efforts such as the Coalition for United Methodist Accountability. "Evangelical legislation," he writes, "is a dead letter in a denomination so bloated with bureaucracy that accountability has long been a joke" (Gibson 1999).

His distaste for any mode of institutionally oriented reform extends even to the election of evangelical bishops within the UMC. In 1996, while he initially lauded the election of G. Lindsey Davis as the bishop responsible for the North Georgia Conference as one "widely hailed by evangelicals, including leaders of Good News and the Confessing Movement," the blush quickly left the rose (Gibson 1999). In 1998, a select committee of the 5,000-member First United Methodist Church (FUMC) of Marietta, Georgia, pastored by the Reverend Charles Sineath, published a 75-page document (First United Methodist Church [Marietta] 1998) titled "Report on the Doctrinal Integrity of The United Methodist Church," in which the committee detailed what it believed were substantial "instances of unfaithfulness to the apostolic faith and the denomination's Doctrinal Standards, and to church law and discipline." As a result of these findings, and in protest of them, the FUMC Marietta elected to redirect a certain percentage of its apportionment (the amount each congregation pays annually to the parent denomination), totaling nearly $60,000, away from areas it believed tainted by unfaithfulness and toward ministries which were more in line with its conservative theology and evangelical missiology. As a result of this, rather than support his evangelical pastor and congregation, Bishop Davis questioned Sineath's pastoral effectiveness, despite protests from the congregation that there were far more people involved in the investigation and reporting process than simply the pastor. A year later, after 22 years in ministry at FUMC Marietta, Sineath was informed by Davis that he would not be reappointed there.

Although Gibson wrote his article prior to Sineath's removal, it seems clear that he saw the handwriting on the sanctuary wall at FUMC Marietta. What incensed him further was the perception that "eminent evangelicals are willing to tolerate a bishop threatening, bullying and intimidating a local evangelical congregation which has taken a conscientious action against the subversive activities of church agencies" (Gibson 1999). The "eminent evangelicals" to whom Gibson referred are the same reform and renewal elite from which he and his conservative colleagues feel so alienated. Rather than fight for the renewal of his denomination alongside those he feels have patently capitulated, "a new generation of evangelicals is desperately seeking to articulate a new vision" (Gibson 1999).

In his call for submissions to *Josiah*, Gibson included a somewhat ironic editorial condition: "Articles should exhibit the highest standards of journalistic integrity and ethics" (Gibson n.d.). In their often acerbic rhetoric, however, his own articles often reveal the depth of frustration and anger he feels toward the denomination of which he is a part, and to which he has dedicated his life as a pastor. Comparing the official response of the United Methodist Women's Division to its participation in the 1993 Re-Imagining Conference to "a bad television situation comedy," Gibson notes that "there is nothing funny about it, except its insipid ineptitude" (Gibson 1994a). Responding to a document titled "A Critical Challenge to the Confessing Movement," apparently written by "seminary presidents, prominent clergy, and theologians" (Green 1997), Gibson calls the document "a pathetic, poorly written treatise issued from a typewriter in 1996 by a group of liberal theologians who apparently did not have access to modern computer word-processing technology" (Gibson n.d.). Arguing that the influence of the UMC's radical fringe has peaked, he continues:

True, this radical fringe controls large sectors of official Methodism. But those sectors are mostly unnecessary appendages of an unnecessary and increasingly irrelevant bureaucracy. Radical control of boards, agencies and other entities merely insures the eventual dissolution of much of what we know as "official" Methodism. Evangelicals will shed no tears when the General Board of Church and Society, Commission on Status and Role of Women and Commission on Christian Unity and Interreligious Concerns collapse of their own weight; and radicals will not shout for joy. (Gibson n.d.)

Vocationally, Gibson is in a definite minority in his church. According to Louisville Institute associate director David Wood, less than 7 percent of ordained clergy in the UMC are 35 years of age or younger, those for whom ministry is a first career choice, rather than a second or third; similar, often lower figures obtain for other mainline Protestant denominations. For the United Methodists this constitutes a drop of 20 percent over the past 25 years (Wood 2001, 18). One of the reasons, suggests Wood, is the alienation younger clergy feel when they compare themselves to their peers in secular employment. Rather than recognition and reward for creativity and innovation, these younger clergy "feel a strong sense of marginalization—not only in relation to the culture at large but in relation to their own congregational and institutional cultures as well" (Wood 2001, 19). This clearly describes young evangelical clergy such as James Gibson and, following certain aspects of status inconsistency and structural strain theories, contributes to an explanation of their dogmatic commitment to objectivity in the vocational domains of theology, doctrine, and liturgy.

If experimentation in any of these domains increases the strain felt at the local professional level—as it certainly does in instances such as the Re-Imagining Conference, the re-evaluation of doctrine in light of denominational debates over sexuality, and the introduction of such worship modes as seeker-sensitive infotainment and edutainment—then the way to reduce the strain is to seek solid, objective criteria for each. For conservative reform movements in the UMC, those criteria reside in dogmatic affirmations about the Bible and its interpretation, the *Book of Discipline* and its jurisdictional deployment, and the *Book of Worship* and its immutable convention. Similarly, Gibson sees the strain evident in "the intimidation placed upon local pastors and churches to conform to the principles of pluralism and diversity, as decreed by the elite brood who have appointed themselves the exclusive arbiters of truth for the church today" (Gibson 1996). "The Body of Christ," he wrote elsewhere, "is infected with a cancer known as liberalism. Worse yet, this cancer has now mutated into numerous deadly strands, variously called pluralism, diversity and inclusiveness" (Gibson 1995). His response, like others in conservative reform groups, is to reduce the strain of disease through a therapeutic appeal to objective authority beyond the reach of mutable social construction. As Patricia Looper, who was listed by Gibson as the managing editor of *Josiah*, declared: "We must stifle, muffle, smother and squash any other teaching within the United Methodist Church" (Looper 1995).

Early in their careers, both Gibson and his colleague, Paul Stallsworth, another young evangelical UMC pastor and occasional contributor to his e-zine, believed that doctrinal adherence was the path to renewal in the church. Though the church had not "heard the last of 'Sophia' and other such faddish heresies," wrote Gibson in 1994, "the folly of such irresponsible theology has now been exposed for all the church to see" (1994). In a similar piece, and echoing Gibson's condemnation of "the absolute corruption of the easy pluralism of our church and old-line Protestantism in America," Stallsworth (1994) drew an important working distinction between theology and doctrine. While theology, "undertaken by individual clergy and laity, is experimental and exploratory, . . . church doctrine is settled. Doctrine is constitutional for the whole church." Vagrant theologizing aside, "church doctrine is what is now called for." By 1997, however, Stallsworth's sentiments had shifted. Like statutory renewal in the face of those who flaunt the statutes, doctrinal renewal had proven itself somewhat less than effective in the face of those who reject the binding nature of doctrine. A true grassroots renewal, they reasoned, a reformation of the church that finds its life in the people who constitute the church, must begin with worship, with the liturgy, with the central act of the church's life (Stallsworth 1997).

While Stallsworth acknowledged that the "Confessing Movement is now providing a helpful and hopeful address to our doctrinally challenged denomination" (Stallsworth 1997), he pointed out that that address may prove ineffectual in light of the "timidity" with which many United Methodist pulpits are currently occupied. "It seems that we United Methodist preachers do not have the ability to say Yes to the Gospel of Jesus Christ and No to the many false gospels that are being peddled out there in the religious marketplace." For Stallsworth, the answer to the weakness he perceives in the pulpit is a return, not to doctrine, but to the Service of Worship as it is laid out in *The United Methodist Book of Worship.*

The weekly Service of Worship—including the preaching of the Word of God and the faithful administration of the Sacraments—is not open to cutting and pasting, subtracting and adding, based upon the whims of the pastor and/or the congregation. The Service of Worship is not open to manipulation for the sake of pleasing discriminating (or non-discriminating) consumers or religious goods and services. The Service of Worship is a given. It has a given order. It has a set form. The Christian Year, the order of service, the rituals for Holy Baptism and for Holy Communion, and the Church's prayers are not just for fussy Episcopalians or liturgical fundamentalists to employ. Rather, they are liturgical structures—given by God for the benefit of the whole Church, including The United Methodist Church—to witness to Jesus Christ as the People of God. (Stallsworth 1997)

Of most interest in this passage is the stipulatory nature, not of Christian worship as a religious concept, but of the specific liturgical form which that worship must take. The Service of Worship is "given by God," and "not open to manipulation"; it has a "given order," a "set form," a structure apparently open neither to liturgical interpretation nor formulary experimentation. In the movement of reform and renewal from the primacy and unalterability of the biblical witness, to the immutable nature of church doctrine, and finally to the permanent conformation of worship, it is the search for some measure of certainty that stands out most clearly. Because worldviews are inherently unstable, wrote Berger and Luckmann, they are ever in search of support for their shaky plausibility structures (cf. Berger 1967; Berger and Luckmann 1966). By its very nature, then, experimentation, whether theological, doctrinal, or liturgical, challenges the essential nature of the accepted forms and must be met with a renewed commitment to the "faith once delivered unto the saints" (Jude 3). While one might make a case for biblical inspiration, and either an infallibility or inerrancy based on it, and while one might derive from that inspiration both theology and doctrine to which one could ascribe a measure of immutability, to suggest for the Service of Worship both a similar inspiration and a similar permanence seems to ignore anew the constructed nature of religious thought and practice. However, in language strikingly reminiscent of the Episcopal traditionalists who are opposed to new versions of the *Book of Common Prayer,* and whom we will consider in the next chapter, Stallsworth concludes that "liturgy is taken as a given, and its participants are shaped to conform to it. People and their needs are not taken as given; they are not allowed to shape the liturgy" (Stallsworth 1997).

Forgetting, of course, that it is precisely people who *have* shaped the liturgy over the entire life of the Christian Church.

CHAPTER 6

Dissensus Fidelium: The Anglican Communion in North America

As have their Presbyterian and Methodist colleagues, Anglican and Episcopalian churches—those denominations that maintain their episcopal communion through the See of Canterbury—have also struggled with liberalism in theology, as well as changes in the way the church deals with issues of sexuality, the ordination of women, and the perceived abandonment of traditional Anglo-Catholic liturgical foundations. Recent conservative reform movements within these church communities in North America have organized themselves in opposition to four basic issues: the introduction of new and revised liturgical resources, the ordination of women, denominational discussions around same-sex unions, and the possibility of the ordination of gay men and lesbians. An alternative Anglican province in North America, one dedicated to theological and liturgical traditionalism, has also emerged. Since the precipitous moments generated by discussions over homosexuality in the church are treated at length in other chapters, the recent election of the Reverend Gene Robinson as the first openly gay bishop in the Episcopal Church notwithstanding, in this somewhat shorter chapter, I would like to consider the Anglican communion in terms of the situation suggested at the end of the preceding chapter: deviance from liturgical traditionalism, and traditionalist responses to it.

LITURGICAL TRADITIONALISM: PRAYER BOOK SOCIETIES

Dispute over what constitutes the appropriate and authoritative Anglican liturgy has been one of the main controversies to shake the Anglican communion worldwide. In recent years, liturgical expression ranging from Thomas Cranmer's *Book of Common Prayer* (*BCP*, complete with archaic language) to Matthew Fox's technocosmic mass (complete with light show and liturgical dancers) have competed for Episcopalian attention. Fox's innovations notwithstanding, in North America, specifically the Episcopal Church (USA) (ECUSA) and the Anglican Church in Canada, the following two fictional episodes (based on Curry 1998) illustrate the problem as it is perceived by many of "God's chosen frozen."

For as long as any of the members could recall, the Episcopal parish of St. Swithin's-on-the-Green had been a prayer book congregation. Worship every Sunday was conducted much as it had been in Anglican churches since the time of Thomas Cranmer. Indeed, despite the thousands of miles that separated them, that one Holy Rite of the Eucharist bound the tiny congregation of St. Swithin's to every other Anglican church around the world. Their eucharistic prayers the same, their readings and collects identical—all announced through the time-honored phrases of the *Book of Common Prayer* that St. Swithin's-on-the-Green was a religious community that held its doctrine and worship life in *common* with every other congregation that followed Cranmer's venerable liturgical system. That remained true even when the parish got its new priest, the Reverend Allan Abernathy. Educated at one of the more liberal denominational seminaries, conversant with the latest biblical hermeneutics, cutting-edge theology, and liturgical innovation, the Reverend Abernathy sought to move the congregation in the direction of a more progressive (read: "sophisticated") liturgical and theological life. His homilies laid before his congregants the latest news from the Jesus Seminar, the most up-to-date ecumenical speculations, and continual calls to move beyond the boundaries of what he regarded as their staid traditionalism.

The one thing the congregation would not give up, however, was its devotion to and use of the *Book of Common Prayer* in Sunday worship. Every attempt by Abernathy to introduce alternative liturgies, whether based on the Anglican Church in Canada's *Book of Alternative Services* or provided by his own denominational worship committee, was met with stoic refusal to change. "Allan's a nice enough guy," said one longtime member of the congregation. "But we know what we believe, and it's in the *BCP*. No one can take that away from us."

Consider, on the other hand, St. James Anglican, a large urban parish, with a great number of outreach programs, a wide range of educational opportunities both for congregants and for members of the wider community, and a reputation for beautiful music and liturgical experimentation. When the Reverend Rita Thomas came to St. James, however, she wasn't quite sure what to expect. Even though she had been educated in a similar institution as Abernathy, one which de-emphasized if not ridiculed the place of the traditional *BCP* in the worship life of the modern church, she has maintained her own devotion to the *Book of Common Prayer* as the sole repository of Anglican doctrine and liturgical practice. More than 400 years after his untimely passing (he was burned at the stake during the reign of Mary Tudor), Cranmer's liturgical system still guided both her daily devotions and her understanding of what it means to *be* an Anglican. Her efforts to introduce the *BCP* into the life of St. James, however, met with no more success than that of Abernathy to move St. Swithin's away from it.

Early on Wednesday mornings, before the round of regular St. James activities begins, a few parishioners meet with her to celebrate morning prayer according to the *BCP*. The ancient prayers are read; the prescribed readings offered; a sense of Anglican connection— communion—is maintained. While they tolerate it, though, not a few of St. James more prominent members look down on the Wednesday morning meetings as an ill-considered return to a less-enlightened period in Anglican history. "If they want to live in the sixteenth century, let them," opined the chair of the Altar Guild. "St. James is committed to moving forward in faith, and no one can stop that."

Of these two examples, Curry (1998) notes: "With the first, the faith is proclaimed and participated in by the faithful regardless of the intent of the celebrant; with the second it is altogether ambiguous what is being proclaimed and what is being participated in despite the intent of the celebrant." To save the *BCP*, which is seen by many as the sole touchstone of Anglican identity, prayer book societies have been formed in Canada, the United States, Great Britain, and Australia. In many ways, the situation that gave rise to the prayer book societies is the polar opposite of those that precipitated, for example, the Institute on Religion and Democracy, and its Anglican counterpart, Episcopal Action. While these latter are concerned primarily with political stances and positions taken by mainline denominations, and only secondarily with issues of theology, the prayer book societies exhibit little or no primary interest in social or political issues. Nuclear disarmament, the problem of environmental degradation, issues of social and economic injustice, and even the preoccupation that mainline denominational hierarchies are perceived to have with these impact the prayer book societies only insofar as they affect the established liturgical tradition of the Anglican communion as laid out in the *Book of Common Prayer*.

A Freedom Virtually Forbidden: Prayer Book Society of the USA (PBS-USA)

In 1971, word began circulating among members of the Episcopal Church, USA—also known as the Protestant Episcopal Church—that the denomination's Standing Liturgical Commission was planning a revision of *The Book of Common Prayer*, the form of Anglican liturgy that had been in use in the church since 1928. According to William Ralston (2001), one of the founders of the Society for the Preservation of the Prayer Book (the PBS-USA's original, slightly unwieldy title), this prospect provoked "a lot of distressed conversation and 'weeping and gnashing of teeth,' " and a number of lay members and clergy gathered to discuss contesting the revision. However, not unlike the original members of the Presbyterian Lay Committee, these founders of the PBS-USA could hardly be considered garden-variety Episcopalians. Three faculty members of the English department from Vanderbilt University joined with colleagues from the University of the South at Sewanee, including the chair of the Sewanee English department, Charles Harrison, and the vice chancellor of the university, Edward McCrady, to discuss what they would do about the situation. Uncertain initially which direction to take to save their beloved *BCP*, the society developed an introductory statement of purpose and began their fight from a rented mailbox in Nashville, Tennessee (Ralston 2001). While "support from the Bishops and clergy was minimal," Ralston contends that, in the years following, the PBS-USA grew to "become the largest voluntary association of laypersons in the history of the Episcopal Church."

Five years later, when the ECUSA introduced the draft edition of its new prayer book, traditionalists continued to react vigorously, arguing that the updated language and multiple service format in the new liturgy should be more appropriately called a "Book of Alternative Services," a potential addition to the *BCP* but in no way a replacement for it. What worried liturgical traditionalists even more was the possibility that any use of the 1928 *BCP* would be forbidden by the church hierarchy, and that the new service book would be imposed on parishes as the sole resource for worship. A review of suggested amendments to the original General Convention resolution proposing adoption of the new prayer book indicates that the PBS-USA's concerns were not entirely unfounded. Initially, the new prayer book was to be adopted in draft form for use in the triennium between General Conventions (that is, between 1976 and 1979) and "declared to be The Book of Common Prayer of this Church" pursuant to a ratification vote in 1979 (General Convention 1977, C-11).

When that resolution was brought to the floor of the 1976 General Convention, the first proposed amendment called for debate on the various sections of the new prayer book to be conducted *seriatim*, an exhausting, time-consuming, and potentially disastrous process for those who sought to introduce the new prayer book as a complete entity. Following the defeat of the *seriatim* request, a Maryland delegate tried to protect the existence of the 1928 *BCP* through an amendment authorizing it as an option in parishes that did not want the new liturgy. That amendment was also defeated. Then, a Pennsylvania delegate tried a different tack:

amend the denominational canons so that bishops could authorize use of the 1928 *BCP* once the new resource had been adopted. If a blanket permission for the church to retain the 1928 *BCP* (which would have called into question the very necessity for the church of a revised prayer book) had been defeated, perhaps prevailing on the individual authority of bishops would succeed. That amendment failed as well. Next, if its presence as *the* Book of Common Prayer for the Episcopal Church would not be permitted, a Virginia delegate sought to include provision that the services, rites, and rubrics of the 1928 *BCP* be allowed to remain, perhaps contained as an appendix within the new prayer book. That amendment failed. Finally, in an attempt to retain traditional liturgy in the face of what proponents of the new prayer book called worship renewal, a New Hampshire delegate asked to have the rite of Holy Communion from the 1928 *BCP* substituted for one of the rites available in the draft prayer book. That way, if the 1928 *BCP* would not be permitted, at least the central liturgical rite to which traditionalists were devoted would be retained and available for use.

While various members of the court voiced their support or opposition to this proposal, one delegate sought to forestall further debate entirely, moving that the president of the House of Bishops "be given the privilege of ruling out of order amendments of like substance that the House had previously determined" (General Convention 1977). Put differently, no amendments seeking to retain either all or part of the 1928 *BCP* would be permitted on the floor of the convention. Such discussion would simply be ruled unconstitutional. Even though that somewhat draconian motion was defeated, the original—to retain the 1928 rite of Holy Communion in the new resource—failed as well. In the wake of these defeats and the provisional acceptance of the new prayer book, wrote Jerome Politzer, a number of PBS-USA leaders, including the original members from Vanderbilt University, resigned their positions in the society and left the Episcopal Church entirely (Politzer 2001).

Three years later, the 1979 General Convention considered the draft prayer book once again and adopted it finally and officially as "the Book of Common Prayer of this Church" (General Convention 1980a, C-8). Two bishops requested that their negative votes be recorded, and a third, who had voted for its adoption three years prior, this time submitted a minority report citing a personal preference for the 1928 *BCP* and thus dissented from the decision. These voices notwithstanding, the convention vote to accept the new prayer book was overwhelming.

This time, however, the Prayer Book Society sought assurances from the Liturgical Committee of the House of Bishops that worship according to the 1928 *BCP* could continue unobstructed in those parishes that still declined to use the new book. A somewhat confusing resolution resulted. While the new prayer book had been designated "the official liturgy of this Church," the court agreed that "liturgical texts from the 1928 Prayer Book may be used in worship, under the authority of the Bishop as chief pastor and liturgical officer, and subject to the directions of the Convention" (General Convention 1980b, C-11). These directions included a parish commitment to "continuing study" of the new prayer book, the use of the liturgical calendar and lectionaries from the new resource, and the two most important guidelines: (a) that "Copies of the 1979 Book be available for congregational study and worship"; and (b) that "Provision shall be made for the regular and frequent use of the 1979 Book." While addressing many of the amendment issues raised (and defeated) three years earlier, these concessions ensured that neither traditionalist congregations nor clergy could simply ignore the new prayer book, now known as *The Book of Common Prayer, 1979*.

The confusion that followed is easily explained by the final caveat in the General Convention's resolution, that is, "That this action in no way sanctions the existence of two authorized Books of Common Prayer or diminishes the authority of the official liturgy of this Church as established by this Convention" (General Convention 1980b, C-11). That which had for 50 years been authorized as official was official no longer, but could still be used; that which was now authorized as official need not be employed, but must be available for use. Jerome Politzer, president of the Prayer Book Society from 1981–91, reminisced that, even with these somewhat ambiguous concessions, the liturgical flexibility suggested by the resolution "was not to be the case." Despite the agreement to allow continued use of the 1928 *BCP*, "following the Convention, the House of Bishops unleashed a nationwide program attempting to stamp out all use of the classic and traditional *BCP*. Traditional clergy and parishes were forced into compliance. Those who resisted were demonized and subjected to intense pressure. During this period of what was called 'liturgical renewal' the Church lost one third of her membership (from 3.6 million to 2.4 million)" (Politzer 2001).

While Politzer does not specify in what this "nationwide program" consisted, nor how compliance with the new prayer book was "forced" or dissenters "demonized," that a number of Episcopalians were unhappy with its introduction is clear. Ralston (2001) reports that by the time of the 1979 General Convention, the PBS-USA had a membership of nearly 100,000, although Toon (2001b) claims that "it had the general support of one-quarter of the laity"; in the few years following 1979, its mailing list (and "fund raising capability") grew sevenfold (Politzer 2001). Membership waned through the 1980s and 1990s, however, a circumstance Peter Toon, the current director of the PBS-USA, attributes to the abandonment of the ECUSA by traditionalists or their capitulation to liturgical change, their willingness "to make do with Rite 1 in the 1979 prayer book" (Toon 2001b).

Rather than dissolve after the implementation of the 1979 prayer book, and still fearful that the traditional *BCP* would disappear either through parish disuse or episcopal fiat, the Prayer Book Society settled in for the duration. Though the ECUSA never allowed the 1928 *BCP* to go out of print, the PBS-USA's first priority was to ensure its continued publication and availability "for parishes inside and outside of the Episcopal Church" (Toon 2001b). Pedagogically, their mission was to educate people in the differences between the two books of prayer, and "to point out the doctrinal weaknesses and errors of the new form of services for the ECUSA" (Toon 2001b; cf. Toon 1992, 1999a). Finally, though, admitting that a recall of the 1979 prayer book and a communion-wide reinstatement of the 1928 *BCP* was unlikely, the Prayer Book Society vowed "to fight for the full rights of Episcopalians to use the 1928 *BCP* not only on Sundays but for weddings and funerals, and so on" (Toon 2001b).

Thirty years after its inception, members of the PBS-USA now realize that they face a crisis of generational transmission, as Toon notes, "a whole generation of Episcopalians now exists who has [sic] not known the classic worship 'in the beauty of holiness' " using the historic *BCP* (Toon 2001b). As such, rather than remedial guidance, the PBS-USA now faces the task of primary education in the Episcopal Church: teaching a crop of younger Episcopalians that which they have not to this point learned and convincing them of the fundamentally flawed nature of that which they have.

As a brief excursus, it might be useful to consider the actual differences between the two prayer books. That is, what are the issues about which prayer book societies across the Anglican world are so aggravated? Briefly, the particular problems traditionalists perceive in the *BCP, 1979* arise in three basic areas: structure, doctrine, and aesthetics.

Structurally, the most obvious difference is that the 1979 prayer book inserts a measure of choice into the celebration of liturgy that was present in neither the 1928 edition nor those by which it was preceded. The 1928 and earlier editions provided only one order of service for daily morning and evening prayer; one order each for the celebration of marriage, the sacrament of baptism, the rite of burial; and, most importantly, one order for the Sunday service of the Eucharist. From Hollywood to Hexham, from Sydney, Australia, to Sydney, Nova Scotia, and from Bangladesh to Venezuela, wherever Anglicans gather in worship according to *The Book of Common Prayer*, the faithful could trust that they gathered around the same liturgy, the same readings, and the same basic prayers. While individual collects—short prayers that generally precede the reading of a lesson during the service—may differ, the fundamental structure of the service was identical.

The 1979 edition, on the other hand, offered the church a choice of liturgies: two rites each for morning and evening prayer, the sacraments, and the service of Holy Communion. Further, though there are only two

overarching rites, within the services of Holy Communion the *BCP, 1979*
provides for six variations on the eucharistic prayers offered at the altar.
In contrast to the one eucharistic prayer from the 1928 *BCP*, and using the
metaphor of a newly launched ocean liner, Toon characterizes these alternative prayers as "appearing to be furnished in a rather cheap way with
inferior materials which soon crack, rust or look worn" (1999a, 40).

According to Toon, liturgical inferiority or superiority notwithstanding,
the most basic problem with the *Book of Common Prayer, 1979* is that it is
not "common" at all. That is, because it offers (albeit limited) choice in
the worship service, it has departed not only liturgically but also theologically from the Anglo-Catholic tradition extant since the sixteenth century
(Toon 1999a, 44–49). Like many denominational traditionalists, Toon laments the decline in Episcopal membership during the 1960s and 1970s
and asserts that many of those who left "were custodians of the received
tradition of the Common Prayer" (Toon 1999b, 13). Into the vacuum left
by their departure have stepped those who would see the 1928 *BCP* abandoned in favor of more contemporary resources. Interpreting the concept
of common in its most literal sense, Toon's argument is that since the new
prayer book offers more than one option for the celebration of the eucharistic liturgy, any practical notion of commonality is lost. The functional calculus here is simple: since there is no way to ensure that all
Anglican churches will be using the same service on any given Sunday,
there are no grounds to allege or claim commonality.

"To remain The Common Prayer," he writes in a discussion paper
drafted for the PBS-USA's official newsletter, *Mandate*, "there must be one
and one only Rite for each occasion, sacrament and office and there must
be a uniform doctrine throughout the whole book" (Toon 1999b, 14). Because the *BCP* is not only a worship resource for congregational use, but
draws on doctrinal standards set by the Anglican Formularies—the classic
BCP, the Ordinal (the 1662 rite according to which bishops, priests, and
deacons are ordained), and the Thirty-Nine Articles of Religion (originally
published in 1571 and to which assent is still required of Anglican
clergy)—and functions as a liturgical mainstay for those doctrines, to
move away from the classic order of the worship service is also to abandon
the anchoring tradition expressed in those doctrines. In the eyes of Toon
and the various prayer book societies, forsaking this central symbiotic
relationship between doctrine and liturgy renders the Episcopal Church
"no more than just another Protestant denomination much along the lines
of modern Methodism or Lutheranism" (Toon 1999b, 14)—that is to say,
adrift and ultimately awash on a sea of relativism.

Thus, the second difference, the second problem traditionalists raise
with the new prayer book: by tampering with the language in which worship is presented, the revisers of the prayer book have modified the church
doctrine enshrined in that language. For Toon, as for other traditionalist

Anglicans (cf., for example, Morrow 2001a, 2001b), the *BCP, 1979* "loosens the Church's commitment to classical trinitarianism . . . through the use of the principle of relativism. That is, they do not set aside the traditional, received doctrine, but they place alongside it variations which look and sound like it" (Toon 1999a, 89). For Toon, this amounts to the imposition of "minimal trinitarianism" as opposed to "orthodox or classical trinitarianism" (1999a, 96–111). While many readers would be at a loss to understand the difference, or the significance of the difference (a reality that he readily admits), in *Proclaiming the Gospel through the Liturgy: The Common Prayer Tradition and Doctrinal Revision,* Toon spends a great deal of time pointing out the importance hidden within the subtleties of language. Unless the Trinity is not represented in the precise form bequeathed to the Church by the ecumenical councils and creeds, he concludes, then there is no authentic Christian Church (Toon 1999a, 111–114). "In fact," he writes, and he is by no means alone in this, "all the major doctrines of the Christian religion fall like a pack of cards if there is no dogma of the Holy Trinity" (1999a, 112). When the revisers' attempt to render Trinitarian theology in language other than the strictly traditional, they have abrogated any claim to a classical Christian authenticity.

Finally, aesthetics. In his dissenting opinion from the second reading of the proposed new prayer book in 1979, General Convention delegate Walker Taylor declared that while he "[recognized] the great value of the Proposed Book," while he "[appreciated] its lasting contribution to the worship of the Church," and while he had "[diligently] studied and used it since 1976," his "personal preference" was for the retention of the 1928 BCP, . . . largely for the reason that 'a thing of beauty is a joy forever' " (General Convention 1980a). Quintin Morrow (2001c), a young Episcopal rector from Texas, concurs, "[commending] the classic prayer book to the Church and the Christian world because *it is beautiful.*" While he provides no specific examples, Morrow draws a clear distinction between the language of the traditional 1928 *BCP* and what he considers its modern imitators: liturgy focused on edutainment and seeker-sensitivity.

Modern worship is man-centered and focuses on entertainment and the meeting of our felt-needs. It drags God down from His throne and makes Him our celestial therapist, if not our equal. The classic prayer takes us rather to heaven, with the angels and archangels, and all the company of heaven, and causes us to fall down before this great and mighty God, and to offer Him our sacrifice of praise and thanksgiving with wonder, love and praise. (Morrow 2001c)

Morrow maintains that he is a traditionalist, "in that I do not believe that women should be presbyters [that is, ordained as priests] and that I hold to biblical norms of sexual relations and behavior," and that he "[believes] that the Bible is the Word of God written and I am thus a biblical literalist and inerrantist" (Morrow 2001b). In a conflation not uncommon among traditionalist Anglicans, Morrow blurs the distinction between Scripture and the 1928 *BCP*. While he admits that one "dare not draw too fine a point in comparing The Book of Common Prayer with the two-edged sword of Holy Scripture" (Morrow 2001a), he argues that in its conceptualization and execution, Cranmer's prayer book is "essentially an amalgamation of Scripture and sound doctrine" the purpose of which was "to indoctrinate its regular users with the truths of God's Word in Scripture" (Morrow 2001a). Elsewhere, in his contemplation of the beauty of the 1928 *BCP*, which he considers "the most potent vehicle for a life of genuine love and godliness" available (Morrow 2001c), this distinction blurs even further. "So, then," he writes, "while the modern liturgical scholars and theological revisionists scurry hither and yon to multiply liturgical texts and try to represent every human condition under heaven with a rite, we shall remain wedded to and in love with the classical Book of Common Prayer. *It is* Gospel. And where else can we fly? It contains the words of eternal life" (Morrow 2001c; emphasis in the original).

As for so many reform and renewal movements, what is at stake here is the politics of Anglican identity (a concept that will be discussed more fully in chapter 9). Who gets to decide what constitutes an authentic Anglican? Limits to the articulation of Anglican doctrine, as provided in the *BCP* and the other Formularies, are essential in order to maintain the distinction between "the Anglican Way" and "the generic way of modern American Protestantism," declares Peter Toon (1999b, 14). In the current situation, there are no boundaries between one thing and the other. In the same statement, Toon writes that "some in the ECUSA who view themselves as orthodox, Biblical Christians believe that their priests can and should cobble together liturgies from the 1979 book and elsewhere to produce services with which they and their congregations are as comfortable as are those using the classic liturgies of the historic B.C.P." While they may regard themselves as "orthodox, Biblical Christians," he asserts that "they do not understand or value the notion that the catholicity of the Anglican Way is related to the commitment to certain forms, the Formularies, to mould her life, worship and doctrine. . . . To be Anglican," he concludes definitively, "(with a substantial meaning from the Common Prayer Tradition) simply is not important anymore for most of the leadership and people of the ECUSA."

While the PBS-USA is not opposed to new liturgical forms, it makes the case that any new worship resources introduced into the Anglican communion must be introduced as adjuncts to and not replacements for the classic *BCP*. To do otherwise is simply to abandon the historic Anglican heritage. Throughout all of this, Toon admits that these are merely the presenting issues of much deeper change and conflict within Anglicanism. Slowly but surely, he believes, the denomination is moving away from the concept of a wholly transcendent God who chooses immanence through grace to a God who is primarily immanent "with only traces of transcendence" (Toon n.d.). For traditionalists like Toon, this represents a shift "from classical Trinitarian Theism to forms of Panentheism and Pantheism" and a revival of the adoptionist heresy, a teaching prominent in the seventh and eighth centuries that Christ was divine only by God's adoption not by divine ontology. Other traditionalist Anglicans (for example, D. Mills 1999, 7) contend that the adoption of alternative credal forms in worship "may actually be heretical," that it "seems to teach the heresy called modalism," an early interpretation of the Trinity that denied the permanence of any distinction between the three Persons of the Godhead. While traditionalists are less forthcoming about precisely how these characterizations obtain as a result of the *BCP, 1979, that* they obtain is not in question.

Twenty-one years after its introduction, the General Convention officially recognized that the transition from the 1928 *BCP* to the *BCP, 1979* had not been smooth. Brought by the bishop of Bethlehem, Pennsylvania, Paul V. Marshall, " 'the simple resolution acknowledges the fact that as flawed human beings the liturgical leaders of the Church occasionally hurt people, most of the time despite their good intentions, and perhaps sometimes out of arrogance and insensitivity" (Marshall, in Toon 2000a). In the resolution the convention issued an apology "to any members of this Church who were offended or alienated by inappropriate and uncharitable behavior during the time of transition to the 1979 Book of Common Prayer" (Resolution B034, in Toon 2000a). The second part of Marshall's resolution reaffirmed the 1979 decision to allow the continued use of the 1928 *BCP* within the ECUSA.

In the face of this albeit qualified and tenuous support, "why then does the Prayer Book Society continue?" asks traditionalist Marilyn Ruzicka (2001). Simply put, because she regards the PBS-USA as the sole guardian of an authentic religious identity. "Prayer Book Society members believe in orthodoxy and conservation of classic Anglicanism. This straight path consists of old-fashioned morality, an all-male ordained ministry, and the timeless excellence and beauty of worship from the traditional prayer book."

"Doctrine in Devotion": Prayer Book Society of Canada (PBSC)

Like its American counterpart, in 1985 the Anglican Church in Canada added to its liturgical roster a new resource, the *Book of Alternative Services* (BAS), the first of its kind in Canada and the first change for the church since the 1962 revision of the Cranmer *Book of Common Prayer*. Although the Canadian church also maintains that it is not a replacement for the

BCP, functionally, in many Anglican parishes this is exactly what has happened, touching off what the former president of the Anglican seminary in Toronto has called a "liturgical Cold War" (Stackhouse 1999). Cranmer's familiar cadences have been exchanged for unfamiliar prayers, readings, and responsories, liturgical innovations that at least one commentator has referred to "gently" as "shallow, boring, sometimes vulgar, and altogether too eager to pander to the easily-offended, spiritually obtuse sensibilities of the age" (Jones 1997).

Two years prior to the publication of the *BAS*, when excerpts, trial liturgies, congregational resolutions, complaints, and accusations flew back and forth throughout the church, concerned Anglicans gathered together and formed what eventually became the Prayer Book Society of Canada (PBSC), "a committed group of laypeople and clergy working for the re-evangelization of our church and society" (Prayer Book Society of Canada n.d.). Through lectures and conferences, news releases, commentaries, and an occasional journal, *The Machray Review* (named after the nineteenth-century Anglican bishop who was instrumental in the creation of the Anglican Church in Canada), takes its traditionalist message to the church. Since its inception in 1985, local branches of the society have appeared in almost every province, from Newfoundland to British Columbia, with 12 branches in Ontario—Canada's most populous province and a historical stronghold of Canadian Anglicanism.

While many of the objections to the *BAS* have centered around the use of updated language, what some fear (somewhat justifiably) may lead to the use of so-called inclusive language in describing the Divine (cf., for example, Bright 1992; Carreker 1994; Ralston 1992), the PBSC has always maintained that the dispute is fundamentally doctrinal in nature. In the words of the Reverend David Curry, vice president of the PBSC, it is about "doctrine in devotion" (1996). Because the Anglican Church has no magisterium, no teaching authority analogous to the Roman Catholic Sacred Congregation for the Doctrine of the Faith, doctrinal standards have to be located elsewhere and weighed according to different standards. For those opposed to liturgical revision, innovation, and experimentation, that "elsewhere" is the *Book of Common Prayer*. Even the proposal of a combined worship resource for the Anglican Church in Canada, retaining elements of both the *BCP* and *BAS*, is seen as the de facto abolition of the Common Prayer tradition and the consequent abandonment of historic Anglicanism (Curry 1999b; cf. Burton 1998). This is because many of its supporters maintain that the *BCP* is not merely a book of worship; it is not a service book in the same fashion as the *BAS*, the Presbyterian *Book of Common Worship*, or the United Church of Canada's *Service Book*. Rather, more than a collection of liturgies under one cover, the *Book of Common Prayer* is a "spiritual system" that "embodies a religious position with a particular view of the Bible, tradition, and worship" (Curry 1999b).

It is this religious position, this particular doctrinal stance embedded and transmitted in set forms of liturgy, that the PBSC and its associate organizations seek to maintain. While supporters of the *Book of Alternative Services* suggest that the systematic theology represented by the *Book of Common Prayer* ought to be treated as a treasured repository of faith, it must be recognized as contextually organized and conditioned, and now subject to the exigencies and demands of a world and a pastorate vastly different than those encountered by Cranmer and his contemporaries. Their opponents, on the other hand, argue that the world is not so very different 450 years later, and that the *BCP* lays out its doctrinal foundation to preclude just such contextual revisions as the *BAS* provides. Alternative liturgies that depart from the Common Prayer tradition, and more importantly the understanding of Christian doctrine explicit in that tradition, open the door to a slippery slope of theological ambiguities ranging from questions around the omission of the *filioque* (literally "and the son") in certain parts of the new liturgies to, as noted by the PBS-USA, the implication of those liturgies in such early Christian heresies as adoptionism and modalism (Averyt 1992).

Shortly after the *BAS* was published, the Anglican Church in Canada instituted an evaluation committee to assess the reception of the new liturgies by the denomination. In response, the PBSC submitted a 70-page report detailing the shortcomings of the new resource. According to the report, "the most telling feature of doctrinal inadequacy appears in the *BAS*' use and understanding of the classical creeds" (PBSC 1991). Critics of the *BAS* see this as diminishing the importance of the Apostles', Nicene, and Athanasian creeds in the life of the church. Of concern, for example, is the change in the location of the Apostles' Creed.

In the *Book of Common Prayer*, during the service of Holy Communion the congregation stands for the reading of the gospel, and follows that immediately with a joint recitation of the Apostles' Creed. Then, only after the creed, is the sermon delivered. That is, in the proper order of worship the creed stands between the gospel and the sermon; church doctrine stands between the Word of God and the proclamation of that Word to the people of God. This rather important symmetry is not lost on members of the Prayer Book Society. In their interpretation of the *BAS*, the creeds have become optional rather than normative in the worship life of the church; they have become temporally descriptive of particular faith stances, rather than perpetually prescriptive of orthodox Christian belief. Put differently, the creeds are not simply a set of doctrines learned by a catechumen, and then recited to the parson prior to one's confirmation; they are the enduring boundary against theological, liturgical, and ecclesiastical aberration. As such, they must be placed before the people on a regular basis, and in such a way that their liturgical position adequately reflects their ecclesiastical importance.

"The creeds," argues the PBSC (1991), "are not only critical in making Christians but also in maintaining Christians in the faith." That is, they are not only evangelistic and catechetical, they also maintain the boundaries of acceptable Christian belief. The liturgical and theological calculus here is clear: if doctrine is not expressed regularly and properly in devotion, that doctrine runs the risk of dilution, alteration, and divergence—in the long run, heresy. Rather than this principle of doctrinal maintenance, contends the PBSC, the compilers of the *BAS* are governed by the desire to recover a primitive, hence authentic shape of liturgy, rather than one that conforms to and supports the doctrinal integrity of the church. "The incantory prayers of the *BAS*," continues the report, "cannot replace the creed as the necessary and sufficient statement of the faith" (PBSC 1991).

Arguing that "there is actually no liturgical precedent, properly speaking, for having the creed follow the sermon," the *BAS* appeals to a "hypothetical reconstruction of an aesthetic ideal of the liturgy" (PBSC 1991). An aesthetic, traditionalists are at pains to point out, that has no basis in the historical record of the church, or in its tradition of worship and devotion. It is not simply a matter of what words get said where. Without the creed acting as a doctrinal hermeneutic through which the words of Scripture are filtered in the sermon, the theological anchor that has sustained Anglican identity is pulled loose. "The place of the creed in the *BAS*," declares the report, "means that the sermon comes between the gospel and the creed. Consequently the sermon no longer properly stands under the authority of Scripture expressed in the creed; in short, under the rule of Scripture doctrinally understood." As a result, "with the *BAS* the creed is left hanging in the liturgical breeze, either an unwelcome and disquieting appendage or a possible moment between the liturgy of the Word and the liturgy of the Sacrament." Doctrine, therefore, is no longer expressed in devotion, and control over the popular absorption of that doctrine slips away.

According to the Prayer Book Society of Canada, however, the creeds are not the only components of doctrinal Christianity given short shrift by the *Book of Alternative Services*. The final section of the PBSC submission (1991) to the *BAS* evaluation committee comments on a number of "significant theological themes" to which the *BAS* gives "insufficient emphasis." In the Anglo-Catholic tradition, for example, penitence has always occupied a primary place in devotional life, whether private or corporate. By making use of the various penitential rites liturgically optional rather than devotionally pivotal, many of its critics have claimed that the *BAS* does not give the theological principles of sin and repentance nearly the same prominence as its venerable predecessor. "While the *BAS* mentions penitence and provides penitential rites," the report concludes, "it has failed to integrate penitence into the structure and pattern of public prayer so that it is a central and essential element."

Liturgically, the cold war between the supporters of the *Book of Common Prayer* and the *Book of Alternative Services* is not limited to these volumes alone. Another contestant has recently entered the field: *Common Praise,* a new hymnbook for the Anglican Church in Canada that is designed to replace both the 1938 *Book of Common Praise* and the 1971 *Hymn Book,* which was published jointly with The United Church of Canada. Of course, as one Anglican cleric and academic wonders, the real issue is: Is the new hymnbook really "something to sing about" (Crouse 1998)? For traditionalists, apparently not. Because *Common Praise* introduces new metaphors for the Divine, because some favorite metaphors have been dropped, and because the new hymnbook simply omits many of the hymns that have sustained the faith of dedicated Anglicans for decades, traditionalists argue that it is, rather, "a book of un-common praise, some parts of it having less and less in common with the Scripture, with authentic patterns of Anglican Worship, and with the original hymns" (PBSC-NS/PEI 1999).

In rewriting many of the venerable hymns of the church to ameliorate what the hymnary editors believe to be either offensive language or offensive theology, the PBSC argues (quite correctly in many cases) that the basic meaning of the hymn has been changed. Postmodern arguments about the priority of the present reader notwithstanding, these changes violate what many Anglicans believe to be the core principles by which their faith is defined. Similar attempts to balance gender-oriented metaphors for the Divine similarly anger traditionalists. Recalling arguments made against denominational participation in the Re-Imagining Conferences, the Prayer Book Society concludes that this "is the next stage of what will follow *Common Praise* and we are not far from the fertility cults which so often ensnared Israel: the goddess religion in modern dress, so to speak" (PBSC-NS/PEI 1999).

Lest readers think that these debates within the Episcopal Church (USA) and the Anglican Church in Canada are merely the arguments of those who have exhausted their exegesis of the more gripping passages of Hooker's *Laws of Ecclesiastical Polity*, they are not. As will be discussed more fully in chapter 9, it is not merely theology that is at stake, nor doctrine. In the eyes of many, these debates have at their core the politics of Anglican identity. For traditionalists, the Anglican Way is predicated on adherence to the liturgical forms of the *Book of Common Prayer*. There are any number of ways to construct one's religious identity, few of which are mutually acceptable to adherents. Roman Catholic identity is a function of baptism into the church, and participation in the sacraments of the church. Other denominations require intentional professions of faith along specific confessional, and in some cases experiential lines. In many Pentecostal churches, a conversion experience is insufficient by itself to demonstrate one's membership in the true Christian church; real conversion is only evident when one's confession of faith is married to an experiential display of glossolalia. Finally, in the most liberal denominations—like The United Church of Canada—infant baptism, a dim remembrance of attendance at Sunday School, or the mere claim to adherence because one knows one is not Catholic, Buddhist, or Druid is sufficient to declare identity.

In a joint statement issued after Lambeth 1998, the four main international prayer book societies condemned the move away from a Common Prayer tradition to one of common worship, the manner of liturgical life implied by efforts to produce a variety of composite worship resources. The prayer book societies argue that use of the word "common" is merely a ploy to retain the favor of those attached to the traditional *BCP* while quite self-consciously moving away from it. In a sermon delivered in Montreal, PBSC vice president David Curry said, "we face, dare I say, almost a kind of ethnic cleansing in our church, an unchurching of the ethos of the Common Prayer tradition, in the idea of a composite book—a combination of the *Book of Common Prayer* and the *Book of Alternative Services*" (Curry 1999a). However hyperbolic one might find Curry's use of "ethnic cleansing" to describe the move from one prayer book to another, it does highlight the seriousness with which the issue is regarded by Anglican traditionalists.

CHAPTER 7

Defending Orthodoxy in the Great White North: The United Church of Canada

INTRODUCTION

Formed in 1925 from the union of the Methodist, the Congregational, and most of the Presbyterian Churches in Canada, The United Church of Canada (UCCan) brought together a broad range of theological opinion and interpretation in its efforts to mold a new Protestant mission in the Great White North. Union was the culmination of a process that had been under way since the turn of the twentieth century, that had survived the interruption caused by the First World War, and that sought as a denomination to embody the principle of its motto: "That all may be one" (cf. Dow 1951; cf. Fraser 1915; Grant 1963; Kelly 1917; Mann 1963; Moir 1966, 1975; Morton 1912; Oliver 1930; Pidgeon 1950; Scott 1928; Silcox 1933).

As the essential first step toward an organic union of the three denominations, Methodist delegates argued that a joint Basis of Union needed to be prepared. In addition to producing that Basis, they suggested that the discussions "would also educate the people interested into a deeper *spirit of unity*, and into that *spirit of reasonable concession* on which the successful consummation of such movements ultimately so largely depends" (Thomas 1919, 259; emphasis added). While a "spirit of unity" might be a wonderful ideal, it was the "spirit of reasonable concession" that both motivated and stalled the proceedings that finally led to union. What constituted reasonable concession? Where did one draw the line between fidelity to the traditions and doctrines of one's own denomination—whether Congregationalist, Arminian, or Calvinist—and their possible concession for the sake of a greater union?

Called simply the Articles of Faith, the doctrinal portion of the Basis of Union was completed first. While they were eventually accepted by the uniting churches as "setting forth the substance of the Christian faith as commonly held among us," in their most basic form the Twenty Articles, as they are also known, originated almost entirely in two Presbyterian statements: The Articles of Faith of the Presbyterian Church in England (ca. 1890; cf. Morrow 1923); and The Brief Statement of the Reformed Faith, prepared in 1905 by the Presbyterian Church (USA) (cf. Clifford 1984, 1985; Morrow 1923). As it stands, the doctrinal portion of the UCCan Basis of Union reflects with few changes far more the accumulated credal statements of those Presbyterian churches than it does either of the other two uniting denominations. What then kept The United Church of Canada from simply growing as another branch grafted onto the Presbyterian tree? One answer, and one that cuts to the quick of many controversies that have arisen in the UCCan since union, is the issue of credal subscription and the academic and theological freedom afforded members of the church by the defeat of the Presbyterian motion requiring subscription to the Articles of Faith.

In the Presbyterian tradition, a candidate for ordination was asked first if he "believed the Scriptures of the Old and New Testaments to be the Word of God, and the only infallible rule of faith and life" (Morrow 1923, 131). As a subordinate authority, he was asked: "Do you believe the Westminster Confession of Faith, as adopted by this church in the [1875] Basis of Union, to be founded on and agreeable to the Word of God, and in your teaching do you promise faithfully to adhere thereto?" For many Presbyterians, credal subscription to the Westminster Confession was the sine qua non of the Protestant tradition. Methodists, on the other hand, were asked simply if they would "teach nothing as required of eternal salvation, but that which you shall be persuaded may be concluded and proved by the Scriptures?" (Morrow 1923, 130). Arguably a less stringent obligation. In Congregationalist polity, though, candidates for ordination were required only to make a "statement of belief to a council or association of local churches, and the living faith of the church in the community is made the test of . . . doctrinal fitness for the office" (Morrow 1923, 133).

For many Presbyterians, however, either of these lesser covenants was unacceptable. If subscription was not required, how would the church monitor, maintain, or enforce what it regarded as orthodoxy? There would be no officially sanctioned grounds upon which to question those either suspected or accused of preaching and teaching outside the pale of legitimate belief. Indeed, Ephraim Scott, then editor of the *Presbyterian Record* and one of the most ardent opponents of union, argued that wherever churches in the new world had abandoned credal subscription, "not a little of that Church drifted into Unitarianism . . . 'Universalism,' 'Christian Science,' 'Esoteric Buddhism,' 'The New Thought,' and other kindred errors" (Scott, in Morrow 1923, 141).

For their part, the Congregationalists, who by their very presence in the negotiations were compromising their tradition of absolute congregational autonomy, objected strenuously to the inclusion of any required subscription in the Basis of Union. In fact, because "subscription merely puts a premium on hypocrisy" (Morrow 1923, 135), and ministers come to preach a gospel in which they do not really believe, its absence was considered by some to be the great achievement of the new Basis. Supporting the Congregationalist position, Methodist Ernest Thomas argued that, since The United Church of Canada's Basis of Union was a comprehensive statement, rather than a definitive one, any attempt to impose subscription would create far more problems than it would solve. Many saw subscription, and the ecclesiology that underpinned it, as the mechanism that allowed "the thumbscrew, the boot, [and] the fires of Smithfield" (Morrow 1923, 136). On the other hand, by opposing subscription, they believed a new age was dawning on the church, an era free from the doctrinal uniformity that belonged to "a credal age, the age of the Book" (Morrow 1923, 135), a time in which varied interpretations of Christian doctrines were now possible. And, in the emerging United Church, this freedom rested less on the confluence of Calvinism and Arminianism than it did on the suffrage of members not to subscribe rigidly to either. As I noted earlier in the book, instead of subscription, ordinands and commissionands within The United Church of Canada are now asked whether they are in essential agreement with the Basis of Union—a concept whose elasticity has resulted in no little controversy over the years.

Like the United Methodist Church, the UCCan sought to respond to the countercultural crises of the 1960s by offering a theology it believed more relevant to the times and more cognizant of a century's worth of biblical scholarship and criticism. And, like the United Methodist Church, the entry point for this was the introduction of what became known as the New Curriculum, published between 1962 and 1964. While the New Curriculum was welcomed by some, traditionalist church members, both clergy and lay, saw it not as an expansion of scriptural and theological vision, but as another example of unacceptable denominational accommodation to secular culture. Like other reform and renewal movements, early members of the UCCan conservative reform groups equated what they perceived as the erosion of the biblical witness with a concomitant reduction in moral standards, family life, and the good order of society. Where the authority of Scripture and the personhood of Christ (however these were understood by traditionalists in the pews) had once been held inviolate, questions about the literal truth of the gospel miracles, the historicity of the Virgin Birth, and a substitutionary atonement as the only possible soteriological paradigm now began to tear at the foundation on which the faith of many had been for years somewhat imprecisely built.

THE GRASS ROOTS AT PRAYER: THE UNITED CHURCH RENEWAL FELLOWSHIP

Recalling the birth of the United Church Renewal Fellowship (UCRF), the first of the UCCan's conservative reform groups, Lloyd Cumming defined the problem of practical life for the United Church in the 1960s as a drift away from firm and clearly defined doctrine. In preparation for ministry, for example, seminary students were not being taught to regard the Bible as the solely authoritative Word of God, but rather to treat it critically and contextually; under the influence of higher criticism, Holy Scripture became merely a tool through which ministry might be carried out instead of the standard against which it was to be measured. Miracles were explained away in naturalist terms; evangelical doctrines of atonement and salvation were questioned and ultimately discarded. In terms of the wider church, "it had become socially popular to attend churches which proclaimed an intellectual secular-humanist philosophy" (Cumming 1990, 27). According to Cumming, the real crisis appeared when "many of the people who flocked into our churches during the 1950s [became] disillusioned by an absence of clear scriptural teaching. They said, in effect, 'If that's all the church has to offer, it is not worth taking seriously' " (Cumming 1990, 26; cf. Cowan 2000).

On March 12, 1966, in response to some pointed challenges laid down by a visiting missionary, the United Church Renewal Fellowship was officially organized. At the time, Cumming and his wife, Edna, had been praying to be led "out of the United Church to a denomination where we could enjoy the fellowship of Christians who shared our desire for scriptural, evangelical ministry" (1990, 28). The formation of a group dedicated to intentional conservative reform, however, convinced them that God's plan was for them to stay. Five years later, Cumming became the UCRF's first full-time employee, serving for many years as its traveling field secretary and executive director.

In those early years, discussions quickly focused on what would become the UCRF's organizational leitmotif during the nearly three decades of its existence, the controlling idea it would pass on to the next generation of United Church reform and renewal: doctrinal integrity in the face of theological pluralism. In a 1969 issue of the group's magazine, *The Small Voice*, for example, UCRF member Michael Tymchak responded to then-moderator Robert McClure's characterization of the United Church as enjoying "a healthy theological pluralism." If this is the case, Tymchak asked, then what *defined* those brought together in United Church fellowship? If anything is permissible doctrinally, how could one be identified as a Christian, let alone a United Church member? The answer, he insisted, was that one could not; the category would be empty, void, meaningless. "Many clergy today," wrote Tymchak, using a nautical metaphor to which the UCRF would return time and again, "disagree on essential points with these doctrines on which our church has been founded. Clearly, the loyalties of some of our crew belie the flag under which they are sailing!" (1969, 10).

As its first order of business, then, the nascent reform movement set about clarifying where the loyalties of faithful United Church people ought to lie. "As we tried to diagnose the condition of the church," Cumming wrote more than two decades later, "we studied the Basis of Union on which the United Church had been established in 1925. (Many of us did not know it existed)" (1990, 28–29). While there are other sections of the Basis of Union, dealing with denominational polity, administration, the ministry, and church membership, conservative reform groups concentrate principally on the doctrinal portion—the Twenty Articles of Faith—and tend to use the two phrases interchangeably. That the Twenty Articles are not well known in the United Church would become a continual refrain in reform discourse, and the UCRF ought to be one of the groups credited with bringing them into popular denominational consciousness. In 1984, the group published *We Have an Anchor*, a collection of essays expounding their understanding of the church's doctrinal foundation (United Church Renewal Fellowship 1984b; cf. Chalmers 1945; United Church Renewal Fellowship 1975). Not surprisingly, after examining the Twenty Articles in some detail, the UCRF "concluded that the church had drifted away from [the foundations on which union took place]. The result was that policy decisions were being made on the basis of man's wisdom rather than according to the admonitions of the Scriptures to which we had committed our allegiance in the Basis of Union" (Cumming 1990, 29).

This reiterates the somewhat complicated relationship that often exists between conservative manifestos and the Bible in reform and renewal discourse. In this case, it is not, in fact, the Bible that provides the organizing doctrinal framework for the UCRF (and other UCCan reform groups). Rather, it is a particular interpretation of the Bible read into the doctrinal principles of the Twenty Articles. Cumming, for example, describes the state of the church as he found it when he assumed the job of field secretary as "continuing to emphasize a secular-humanist, social-political liberal theology that was diametrically opposed to the scriptural base to which our pioneers had committed us in our Basis of Union" (1990: 47). Note how the primary emphasis here is laid, not on Scripture, but on the Basis of Union, a theological compilation woven together from different interpretive strands, but often held all but equal to Scripture itself. Although the UCRF would never explicitly claim an equivalence between the UCCan's doctrinal statement and Holy Writ, functionally and rhetorically, like the Anglican *Book of Common Prayer,* the boundaries often blur. "When the United Church of Canada came into being in 1925," wrote Cumming in a 1984 *Small Voice* editorial, "our founders established a point of reference. They called it 'The Basis of Union.' We maintain that all our decisions should be reconciled with that point of reference" (1990, 101). For all intents and purposes, then, it is fidelity to the Articles of Faith, not the Bible per se, to which the UCRF has consistently called the church. This emphasis has led many critics to contend that the UCRF, as well as its reform and renewal descendants, have made a "damned idol" out of the Twenty Articles. During the debates that raged over the place of homosexuality in the church, for example, the UCRF blurred the distinction between Scripture and the Basis of Union even further, referring at times to "the scriptural *Point of Reference* which was the *Basis of Union* of The United Church of Canada" (Cumming 1990, 105; emphasis in the original).

Early UCRF efforts at church renewal followed two different tacks: (1) prayer, which was supported by occasional newsletters and (2) personal evangelism, using *The Master Plan of Evangelism,* written by Robert Coleman, a professor of evangelism at Asbury Theological Seminary (see Coleman 1993). As Cumming notes, "we distributed hundreds of copies of that book to UCRF members and friends. It became a textbook which set a course and a goal for the Renewal Fellowship" (1990, 33). According to Cumming, though, Coleman's book also gave the UCRF some much needed perspective on the role they were seeking to play in the evolution of the United Church. For some time, they had wrestled with the question of the most effective way to facilitate denominational reform. Should they work through the political structure and try to effect change from the top down? Or, should they concentrate their efforts on grassroots witnessing and organizing? Coleman's work convinced them that if renewal was ever going to take place in the church it would be through God's activity, not theirs. This realization "was a fundamental change in the course of the whole ministry of The United Church Renewal Fellowship. The basic lesson we learned was that the renewal of the church was God's responsibility—not ours" (Cumming 1990, 38). Rather than "political action from the top down" (Cumming 1990, 38), making disciples—for Coleman, a crucial conceptual distinction apart from ordinary Christians—and supporting those disciples through continual prayer became the UCRF mandate. Despite the fact that many in the church came to view them in just that light, "our calling was not to be a negative, critical, protest group" (Cumming 1990, 47). The rigidity of the UCRF worldview, however, its unwillingness to compromise in the face of alternative biblical and theological interpretations, often contributed to perceptions of it as a narrow, intolerant, conservative interest group. For its part, the UCRF was clear that borders, boundaries, and limits are precisely the issues at stake in its

struggle; authentic Christianity resides within and only within appropriate doctrinal limits, limits defined according to an evangelical interpretation of the Twenty Articles of Faith.

Early in its career, however, the UCRF embraced another aspect of renewal in the church. In similar fashion to churches across the mainline
spectrum, neo-Pentecostal experiences began to manifest. In a number of
United Churches, members were beginning to speak in tongues, to display
spiritual gifts of healing and prophecy, and to exhibit a joy in their religious experience that was quite unfamiliar to many in the denomination.
At first, since they had anticipated a strictly evangelical reform, with salvation through a personal commitment to Jesus Christ as its chief indicator, this new charismatic manifestation concerned the UCRF. "We had
not bargained on an unprecedented movement that led Christians into a
New Testament experience of gifts and healing," wrote Cumming. Like
the Good News Movement in the UMC, "the result was some confusion
and reluctance on the part of many Church members to accept the authenticity of the Charismatic Renewal" (1990, 50).

To its credit, though, while many of its members were clearly uncomfortable with this new spirit in the church, and some rejected its authenticity outright, the UCRF did not splinter over it. The governing board
did feel it necessary to issue a statement on the phenomenon: a brief re-
hearsal of the experience, its scriptural basis, and their inability to understand it completely. However, in a decision that might have drawn
legitimate comparison to the withholding of information by the official
denominational hierarchy, the "statement was not published or circular-
ized to our members but copies were made available to those who raised
the question, 'Where does the UCRF board stand regarding the Charismatic Renewal movement?' " (Cumming 1990, 56). In retrospect, given
the rigidity with which many in the UCRF drew their doctrinal boundaries, the less openly the issue was discussed, the less likely the UCRF
was to experience fracture and the more likely it was to maintain a unified
face to the denomination at large.

For nearly 20 years, personal evangelism and prayer (whether charismatic or not) were the mainstays of UCRF activity. Following their early
missional perspective, they did not try to affect denominational policy
through political action at the various conciliar levels of the church. That
changed in the mid-1980s, however, when debates over homosexuality
and inclusive language rocked the denomination. In the wake of the 1988
decision that sexual orientation would not stand as an a priori barrier to
ordination or commissioning, membership in the UCRF began to drop
dramatically. Traditionalist church members who had fought for years
recognized that, in The United Church of Canada, the day finally belonged
to the denominational liberals. By 1996, the decision was made to merge

the United Church Renewal Fellowship with the National Alliance of Covenanting Congregations, and continue the battle under a joint flag.

THE ACADEMIC ARM: CHURCH ALIVE

Few reform or renewal movements start out self-consciously so; more often than not, like the UCRF, they find their origin in like-minded individuals gathered initially at a restaurant or around a coffee table, comparing notes, discovering common concerns, and proposing possible responses. When, as C. Wright Mills (Mills [1959] 2000, 226) pointed out, private troubles must be understood in terms of public problems, social countermovements begin to take shape. Gathered around the emerging problem of liberal theology, this nicely describes the beginning of Church Alive, the most academically oriented reform movement in the UCCan. Alarmed at the directions the church was taking in the 1960s and early 1970s, a number of clergy in the Montréal and Ottawa area began to talk with each other about ways to shift the course on which their denomination seemed set. Three senior clergy in the area—Campbell Wadsworth, Victor Fiddes, and Daniel Mathieson—were joined in their deliberations by three younger colleagues: Graham Scott, who had done doctoral work at Strasbourg, C. Gordon Ross, a pastor and lawyer, and Kenneth Barker, a minister who moved back and forth between the UCCan and the Presbyterian Church in Canada (Riordan 1990; Ross 1999; Scott 1989).

According to Riordan, in addition to the New Curriculum, Scott read the signs of the denominational times both in a 1966 missions report, and in the 1968 New Creed of the UCCan. Whereas the missions report declared that God was "redemptively at work in the religions of the world," Scott argued that such a theology challenged the uniqueness and exclusivity of Christianity. "To suddenly say that redemption is possible through Buddhism, Hinduism, and those other religions," he contended, "you're giving up the catholic doctrine of the atonement" (Scott, in Riordan 1990, 34). Calling the New Creed "sub-Christian and implicitly heretical" (Scott, in Riordan 1990, 35), he insisted that it diminished the divine nature of Christ and encouraged an incipient unitarianism and universalism. Scott's colleague, Campbell Wadsworth agreed. "Wearing his Trinitarian faith on his shirt sleeve," writes Gordon Ross in retrospect, "he fretted presciently about the serious risk that the United Church might soon end up as an unacknowledged proponent of Unitarianism" (1999, 4).

When asked why he did not simply join the UCRF and work for renewal through them, Scott illustrates part of the theological spectrum often embraced by conservative reform and renewal, a spectrum that is just as often ignored by their critics. "The UCRF was inclined to see the Scriptures as infallible. While I believe the Bible to be trustworthy, I cannot accept that it's infallible" (Scott, in Riordan 1990, 35). An important hermeneutic and sociological distinction, Scott highlights here the difference between church members who are concerned about the theological drift in the denomination toward an ill-defined liberalism, and those who fear the abandonment by the denomination of foundational authorities. Over time, this distinction blurred, and the theological drift came to be perceived as rooted in the abandonment of these authorities—first, the Bible, and second, the Twenty Articles of Faith. At first, however, many of those opposed to the liberalization of the church were not any more comfortable with the kind of biblical literalism proposed by the UCRF than they were with the neo-orthodoxy advanced by the denominational hierarchy.

In early March 1973, Wadsworth gathered his colleagues together to discuss a proposed manifesto for their organization. While some were concerned that such a pronouncement would polarize the church, splitting it into factions defined by and aligned with particular doctrinal stances, others saw it as a necessary first step toward reclaiming the church for orthodoxy. Like the UCRF, all agreed that they did not want to be a negative force in the church. Rather than criticizing the theological and doctrinal faults they saw all around them, they would instead witness positively for a traditional and historic Christianity. Nearly a year after the first draft of the manifesto had been circulated, Scott wrote Barker, "I am simply overwhelmed by the quality of the draft. It is a real breakthrough and was so inspiring that I actually got off my sick-bed and hammered out a revision, which I am enclosing for your consideration" (Scott 1989, 5). On February 24, 1974, meeting as the Ad Hoc Committee for Affirmation of the Faith, the group gathered once again in Montréal to finish its theological statement: 15 Affirmations by Concerned Members of the United Church of Canada.

As its name implies, the 15 Affirmations is a fairly inoffensive restatement of much that its authors found in the UCCan's Twenty Articles. God is seen as sovereign in creation; the uniqueness and exclusivity of Christianity is located and confirmed in the historicity of its defining moments, specifically the soteriological death and physical resurrection of Jesus; the Bible is affirmed as the authoritative norm for Christian teaching and worship; and the Church, as established by God, is seen as "a sacramental community of faith, worship, fellowship, evangelism and service" (Church Alive [1974] 1989, 4).

As we have seen before, though, because conservative reform movements respond to particular problems of practical life as they have arisen denominationally, doctrinal assent is almost inevitably linked to some manner of ethical piety. Thus, woven into the theological warp of the 15 Affirmations (Church Alive [1974] 1989, 3) is the practical woof of its opposition. Because, for example, "man and woman were created by God with freedom and dignity," humanity is "therefore not wholly determined by heredity or environment, but remain responsible moral agents." Here, the group was repudiating both the nature versus nurture debate current at the time, and exemplified in the behaviorism of B. F. Skinner, as well as the publication and subsequent popularization of Episcopal priest Joseph Fletcher's *Situation Ethics* (1966), which argued that moral and ethical decisions could never be made on the basis of a nomic prescription, but only after due consideration of the particular circumstances at hand. The world missions report to which Scott had responded so strongly was likewise rejected. "We believe that Jesus Christ has a definitive significance for all the races and religions of man," read the declaration. "We therefore affirm that Christ is the judge of all faiths, including Christianity. We believe that Jesus Christ is the divine answer to the human longings to which all faiths testify." Thus, while God may be at work creatively in faiths other than Christianity, only in Christianity is God at work redemptively.

Once the 15 Affirmations document was ratified by the Montréal group, it was circulated to every minister in the UCCan with an invitation to join in the protest. According to Scott, "over five hundred Ministers and members" signed, and the manifesto was "reviewed sympathetically in THE PRINCETON SEMINARY BULLETIN" (Scott 1989, 5). Like the United Methodist response to Keysor's article on U.S. Methodism's silent minority, the response to the 15 Affirmations led the framers to organize the ad hoc group on a more permanent footing. A year later, Church Alive was formally incorporated as a nonprofit religious organization. Incorporation, however, was not without its difficulties. In a church that had come into union under the motto, *Ut omnes unum sint* ("That all may be one"), the principal concern raised during discussions over the manifesto had been the potential for the document to be regarded as a polarizing influence and its framers dismissed as schismatics. In the same way Scott distanced himself from the UCRF, he maintained that Church Alive did not want to be perceived as "identifying itself with what might be considered by many to be a narrow conservatism; it called, rather, for responsible Biblical and theological scholarship within the mainstream heritage" (1989: 6). That desire notwithstanding, Kenneth Barker, one of the original framers of the 15 Affirmations, chose not to join the newly incorporated group initially.

Since its incorporation, while Church Alive has not had the media profile of the UCRF or the Community of Concern, it has gone diligently about the work of church reform. Under the editorship of another UCCan minister, Ed McCaig, it published an intermittent newsletter, *Affirmations;* it sent mailings to conference delegates, detailing the conservative position on a variety of issues facing the church; and its members continued to meet for mutual support and planning. A decade after he left, however, convinced that the denominational bureaucracy was "encouraging and funding pressure groups outside of the normal operation of the church courts" (Scott 1989, 6), Kenneth Barker returned and formally joined

Church Alive. The following year, he was asked to stand as the group's president. His condition for acceptance was that he be allowed to extend the organization's reform and renewal publishing, introducing "a modest newsletter which might expand the influence of the group" (Scott 1989, 6). Barker said that he "would be far more interested in acting as Editor of such a newsletter . . . than I would as titular President. In all honesty I must say that without commitment to some such project, I question the continued usefulness of Church Alive" (Barker, in Scott 1989, 6). Put differently, unless Church Alive did something to prove itself alive, it was dead by default. Barker's vision became *Theological Digest*, now *Theological Digest & Outlook*, an important component in the United Church's evolving reform movement.

THE ISSUE: 'EIGHTY-EIGHT AND BEYOND

Victoria, British Columbia, is one of the most beautiful cities in Canada. Located at the southern tip of Vancouver Island in the Strait of Juan de Fuca, it is well known for its charm, hospitality, and magnificent natural setting. In August 1988, the University of Victoria hosted the 32nd General Council of The United Church of Canada, a meeting that was destined to stand as a watershed in the history of Canada's largest Protestant denomination. Despite a full agenda, the only question of moment was whether the church would agree to the ordination or commissioning of gay men and lesbians. Since the mid-1970s, the church had been struggling with this question, and momentum toward the Victoria meeting had been building for years.

Nearly a decade earlier, a 1980 church report on human sexuality, *In God's Image*, recognized the fact that gay men and lesbians were already active in ministry, in most if not every denomination, and had been for a very long time (Division of Mission in Canada 1980; cf. Anderson 1983; Watts 1983). Thus, the question of *acknowledged* ordination and commissioning fell under two broad rubrics: (1) should homosexuality, in and of itself, be a barrier to ordination and commissioning, and (2) given the possibility of ordination and commissioning, how should the church effect the *integration* and *acceptance* of homosexual ministers into congregational life? For many in the church—both those opposed to homosexual ordination and commissioning, and those in favor of it—the nearly 100 pages of the report boiled down to one sentence: "On the basis of this report there is no reason in principle why mature, self-accepting homosexuals, any more than mature, self-accepting heterosexuals, should not be ordained or commissioned" (Division of Mission in Canada 1980, 98). That year, at its 28th General Council, the United Church received *In God's Image* as a preliminary study document to be disseminated throughout the denomination for further discussion. The council directed that a draft statement reflecting the outcome of these discussions be ready for the 30th General Council four years hence.

Among other things, *In God's Image* discussed such topics as the silence of the Gospels on Jesus' sexuality, the biblical witness about angelic sexuality, the place of intimacy as the heart of marriage, and an almost tantric affirmation that "every sexual act has the power to become a disclosure of spirit to spirit" (Division of Mission in Canada 1980, 46). The report made four years later, however, recognized that, out of all the various discussions both surrounding and generated by *In God's Image*, there was really only one question in which most church members were interested: Would the church ordain or commission self-declared, practicing homosexuals? Before that question, all others were quite simply rescindent (cf. Division of Ministry Personnel and Education 1984).

Released as *Sexual Orientation and Eligibility for The Order of Ministry*, the task group responsible for the 1984 report had sought input from groups in favor of homosexual ordination as well as those opposed to it (which, at that point, in an organized sense meant the UCRF and Church Alive), denominational officials and academics, various provincial human rights commissions, as well as other mainline Protestant denominations such as the Presbyterian Church (USA), the United Methodist Church, and the United Church of Christ. Although the task group identified six positions on the question of homosexual ordination and commissioning, ranging from "Don't Know" to "Yes, Now," it reserved its harshest commentary for those clearly opposed to the church ever knowingly admitting gay men and lesbians to its order of ministry. "The majority in this position," said the report, "take a selective legalistic approach to the Bible on this issue; attack or ignore contemporary biblical scholarship; are judgmental and in some cases punitive; are influenced by popular myths and stereotypes; express varying degrees of anger and even hatred toward homosexual persons" (Division of Ministry Personnel and Education 1984, 7–8). Clearly this was not the position the task group was prepared to take nor recommend to the church. Indeed, following *In God's Image*, the task group's "principal conclusion" declared: "After due study, consultation, deliberation, and prayer, the task group has come to the conclusion that, in and of itself, sexual orientation should not be a factor determining membership in the Order of Ministry of The United Church of Canada" (Division of Ministry Personnel and Education 1984, 5). What the earlier report had left as a hanging option for the church, *Sexual Orientation and Eligibility for The Order of Ministry* suggested as a firm denominational direction.

Reaction across the church was swift and predicable. While wondering if the report went far enough, AFFIRM, a national church coalition of gay men and lesbians, cautiously praised it; conservative church members, including the UCRF, roundly condemned it, divining in its principal conclusion the death knell of the denomination. The UCRF published a 10-page critique of the report (United Church Renewal Fellowship 1984a), calling it "myopic," "uncritical," and "biased," "a hasty leap to unsubstantiated conclusions," and pointing out among other things the vast difference in the report's characterization of those who oppose homosexual ordination and those who support it. Indeed, the UCRF critique offered a compelling methodological analysis of the report, which was due for presentation to the church in August 1984.

Meeting in the small Manitoba town of Morden, 20 miles from the North Dakota border, the 30th General Council virtually replayed the events of 1980, receiving the report of the task group and electing to keep The Issue before the church for yet another round of study and debate. The council instructed two of its divisions "to develop an educational programme with thorough and well developed biblical, ethical and theological components reflecting in a balanced way the theological diversity of the United Church of Canada" (United Church of Canada 1984, 99). The niceties of ecclesial language aside, though, it was clear that the Issue was coming to a head. Those who advocated gay ordination would not wait much longer for it to happen; those who opposed The Issue would not wait much longer for it to be laid permanently to rest. The mandate given the two divisions was to "report back no later than the 32nd General Council [that is, 1988] with a comprehensive statement concerning sexual lifestyles of all members of the Church (heterosexual and homosexual) and concerning fitness for ordination/commissioning based on findings which come following consultation with sessions, congregations, Presbyteries and Conferences."

Another task force, this one with the rather unwieldy name of the National Coordinating Group for Programme & Study on Sexual Orientations, Lifestyles and Ministry (NCG), was struck a few months later, and began work on the educational tools necessary to move the discussion forward. Though the General Council motion called for a "comprehensive statement concerning sexual lifestyles of all members of the Church," the NCG knew as other task groups had before it that very few in the church were concerned with anything other than The Issue at hand. While mandated to include a balance of theological perspectives, like so many denominational study programs even a cursory review of the two NCG discussion kits reveals that they clearly privileged (if not fully supported) an interpretation and presentation of data that favored the principle conclusion of the 1984 *Sexual Orientation and Eligibility for The Order of Ministry*, a reality not lost on those opposed to homosexual ordination and commissioning.

Nearly four years after its original mandate, as the UCCan was preparing for what many in the denomination believed would be the most important General Council since union, data from the consultation was collated and prepared for release to the church as *Toward a Christian Understanding of Sexual Orientation, Lifestyles and Ministry,* known colloquially as the *SOLM* report (National Coordinating Group 1988). Statistically, the response rate to the two discussion resources provided by the NCG was abysmal. By the deadline for submissions, only 17 percent of pastoral charges had responded; out of more than 3 million members and adherents in the denomination, less than 200 sent personal letters to the NCG either supporting or opposing the initiative.

A number of reasons could explain such a low response to such a volatile issue: (a) many who saw the NCG discussion resources also saw through them, recognizing the biases that had been built into them and suspecting the futility of opposing their direction; (b) in many ways, those resources were complicated and unwieldy, requiring a far greater level of commitment and intentionality than many members were willing to invest; (c) many church members—both clergy and lay, on both sides of The Issue—had already made up their minds about the question of gay and lesbian ordination. Not to put too fine a point on it: the church could conduct studies and discussions until hell froze over without changing the opinions of either group. (d) A number of long-term members of the church suggested that apathy was the reason; that is, the majority of rank-and-file members knew that a decision either way would not really affect them or their congregation, and thus they saw little reason to concern themselves. Finally, (e) many in the church, again both clergy and lay, again on either side of The Issue, had already been through numerous official study processes and focus groups at all denominational levels, had participated in innumerable unofficial, watercooler discussions, had watched as the United Church of Canada was alternately pilloried and praised in both the mainstream and the Christian media, and were quite simply exhausted by it all. Whatever the decision, ultimately, a great many in the church simply wanted The Issue to go away.

The NCG studies asked respondents to submit Affirmation Statements, a rather transparent bid to avoid the kind of negative feedback that is so scorned by many mainline Protestants. These Affirmation Statements were then collated in an attempt to plumb the collective mind of the denomination. In those sections of the collation devoted to issues of sexual orientation and the order of ministry, the majority of statements either declared outright or could be construed as declaring their opposition to The Issue. Other comments indicated that some participants felt the study a waste of time, that The Issue would destroy the church, that the study materials were "biased and manipulative" (National Coordinating Group 1988, 88), and that the church ought not be discussing the Issue at all. Regardless of the responses, and corroborating somewhat the conservative position that a decision to ordain gay men and lesbians was inevitable regardless of denominational will, the recommendations made by the

NCG included a clause virtually identical to the 1984 report's principal conclusion. At its 32nd General Council, the church would be asked to "affirm that sexual orientation in and of itself is not a barrier to participation in all aspects of the life and ministry of the Church, including the Order of Ministry" (National Coordinating Group 1988, 4).

This time, it seemed, the church would vote.

When Donald Collett was selected as a commissioner to the 32nd General Council and asked to sit on Sessional Committee 8, the group delegated to deal with the *SOLM* report and its implications for the church, he had some idea what lay ahead. Then serving his third pastoral charge, he had already participated in many of the debates over the past several years. More than that, he knew that he carried with him the weight of conservative expectation from both his congregation and his presbytery.

With the other 23 members of the committee, Collett arrived in Victoria three days earlier than most council commissioners. While there were a host of other items on the biennial council's eight-day agenda, none would generate the controversy and the emotion of the *SOLM* report. For those initial three days, however, Collett and his colleagues pored over more than 1,800 petitions that had been received by the General Council about the report. Of those petitions, sent in from across the church by individuals, both clergy and lay, congregations and their official boards, committees, presbyteries, and conferences, the vast majority registered strong opposition to the only recommendation in the *SOLM* report that ultimately mattered.

Long days of work followed for Collett and the committee, with many sessions extending into the early morning hours. They struggled not only with the various implications of the report itself, but with the broad spectrum of opinion that existed within the committee itself, with the wide-ranging, often acrimonious debates on the floor of the council, with the appearance of "obscene, violent, anti-homosexual graffiti scrawled across several blackboards" in the university classroom that had been designated as their workroom (Riordan 1990, 136). In an effort to negotiate some measure of common ground, some compromise position from which the church could move forward, overtures were made by and to each of the main caucuses: AFFIRM in favor of *SOLM*'s recommendations, and the conservative reform groups that opposed them. Not surprisingly, no matter how hard they worked, no matter how much good will they brought to the table, no such rapprochement was forthcoming.

Finally, based on the enormous amount of feedback they had received, the members of Sessional Committee 8 decided that they could not bring the *SOLM* report before the council and expect anything more than acrimony, rancor, and deadlock. Instead, in a bold move, they took the prerogative afforded sessional committees and decided to write their own statement, setting it before the council in place of the *SOLM* report. After hours of work and numerous drafts, the statement was ready. Under ordinary circumstances, recommendations from sessional committees are presented to the council by the committee chair—in this case, Marion Best, a laywoman from the interior of British Columbia who would herself be elected moderator of the United Church six years later. Sessional Committee 8, however, would not allow her to take the podium alone. They had worked through this together; they would stand with her when she presented what would become known as the Membership, Ministry, and Human Sexuality (MMHS) statement to the nearly 300 commissioners.

In a well-conceived tactical move, Sessional Committee 8 separated the two most contentious components of the *SOLM* report: the link between sexual orientation and ordination or commissioning. Instead, the first declaration of the new statement read: "That all persons, regardless of their sexual orientation, who profess Jesus Christ and obedience to Him, are welcome to be or become full members of the Church" (United Church of Canada 1988, 103). Even in the Community of Concern, few opponents of gay ordination or commissioning had gone so far as to suggest that homosexuals were not welcome in the United Church at all. Separated from this, the first part of the second declaration read: "All members of the Church are eligible to be considered for ordered ministry." While, in practical terms, the separation of the two components is little more than semantics, the symbolic weight it carried, especially in light of the added phrase "are eligible to be considered," was significant.

Hours of debate on the council floor followed the presentation of the new statement. Through a series of motions, the Community of Concern, only a few months old and still struggling to find its own voice in the debate, sought to abridge the obvious implications of the MMHS statement. A definition of what the church meant by "sexual orientation" had to be included. *Defeated.* An amendment was proposed adding to the statement that God expected "celibacy, chastity, sexual abstinence and continence" from all those not in a heterosexual marriage. *Defeated.* An attempt to remove any reference in the statement to injustice against gay men and lesbians on the grounds that it might indicate approval of homosexuality. *Defeated.* A motion to remove the phrase, "regardless of sexual orientation," the heart of the new statement. *Defeated.* Finally, a motion to include the boundary phrase: "in light of Holy Scripture our ideal for all being both faithfulness in marriage and faithful abstinence while single" (see United Church of Canada 1988, 95–112). *Defeated.*

Late on the afternoon of August 24, 1988, the work of Sessional Committee 8 was deemed concluded. Given the emotion of the previous week, the official Record of Proceedings is decidedly understated: "The Moderator expressed sincere thanks to the court for their work on the new Sexuality statement. The Moderator then told the Court a story and Marion Best read from the Psalms" (United Church of Canada 1988, 213).

However ambiguously, the council had spoken, and, as they had over the past several days, newspaper headlines across Canada offered variations on but a single theme: The United Church of Canada has thrown open its pulpits to gays.

THE COMMUNITY OF CONCERN WITHIN THE UNITED CHURCH OF CANADA

"In future years," writes Graham Scott (1989, 5), "a number of Ph.D. theses will undoubtedly be devoted to the crisis which took place in the United Church of Canada in 1988." While, to date this has not been the case, if and when such studies are undertaken, the Community of Concern within the United Church of Canada (COC) will figure prominently in the analysis. Within a decade of its formation, and largely because of its ability to channel various streams of conservative dissent that had been simmering for decades, it has grown into the major theological watchdog organization in the UCCan. Its beginnings, however, were more scattered and decidedly less auspicious.

In February 1988, the Reverend William Fritz was one of those who believed he saw the handwriting on the sanctuary wall for the United Church of Canada. Over the last several years, each of the study documents on sexuality had moved closer and closer to precisely the kind of declarations made in the *SOLM* report. Anticipating the release of the report, Fritz suggested to Church Alive's Kenneth Barker that something proactive needed to be done; reacting after the fact, he argued, would accomplish little. According to Scott (1989), "a well organized push was underway" to approve the recommendations in the *SOLM* report, including support from "the top religion journalists of *The Toronto Star* (Scott 1989, 6–7). Opposition to the report, however, was building across Canada, and clergy in Ottawa, Saskatoon, and on Vancouver Island were preparing a vigorous resistance. Many were already talking about leaving the denomination. Rather than simply meeting to fuss about the impending report, though, Barker sent Fritz a draft dissent, and suggested that a meeting of similarly concerned ministers be called for St. Patrick's Day. At that meeting, an initial Statement of Dissent was prepared, and a public meeting called for April 8—the birth date of the Community of Concern within The United Church of Canada.

Over 250 clergy and laypeople from across the country met at the public meeting in Weston, Ontario, to voice their confusion and concern. Throughout the day, they discussed options and reworked the draft statement supplied by Barker. By the end of the day, the Declaration of Dissent (Community of Concern 1988b; cf. Barker 1988) was ready. Since, like the UCRF and Church Alive before them, the nascent COC wanted to avoid any impression that it was little more than a group of conservative reactionaries, the first article in the Declaration of Dissent was careful to point out that signatories held "a diversity of theological approaches." In stark contrast to later COC statements, both official and unofficial, this diversity is also reflected in the statement's rather broad, even generous language. Those who signed "affirmed the rights of all people within God's creation to be respected as part of the human family on earth," but "expressed our opposition to essential thrusts, directions and conclusions" of the *SOLM* report. An "inadequate understanding of the role of the Holy Spirit operating in Scripture" had led the NCG to a "flawed methodology" and "limited and subjective conclusions." The core of their position, which would remain so throughout the debates of the coming years, was that "we are convinced that the Biblical intention for sexual behavior is loving fidelity for life within marriage and loving celibacy outside marriage." While many were concerned that the position of marriage was being degraded by the report and that sexual activity outside marriage condoned, few at the meeting and after were under any illusion that the real issue was the looming possibility of gay and lesbian ordination.

When the Declaration of Dissent was approved unanimously, the question became: What now? Since the response to their invitation was considerably greater than the organizers had anticipated (Scott 1989, 7), another proposal was put before the group. A national body would be incorporated, to be known as the Community of Concern, and a 15-member steering committee—the vast majority of whom were clergy, a not infrequent occurrence in reform and renewal movements—elected. As its first order of business, the COC distributed the Declaration of Dissent to clergy and congregations across the church. At this point, the COC was a loose coalition of regional groups organized around support for the April 8 Declaration of Dissent, and the steering committee did little more than coordinate the distribution and collection of signed statements.

In less than four months, more than 1,000 ministers and 32,000 members had added their signatures to the document. Scott contends that the actual lay figure was considerably higher given that this number represents "only a fraction of the response for many congregations wrote in registering their dissent without [individual] signatures" (Scott 1989, 7). Thus, it is impossible to know precisely how many opposed the *SOLM* report— or opposed what they thought it was, since few actual copies had been made available, and many church members were reacting to secondhand reports from the media and the pulpit. In signing, though, a number of different groups across the church adopted the name Community of Concern, and the impression of a national, grassroots movement began, one dedicated to a single goal: the defeat of the *SOLM* report at the upcoming General Council.

And it was defeated—soundly—to be replaced by the Membership, Ministry, and Human Sexuality statement. Following the General Council, though, as August passed into September, confusion reigned in the church. While the official position was that "nothing had changed" with respect to standards of ordination and commissioning, few did not realize that, in many ways, "nothing was the same." Technically, nothing *had* changed. The church had made no official statement that gay men and lesbians would be admitted to the order of ministry. Defenders of the decision appealed to the deliberately ambiguous language of the MMHS statement that all full members of the church were "eligible to be considered for ordered ministry," and reiterated to their constituents the long, often arduous process by which prospective ministers were screened, selected, and educated before ordination. As Vernon Wishart, a former member of the denominational Theology and Faith Committee, stated, however, "whether one agrees with the Victoria statement or not, it is less than honest to continue to say the decision represents 'no change.' To perpetuate that myth does nothing but breed distrust and cynicism about our leadership" (Wishart n.d.: 1).

This distrust was exacerbated by the General Council's repeated rejection of suggestions that the Victoria decision be sent to the entire church for approval by remit. For supporters of the MMHS statement, such a move would have proven disastrous; the vast majority of petitions Collett and his sessional committee colleagues digested opposed in no uncertain terms the ordination or commissioning of gay men and lesbians. To this day, Collett is unequivocal in his opinion that if the question had gone before the church in the form of a remit—a vote either by every congregation or by every member—The Issue would have been resoundingly defeated. "Obviously the Church had made a momentous decision," wrote Scott, just a few months later, "and to pretend otherwise seemed to many only a tactic aimed at avoiding a fair testing of the question" (1989, 8).

A variety of responses followed. Some members, both clergy and lay, withdrew from the Community of Concern because they felt they could live with the Victoria decision; they had wanted the *SOLM* report defeated, and it was. Case closed; move on. Others, though, feeling that the replacement statement both endorsed the most controversial part of the original report and confirmed fears that their voices simply did not matter in the evolution of denominational policy, withdrew from the United Church altogether, some advocating a full-scale secession. Others stayed, but moved to boycott the church, withholding funds until the MMHS statement was rescinded.

Eighteen months after the council, for example, Five Members in Faith, a group of retired laymen still outraged over the MMHS statement, urged the church to stop payments to the denominational headquarters. "It is TIME to takes the gloves off!" they wrote in a letter sent to the official board of every congregation (1990). "Armchair protests—Resolutions (1800)—Prayer Vigils—are not enough. Only FISCAL ACTION will stop the 33rd General Council . . . from ramming the current Membership, Ministry and Human Sexuality report down our throats!" Their solution was for churches to withhold congregational apportionments from the denomination's Mission and Service fund (from which the General Council and its divisions draw their operating budgets), and use them instead to fund "outreach projects of our Congregations' own choosing, until such time as we are satisfied that *Ordination of Self-declared Practicing* Homosexuals is **unacceptable** to General Council of The United Church of Canada" (Five Members in Faith 1990; emphasis in the original).

A month after the council in Victoria concluded, though, a general meeting of the COC was called to consider just what to do next. While more than 800 laypeople and clergy attended the meeting, they were told on arrival they would be permitted to participate in the day's discussions only if they first signed a new COC statement, called the Declaration of Intentions (Community of Concern 1988c), which organizers had brought with them to the meeting. The most vocal protest over this came from the Very Reverend Clarke MacDonald, a former moderator and distinguished church leader who had joined the COC out of his concern over the implications of the *SOLM* report. Now that the report had been rendered a historic document, he could not support the increasingly militant tenor of the emerging reform movement, and withdrew. In addition to so high profile a churchman as MacDonald, following this meeting the COC lost other members who either could not in good conscience sign the Declaration of Intentions, or felt manipulated by the emergent COC process that day.

Citing a number of incidents across the church, though, many of those who supported a continued, intensified dissent insisted that any clergy who publicly opposed the directions set by General Council were immediately targeted for harassment by church officials. Feelings around this ran the gamut from a vague discomfort at presbytery meetings to fully orbed conspiracy theories that included a secret blacklist of dissident clergy allegedly kept at the denominational headquarters. Any difficulty encountered by evangelical clergy in pastoral charges was incorporated into this construction of reality, often without regard for the ways in which the clergyperson had either co-created or exacerbated the situation. The realities of individual pastoral relationships notwithstanding, the Declaration of Intentions "called upon the officers and courts of the Church to cease and desist from the harassment of ministers and congregations who are in conscience dissenting from the General Council decision to ordain/commission practicing homosexual persons" (Community of Concern 1988c).

Within months, sometimes weeks of the Victoria decision, numerous presbyteries and congregations, often employing the language of "loving faithfulness in marriage and faithful chastity in singleness," passed motions that they would neither ordain nor commission an acknowledged homosexual, nor would they settle or accept one for settlement. In 1989, the COC produced statistics indicating that nearly 90 percent of United Church membership disapproved of the ordination or commissioning of gay men and lesbians, and that nearly 80 percent were dissatisfied with the way in which the decision had been reached (Community of Concern 1989). Though their accuracy is not outside the realm of possibility, whether these statistics actually reflect the views of the denomination is, in reality, immaterial (recall the VOW survey in chapter 4). More important was the fact that the Community of Concern believed them, that they regarded the figures as justification for their cause, and that they plotted their organizational course on the basis of those beliefs.

A great many in the church, however, were confused about what, precisely, the role of the COC was now that the MMHS statement had been accepted. Should it not, as MacDonald inferred, simply disband now that its stated task—the defeat of the *SOLM* report—was accomplished? In April 1989, GC general secretary Howard Mills issued a statement to the Toronto-Scarborough Presbytery regarding the COC. In part, it read: "Please be advised that the Community of Concern is a movement which is not recognized as an official body accountable to the courts of The United Church of Canada, even though it is made up of United Church members" (Mills, in Ross 1990b, 1). COC executive director Gordon Ross responded to this in early 1990, sending the General Council Executive an open letter, beginning with what was by then a fairly standard encomium of concerns. Recognizing that the 33rd General Council would have to revisit the Victoria decision in some fashion, and choose either to rescind, reconsider, or reaffirm the MMHS statement, Ross (citing Faris 1989) concluded that "the remarkable phenomenon of the extensive dominance of pro-homosexual ideology" in the United Church was clearly documented (Ross 1990b, 4).

This notion of a "pro-homosexual ideology" is an important conceptual shift in the COC's articulation of the problem. Until now The Issue had been sexual orientation, sexual practice, and the suitability of gay men and lesbians for the order of ministry. With publication of Vancouver minister Donald Faris's book, *Trojan Horse: The Homosexual Ideology and the Christian Church* (1989; cf. Faris 1993), which was hailed by denominational conservatives as both a vindication of their position and a manifesto for their struggle, the problem was now one of pro-homosexual ideology, a floating concept deployed more for its symbolic value than its realistic contribution to the debate. "It seems to us," Ross continued, "that the time is overdue for the United Church of Canada to reject this pseudo-orthodoxy that the homosexual ideology currently enjoys within the structures of the church" (1990b, 6).

At that time, a major concern for Ross and the COC, vis-à-vis the trojan horse of pro-homosexual ideology, was the continued appointment of an openly gay minister, the Reverend Ron Coughlin, as the denominational secretary for education and ministry vocations. Ten days earlier, Ross had sent a letter to Coughlin's supervisor questioning the appropriateness of his appointment. In language reminiscent of the McCarthy investigations, Ross wrote: "This is to advise you that we have on file affidavit evidence which attests to reasonable and probable grounds for the belief that the said Ron Coughlin has been and is presently a practicing homosexual, openly and publicly declared and professed in that he has, on at least two occasions, admitted to living in a marriage/covenanted relationship with another male person" (1990a, 3). Calling for an investigation into these allegations, the clear intention of Ross's letter was that Coughlin be removed from the position as soon as possible.

In preparation for the 1990 General Council, and uncertain how the court would treat the Victoria decision, the Community of Concern issued yet and again another statement of its position: the "comprehensive Community of Concern agenda" (Trueman 1990a). While still anchored around the COC's desire to see the Victoria decision rescinded, the 40-point Articles of Concern (Community of Concern 1990) address a considerably wider range of issues. And, although it includes some rather banal suggestions (for example, "Encourage Church members to communicate amongst themselves using Church publications, advertisements, and notices"), it does make a number of pointed demands for denominational reform. The COC called on the church to "Abandon 'affirmuolatry'—i.e. an inability to say no to practices and perspectives at variance with historic Christian faith" (art. 6). This was followed immediately by a request to "Establish a theological college to teach theology consistent with historic Christian faith" (art. 7). Both of these articles highlight a common device in reform and renewal discourse—the concept of the "historic Christian faith." While I will discuss this more fully in chapter 9, here it is enough to point out its deployment as another floating concept, again more useful for its rhetorical effect and its reinforcement of the conservative reform movement's cognitive praxis than for its substantive contribution to the discussion. Under the rubric "On Discipline and Discipleship," the COC wanted the denomination to "Acknowledge the right of free speech within the Church" (art. 16); to "Withdraw intemperate language used to describe those who challenge present church policy" (art. 17); and "Value those ministers who practice legitimate dissent and remove fear of prosecution and reprisal within the Church Courts" (art. 18).

Two aspects of these articles are significant for the cognitive praxis that was evolving, and that led to the rapid entrenchment of the COC's oppositional principles. First, that these items are included in the 1990 manifesto indicate clearly that the COC regarded them as serious concerns by that point in time. In their opinion, free speech *had* been denied to traditionalist members of the church. Notwithstanding the caustic language occasionally deployed by reform and renewal movements themselves (see chapter 9), "intemperate language" *had* been used by church officials. Clergy who dissented from the Victoria decision *did* feel deprecated. And, once again, whether any of these perceptions reflected events accurately is entirely beside the point. Intemperance, bad feelings, suspicion, and acrimony described both sides of the debate, and this perception controlled the development of the COC. Second, they indicate the level of persecution felt by those who opposed the Victoria decision and other recent denominational directions, such as inclusive language, the privileging of feminist and liberation theologies in church seminaries, and the alleged abandonment of the authority of Scripture and the centrality of Christ. This sense of persecution is reflected in a number of articles included under the rubric, "On Just Attitudes." Here, the Articles of Concern called on the church to "Acknowledge that the Community of Concern is a loyal voice within the United Church of Canada" (art. 35); "Halt legal actions against congregations who have withdrawn from the United Church and have kept their buildings and property" (art. 37); and "Convene a public forum to consider these Articles of Concern prior to the 33rd General Council" (art. 40). The COC believed that those in favor of homosexual ordination and commissioning had already had their chance at a public forum, the 32nd General Council in Victoria. Now, the opposition deserved a chance.

When the General Council met again in August 1990, however, Sessional Committee 10 presented a simple motion to the United Church's highest court: "IT IS MOVED that the 33rd General Council affirm the Statement 'Membership, Ministry and Human Sexuality' as adopted by the 32nd General Council" (United Church of Canada 1990). Urging the church to "seek unity in this diversity," and despite the fact that a denominational consultation carried out by the General Council indicated that the majority of the church was opposed to the 1988 statement, the council carried the motion 302 to 74.

The Community of Concern had lost. They had come looking for some measure of compromise, some affirmation that their position was as valued by the church as those who supported MMHS. Both then-COC president, John Trueman, and executive director, Gordon Ross, had been granted corresponding privileges by the court; they could participate fully in the discussions, but could not vote. And they had come away with nothing.

Two days after the decision to reaffirm the MMHS statement, wearing black sashes, Trueman and Ross resigned from the court. In a letter to the moderator, the Right Reverend Sang Chul Lee, they wrote that "in light of the action taken by the 33rd General Council in affirming the recommendations of the Committee without significant amendment, we have no further wish to participate in the proceedings. . . . Accordingly, we would ask that our names be removed from the roll of the 33rd General Council at our request" (Ross and Trueman 1990). Not unlike conservative members of the Presbyterian Church (USA), they declared: "It is our continuing view that the United Church of Canada finds itself in a situation where irreconcilable differences exist between the positions held by significant portions of its membership, as reflected in the MMHS consultation with pastoral charges and those re-affirmed by the Commissioners of the 33rd General Council on Tuesday, August 21st. In our view, the possibilities of dialogue on this question have now been exhausted" (Ross and Trueman 1990).

In a sidebar explaining the situation, Trueman (1990b) expressed his own outrage at the proceedings. "It was impossible to attend the 33rd General Council without realizing that the majority of Commissioners had been hand picked and were perfectly programmed by the administration, before the Council began, to ignore reason, to ignore fact, and to ignore conciliation on the MMHS statement. Not only was the conference decided on this issue, but the conference itself was not conciliatory—it was inflammatory!"

Since 1990, the United Church of Canada has attempted to deal with a number of significant theological, doctrinal, and practical issues, some of which emerged in logical consequence to the MMHS decision: same-gender covenanting; the authority and interpretation of Scripture; ecumenism and its place in the expanding religious economy; the person and work of Jesus Christ; the relationship between Christianity and Judaism; and new liturgical and musical resources for congregational worship. From each of these, the Community of Concern has derived a continuing mandate for theological reform of the church and discovered ongoing validation that their construction of reality is accurate.

THE NATIONAL ALLIANCE OF COVENANTING CONGREGATIONS

As the continued denominational frustration of their efforts propelled the Community of Concern from a single-issue oppositional movement to a full-time theological watchdog in the United Church, conservatives who wanted both to remain in the church and, at the same time, to express their anger at the Victoria and London decisions, began to put other reform measures in place. Six weeks before the 33rd General Council was to meet in 1990, four ministers from rural Alberta met together to draft a set of Articles of Association according to which conservative congregations could align themselves within the church, but in opposition to the directions they feared the London council would reaffirm. This was the beginning of the National Alliance of Covenanting Congregations (NACC).

In very similar manner to statements made by the United Church Renewal Fellowship, Church Alive, and the Community of Concern, the
NACC's "Articles of Association for Member Congregations of The
United Church of Canada Wishing to Maintain the Historic Faith" reit-
erate allegiance both to the Twenty Articles of Faith and to "the Scriptures
of the Old and New Testament as the primary source and ultimate standard of Christian faith and life" (National Alliance of Covenanting Congregations 1990). Like so many similar statements, there is a deceptive
simplicity to the way in which these articles are framed. First, primary
allegiance is given to the Twenty Articles, and given as though these articles are in some way self-explanatory and self-interpreting. Second,
while reform and renewal movements may not be quick to admit it, very
few liberal members of the church would have difficulty offering similar
allegiances. Recall that, in the United Church of Canada, when a minister
is ordained or commissioned, he or she is expected to declare an essential
agreement with the Basis of Union, especially the Twenty Articles. Problems develop, however, when the cognitive and theological elasticity built
into the concept of essential agreement generates mutually exclusive interpretations of those Twenty Articles. The normative dissonance allowed
by essential agreement is considerably more restricted in reform and renewal domains than in liberal sectors of the church. There, a much narrower range of interpretation is considered legitimate. Put differently,
when both the Twenty Articles of Faith and the biblical witness are interpreted according to reform and renewal principles, those interpretations
are considered authentic and valid; when they differ—as, for example,
with homosexuality, inclusive language, and issues of social concern and
the role they ought to play in the life of the church—the interpretation is
considered faulty at best, and often iniquitous or heretical at worst.

Because the MMHS statement was the precipitating moment for the
NACC, it is logical that the central article of association should address
the primary issue at hand: preventing gay men and lesbians from assum-
ing ministry positions in the church. In the context of conservative reform
discourse, this happens both obliquely and at the same time transparently.
Thus, the second article reads: "It is expected that those called to the pastorate of associated congregations will strive to exemplify the highest ideals of faithful service in the exercise of their public ministry and will live
with honesty, purity and charity with all people. Fidelity and marriage
and chastity in singleness, as defined by the 19th General Council, are
among the standards of faith conduct required of pastors of associated
congregations" (National Alliance of Covenanting Congregations 1990).

It is difficult to envision ministers in any circumstance *not* agreeing, at
least in principle, with the first sentence. Try to imagine a minister intentionally exemplifying *less than* the "highest ideals of faithful service," intentionally seeking to live his or her life dishonestly, impurely, or

uncharitably. That this happens, frequently, regularly, and without denominational exception, I take as an axiom of church life; but circumstance and transgression are significantly different social dynamics than intention and strategy. However, because at that time same-gender holy union ceremonies (that is, marriages—although the gay and lesbian community is seriously split on the usefulness of both the term and the conceptualization) were recognized neither civilly nor ecclesiastically in Canada, the second sentence effectively and pointedly excluded from the order of ministry those homosexuals who wanted to live their lives honestly and faithfully. Which was, of course, precisely its point.

Like many similar reform and renewal movements, while the NACC framed its organization around fidelity to theological principles and ecclesiastical traditions, its primary function was to coordinate and facilitate congregational opposition to the Victoria decision. The Commissioner's Covenant, a second statement that was presented for signature to the delegates of the 1990 General Council and which is now a constitutional appendix for the NACC, puts the matter more clearly. Given "loving faithfulness in marriage or loving chastity in singleness," the document states (art. 4.3), "it is therefore a contravention of our faith to solemnize same-gender unions ('marriages'), or to ordain, commission, settle or appoint self-declared, practising homosexuals, however admirable they may be" (National Alliance of Covenanting Congregations 1990). For whatever reasons, the Commissioners Covenant was signed by just 22 delegates out of 400.

While presenting a multipart statement of purpose, the agenda of the NACC breaks down into two fairly simple items: (1) "encourage United Church of Canada congregations that are committed to maintaining the historic Christian faith and life" and (2) "maintain a register of covenanting congregations and regional associations" (National Alliance of Covenanting Congregations 1990). All other activities, national and regional meetings, news items distributed across the covenanting network, prayer requests and calendars, as well as pastoral vacancies and clergy availability lists support those two primary functions. Like vague statements of allegiance to the Twenty Articles of Faith and the primacy of Scripture, "the historic Christian faith" is another floating signifier that NACC adherents interpret within rigorous conceptual boundaries. That which transgresses those boundaries is, by definition, located outside the pale of that historic Christian faith.

The problem with this is that, as a signifier of anything other than that which is interpreted to support and maintain the conservative Protestant vision of Christianity, "the historic Christian faith" is simply an empty concept. Although it is often used this way, history is not an objective circumstance that can be abstracted and made to command fealty for purposes of ideological advancement. There is no one authoritative version of history that can indisputably separate the authentic from the inauthentic. Rather, in terms of its contribution to the social construction of reality, history is an intricate, often murky and inconsistent complex of situations and forces, attitudes and choices, memories and anti-memories, all of which serve the interpretative agendas of those who deploy history as something demanding allegiance. And, in deploying something like "the historic Christian faith" as a binding signifier, reform and renewal movements almost consistently ignore the fact that there is no such thing as Christianity per se; there are, instead, both geographically and across time, multiple, often competing, sometimes mutually incompatible Christianities. The historic Christian faith as it is understood, for example, by the Greek Orthodox monks at the monastery on Mount Athos (at which not even female farm animals are allowed) is considerably different than that embraced by fundamentalist congregations in the Ozark Mountains whose faith is actualized through handling poisonous snakes. Yet, neither would deny they inhabit the historic Christian faith, although they may deny such inhabitance to the other. More pointedly, while the Roman Catholic Church is perhaps the leading contender for an unbroken Christian durability, some other defenders of the historic Christian faith—notably fundamentalist Protestants—consider it to be not only un-Christian, but the leading contender for the One World Religion of the Antichrist (cf., for example, Hunt 1990, 1994). Thus, like most floating signifiers, the historic Christian faith actually conceals more than it discloses, and obscures more than it clarifies. It functions as a code phrase, a primary group sigil for, in the case of each of the UCCan's reform and renewal movements, "like-minded congregations and individuals" (National Alliance of Covenanting Congregations 1990).

PART III

Constructing Dissent as Identity and Community

What should our approach be? Should it again be low-key, with perhaps an information table and a newsletter for commissioners? On the other hand, should we have mass demonstrations on the floor of General Council until it is either brought to a halt or is prepared to move in an acceptable direction? Or should our emphasis fall somewhere between these two extremes?
—Community of Concern within the United Church of Canada

So, who's causing schism? Some leaders of the Presbyterians are accusing evangelicals in the Presbyterian Church (USA) of being schismatic and trying to lay a guilt trip on the Presbyterian Lay Committee because its voice is so dominant. Sorry, that dog won't hunt. What is being ignored in such accusations of "divisiveness" and "schism" is that the denomination and its leaders have been the instigators of schism and division for 36 years—and, regrettably, they have been unimaginably successful at chasing people away.
—The Presbyterian Lay Committee

The Confessing Movement seeks to be a responsible advocate of orthodoxy. The challenge is to engage in such activity in ways that do not treat antagonists inaccurately or unjustly. The history of theological debate reveals the difficulty of this task and the tendency of all sides to violate the ideal along the way. The Confessing Movement is needed at this time to insure that the orthodox position is accurately advocated, and that caricatures by others do not go unaddressed.
—The Confessing Movement with the United Methodist Church

CHAPTER 8

Structuring Dissent: Organizational Dimensions of Reform and Renewal

It seems reasonable to suggest that people respond to situations based on the *perceived meaning* those situations have for them, not necessarily the accuracy of their perceptions. And that meaning is both reinforced and modified according to the various interactions that take place between the various actors, claimsmakers, and stakeholders involved in any given situation. It follows, then, that the same situation will not have the same meaning for all potential participants, and one of our tasks is to understand as far as we can why groups interpret situations differently and why different groups gravitate to the particular interpretations that they do. Understanding this process ultimately helps us understand how the cognitive praxis of particular social groups and movements develops over time, evolves through a process of social dialectic, and, often, is reified as an institutional or quasi-institutional position.

To take an example common to any participant in acrimonious church dispute, if the vote following a particular debate on the floor of a church court does not go the way one group hoped that it would, that group may interpret the decision as an indication that its voice has not been heard by the denomination, that it has been ignored, marginalized, or dismissed. And, of course, that may be the case. On the other hand, it may just be that the rest of the participants in the debate didn't agree with it. Its voice *was* heard; it *did* contribute to the debate; it simply *lost* the vote. In the context of recent contests over issues as volatile as those that have threatened to split mainline Protestantisms, however, the appearance of being proactively marginalized by the denomination carries considerably greater symbolic weight than merely being outvoted on the floor of a General Synod, Council, or Conference.

In situations of competing interest, then, the ability to control meaning, to limit and manage the acceptable or authoritative interpretations of events, to mitigate or eliminate competing perceptions, and to establish and maintain the unique correctness of one's own version becomes paramount. Thus, *how* conservative reform groups choose to present denominational positions and decisions with which they disagree is as important as the reasons they claim for their disagreement. While their more liberal coreligionists are often as rigid and unyielding in their beliefs as are members of these reform movements, in this chapter I would like to pursue some of the ways in which mainline Protestant traditionalists seek to influence the discourse in an attempt to advance their cause. Following a brief excursus into the rationalist character of reform and renewal response to denominational change, in these two concluding chapters I would like to consider this negotiation in light of (a) the structural development of reform movements, (b) the politics of reform and renewal identity, and (c) the prospects for reform and renewal in the context of denominations that seem disinclined to significant changes in their theological, doctrinal, and practical directions.

BRAND BETRAYAL AND THE DENOMINATIONAL MAINLINE

The occasionally overblown claims of their critics notwithstanding, the cognitive praxis of conservative reform and renewal consists of eminently rational actions. That is, they are actions undertaken on the basis of rationally grounded intellectual processes, the adversarial nature of subversive processes and confrontational tactics, and the logical processes of litigation, both civil and ecclesiastical. Put differently, when asked to explain why they do what they do, most reform and renewal participants would have little difficulty articulating their reasons, their rationale for both viewpoint and tactics. In this, they conform to what Jürgen Habermas considers "the central presupposition of rationality: they can be defended against criticism" (1984, 16). This is not to say, of course, that all parties will accept these defenses as valid, coherent, or in any way compelling. That they are so for those who adhere to them, however, is undeniable.

Since church decline, both numerically and financially, is perhaps the most common conceptual framework in which conservative reform movements articulate their various denominational problems, one way of looking at this process is to consider these movements through the lens of a religious economy. In this analytic metaphor, different types of religious organizations function as competing firms within a particular social economy: religious doctrines and experiences are the commodities offered by these competing firms, and religious adherents, both actual and potential, are the consumers these firms seek to attract with their specific brands of goods and services. While this way of approaching a religious economy is not new (cf. Finke and Stark 1992; Iannaccone 1994; Stark and Finke 2000; Young 1997), it is less often applied to conflict and competition within specific denominations.

In many cases, the situation of reform and renewal movements can be compared to brand-loyal consumers who awake one morning to find that the firms with which they have dealt for so long are now carrying a decidedly different product, one often characterized as "new and improved," but which is deeply dissatisfying to many longtime consumers. It tastes like Coke, but it isn't *really* Coke; it's "new" Coke. It reads "Smarties" on the box, but everyone knows real Smarties aren't *blue!* For many denominational traditionalists, this same experience of brand betrayal lies at the heart of what they regard as their faithful resistance.

Consider the actions of the Savannah Presbyterian churches, which argued that changing denominational positions amounted to a breach of the contract under which those churches joined the denomination. Or, consider the conservative protesters outside the meeting halls at the 1992 United Church of Canada (UCCan) General Council. Carrying large banners that read, "They have taken my Lord away and I know not where they have laid him," they registered their dissatisfaction with the denomination's emerging stand on the authority and interpretation of Scripture and what they regarded as its de-emphasis on the centrality of Christ. Or, consider Ted Wigglesworth, a former United Church of Canada minister who claimed that changes in the theological position of the church (which amount to a change in the brand of religion offered or endorsed by the church) actually constitute a breach of contract with him, not only as a religious consumer but as a church employee, and in 1999 filed suit against the church on those grounds. Or, finally, consider the numerous court cases brought by various clergy in the United Methodist Church in an attempt to prevent the celebration of same-sex unions or to punish those who have celebrated them. Their understanding of the faith interprets such celebrations as breaches of faith—and implicitly of ecclesiastical contract. This list, obviously, could be extended considerably.

For many reform and renewal participants, these denominational shifts represent at their core an abandonment of understood and accepted religious commodities. To draw out a different analogy, it is as though customers at a particular bank invested their hard-earned money in American dollars, but unbeknownst to them the bank made a decision to honor withdrawals only in Thai *bhat*. Useful in Thailand, perhaps, but not what the customers here at home had come to expect. As one traditionalist member of the UCCan put it in a 1998 letter (McCartney 1998) to *Fellowship Magazine:* "The United Church has a written contract with its supporters;

it is the *Basis of Union* as amended." Similarly, for traditionalist Episcopalians, Cranmer's *Book of Common Prayer* is the liturgical embodiment of the doctrinal contract between the See of Canterbury and the worldwide Anglican communion. Whatever their rubric, alternative worship resources breach that contract.

As a way of considering these processes a bit further, I would like to suggest a few minor axioms and propositions. While these may seem a bit obvious at first, I think they serve useful heuristic purposes both to remind us of their basic force in society, and to help in understanding the character and motivation of conservative reform movements. The first axiom reads:

A1: Religions are not static entities. They evolve and change over time, in response to a wide variety of social, cultural, even geographical and physical factors. They exist in time, and to exist in time is to exist in change. (see Stark and Bainbridge 1987, 27)

The changes that take place in particular religious traditions vary from the seemingly insignificant—reading congregational announcements at the beginning of the worship service instead of just before the collection of the offering—to the indisputably substantial—women, perhaps even lesbians, ordained as priests and ministers. Traditionalist conceptualization of religious belief and practice, however, often minimizes this evolution in an attempt to regulate or restrict change. Religious belief and practice become reified, located in particular historical and cultural forms, but universalized as though those forms forever define the limits of acceptable belief and practice. Despite clear evidence in the early Church of different oral and textual traditions, despite the various controversies over what should and should not be considered Scripture, and even despite the suggestion that some scriptural materials were deliberately manipulated during the process of canonization to conform to an emerging orthodoxy (cf. Bauer 1971; Ehrman 1993), the Bible as the Word of God has become reified as an object somehow apart from the social and cultural processes of its production. While this reification is perhaps more commonly associated with the evangelical or fundamentalist Protestantisms, "the Bible is a book of absolutes, an infallible book," writes United Methodist pastor Gary Wales (1998). "The Bible claims to be an infallible book, meaning that it is incapable of error." Rather than a series of documents gathered together over time, modified as the church evolved (consider the deuterocanonical books extant in Roman Catholic versions of the Bible, but deleted from Protestant editions), and subject to all the exigencies of transmission, translation, and interpretation, the Bible is regarded as a static entity, the Word of God immune from the effects of these factors, and as such unassailable. And this is so not only for the documentary but also many of the doctrinal artifacts of the Church.

Coinciding with church discussions over the person of Christ, for example, has been the debate over the nature of the Godhead, specifically the Trinity. In "The Trinity: Irrelevant or Essential?," the Reverend Andrew Stirling, a conservative United Church of Canada pastor, illustrates the manner in which doctrinal reification often takes place in response to doctrinal questions and challenges. The article's title itself sets up the first of several false dichotomies: if the traditional doctrine of the Trinity is not essential, then it is irrelevant. That there are other options, other ways of framing the Trinitarian problem that take into consideration the essentially metaphorical character of theological language (cf. McFague 1989, 1997), is not addressed by Stirling. Rather, the argument is framed in terms of artificially polarized choices, neither of which may satisfy Stirling's denominational colleagues. He does admit the socially constructed nature of theology during the first centuries of the Church when he notes that "the Church finally concluded that the Trinity was the best expression of God, and that He is Father, Son, and Holy Spirit" (1999, 5). He then proceeds, however, to argue for that same formulation's essential relevance for the Church sixteen centuries later, when virtually nothing of the intellectual, social, or cultural world of the fourth-century Mediterranean church obtains in mainline North American Protestantism. This he does through a series of derivative false dichotomies. "If Jesus was not divine then nearly all our worship is idolatrous" (Stirling 1999, 6)—avoiding the fact that many Christian churches do not worship Jesus per se, but worship God through Jesus. A subtle, but not unimportant theological distinction. Following on this, though, Stirling continues that "if Jesus is not one with the Father, then the Christian community has simply made Jesus to be another God and we are in error" (1999, 6). Here, in addition to the liturgical difficulty just noted, the problem is what Stirling means by "one with the Father"—a problem that was lost neither on the Eastern Orthodox Churches at the time of the *filioque* split (ca. 1054), nor on the various modern Unitarianisms or modalist Trinitarian reinterpretations. "Take away the Trinity," Stirling concludes, however, "and the love of the Cross becomes a kind gesture or a mistaken act of self-abasement" (1999, 6). Once again, that there are numerous other ways of interpreting the crucifixion and its significance for Christianity is not considered by Stirling. Rather, there is simply the stark choice of a reified theological construct, or the abandonment of all theological grounding.

Both Wales and Stirling illustrate aspects of the second axiom.

A2: Because religions are not static entities, it follows that, when changes take place, these changes will be welcomed by some (those whom the changes benefit in some way) and resisted by others (those whom the changes in some way threaten).

Another good example of this, and which, since they are legion in the history of religion, could form the bedrock for a sociology of orthodoxy and heresy, is the reaction of Roman Catholics to the decision made by the Second Vatican Council. While I have not discussed Catholic reform and renewal movements in this book, I include this very brief example here simply to highlight the fact that Roman Catholicism displays many of the characteristics we find in conservative Protestant reform movements (cf. Cuneo 1997; Dinges 1983; Dinges and Hitchcock 1991; Weaver and Appleby 1995). While many Catholics did greet with great joy the changes brought about by Vatican II, as Pope John XXIII hoped they would when he gave his opening address to the council, the swift opposition from Catholic traditionalists to such documents as *Sacrosanctum Concilium* (The Sacred Constitution on the Liturgy) indicated that such joy was hardly universal.

Finally, as we have seen, the place of gay men and lesbians in the church, particularly in the order of ministry, has precipitated denominational sea changes that draw clear lines around these two axioms. That is, the precise change that is welcomed by one group is the very thing that catalyzes opposition in the other. From these axioms, a number of propositions derive, of which the first two read:

P1: A change in the nature of understood and accepted religious commodities will generate feelings of abandonment and brand betrayal in some portion of the constituent religious consumer base.

P2: Because behavior is not necessarily based on reality as it is, but reality as it is perceived to be, the *perception of change* in the nature of understood and accepted religious commodities will be enough to trigger feelings of abandonment and brand betrayal.

In some instances, change is sufficient to generate a schism within the organization; groups hive off the parent denomination and form subgroups—antigroups, as it were, created in symbolic or actual opposition to the parent group that has exhibited brand betrayal. Perhaps the most obvious example of this is the Protestant Reformation. In other instances, however, denominational loyalty overrides the perception of brand betrayal by the denomination. In these cases, an external schism does not occur, but rather denominational stresses generate the formation of reform and renewal groups, which rally around shared feelings of dissatisfaction, and emerge as opposition movements within the denomination. In some cases, these groups might be considered protoschismatic (for example, the National Alliance of Covenanting Congregations in the UCCan; the Episcopal Synod of America, and the Forward-in-Faith Movement in the ECUSA). That is, they advocate for such measures as a parallel system of theological education, clergy call and placement, and other aspects of life within the larger denominational structure, but do not necessarily support immediate withdrawal from the denomination. Rather, they remain, a remnant witness to the experience of shared brand betrayal. From this process we can propose thus:

P3: If the brand betrayal explicit in denominational shifts in theology, doctrine, polity, or practice is deemed sufficiently egregious, two possibilities present themselves in terms of organized, negative response:

P3a: External schism, or sectarianism. Individuals or groups cannot reconcile their dissatisfaction with changes in the parent denomination with ongoing membership in that denomination.

P3b: Internal schism, or protosectarian organization. Individuals or groups choose to reconcile their dissatisfaction with changes in the parent denomination with their ongoing membership through a process of worldview construction and maintenance that casts them in the role of the remnant faithful. (I call these groups and individuals protosectarian because the option for separation and schism remains live.)

THE ORGANIZATIONAL DEVELOPMENT OF REFORM AND RENEWAL

Even though many of the reform movements I have discussed in this book began as organized responses to particular events or circumstances in the church or denomination of which they are a part, this is not to suggest that there was no dissatisfaction prior to these precipitous moments. Far from it. Rather, these precipitous moments serve as organizational catalysts, galvanizing responses that had been to that point latent or, at least, less well established. While latent dissatisfaction had existed for many years in what became the United Methodist Church, the Good News Movement was catalyzed by the appearance of a new church school curriculum and the perception that that curriculum confirmed the worst fears of denominational conservatives about the liberal direction in which the church was moving. The Community of Concern came into being as a result of the *SOLM* report, and continued because many members saw no significant difference between the recommendations of that document and the MMHS statement that was eventually accepted by the United Church of Canada in 1988. Likewise, the Episcopalian and Anglican prayer book societies emerged in specific response to the possibility that the traditional *Book of Common Prayer* would be abandoned.

In addition to those implied by the analytic metaphor of brand betrayal above, several other reasons suggest not so much why groups like the

Community of Concern, the Good News Movement, the Presbyterian Lay Committee, or the prayer book societies emerged, but why they have chosen to remain within denominations that are clearly disinclined to move in the more conservative doctrinal, ethical, or practical directions that they demand. In broad terms, while each of these groups came into being in response to particular primary issues, each emerged from the debates with mandates that are considerably more comprehensive in scope. Why, though, did they stay at all? I would like to suggest three reasons.

At the most basic level, there are the reasons offered by the groups themselves. That is, taking these groups entirely at their word, within their particular denominations they have become the principal watchdogs of theological orthodoxy and its institutional derivatives, the gargoyles, as it were, on the church ramparts. Whatever practical or political considerations might constellate around them, it is the *faith* concerns of these groups that anchor both their opposition to denominational practice and their critique of denominational position. Understood thus, while the two-year explication of the UCCan's Twenty Articles of Faith by John Niles, a UCCan minister in Toronto, and published in *Fellowship Magazine,* was critical of a number of positions taken by the denomination, the intent of the monthly columns was to call readers back to (or, given *Fellowship's* constituency, reinforce) a more evangelical understanding of the faith. In the face of perceived challenges to its denominational spirituality, particularly through events such as the Re-Imagining Conferences, the Presbyterians for Faith, Family and Ministry "is working to restore the strength and integrity of the PC(USA)'s witness to Jesus Christ as the only Savior and Lord" (Presbyterians for Faith, Family and Ministry 1996). Urging its readers in a double entendre to "raise the standard," advertisements for *The Layman* declare that "the mission of the Presbyterian Lay Committee is simple: to inform and equip God's people by proclaiming Jesus Christ alone as the way of salvation, the truth of God's word and the life of discipleship."

Next, reflecting on the continued presence of conservative reform groups in denominations that are growing less and less responsive to their demands, not a few church members have suggested that less noble, more pecuniary interests lie at the heart of the matter for at least some traditionalists. That is, since in many cases, though certainly not all, leading movement intellectuals are members of the clergy, and are often longtime employees of the denomination, some church members who are suspicious of reform groups have suggested that dissident clergy have remained within their denominations only to protect their pensions and job security. Within these denominations, conservative clergy will almost always find congregations willing to call them, but this may not be the case beyond those denominational boundaries.

Finally, there is what I consider to be the central issue of cognitive praxis and movement identity. That is, as organizational expressions of the concept of a remnant faithful, movement identity is inextricably bound to the conflict that exists within particular denominations. If individuals or groups leave, that notion of movement identity is lost. In this regard, I would like to explore briefly a few further propositions. While these will not apply to all conservative reform movements, nor will they apply to movements at all points across the trajectory of their organizational careers, they do provide some explanation, I think, for the tenacity and durability of these social movements.

First, movement identity is located in circumstantial tension; it is the strain within the denomination that creates an ongoing identity for reform countermovements. If that circumstantial tension is resolved, movement identity either dissolves or attenuates. If, for whatever reason in 1988, the United Church of Canada's General Council had decided to reject the *SOLM* report, as well as the alternatives Sessional Committee 8 offered in its place, if the court had decided that the possibility of homosexual ordination would not be entertained as a live option in the church, and if it committed the church to the pursuit of a doctrinal course more acceptable to conservative reform movements, much of the circumstantial tension that catalyzed the movement would have been resolved. Similarly, if the Anglican and Episcopalian churches had firmly and decisively rejected the possibility of a liturgical replacement for the *Book of Common Prayer*, then prayer book societies as defenders of its denominational position would have become largely superfluous.

For a time, of course, there may be some residual concern, a weather eye kept, as it were, on the denominational quarterdeck. If the denomination stays the conservative course, however, like a nation-state whose security increases following an attack but relaxes as periods of peace lengthen, conservative reform movements would ultimately grow complacent, question their need to exist, and eventually dissolve. Since this has not been the case in any of the denominations I have considered, reform and renewal movements are faced with three basic choices: (1) leave the denomination when it does not acquiesce to their demands; (2) accept the decisions of the church and disband as opposition movements within the denomination; or (3) remain within the denomination and continue the struggle for reform. The third, obviously, is the choice made by groups and movements considered here.

Second, in the evolution of movement identity and cognitive praxis, if the circumstantial tension—the precipitous moment—is resolved, but not to the satisfaction of denominational conservatives, and identity formation has been organized around that circumstantial tension explicitly, then the organization has the choice to expand its mandate, to increase the scope and depth of its cognitive praxis. Otherwise, it may be faced with the rather barren prospect of fighting the battle long after the war has been lost and the winning side retired from the field. The Good News Movement, for example, does feel that it has had some moderate success in restraining denominational use of its precipitating concern: the new curriculum and its reduced concentration on more traditional constructions of the Christian faith. In its efforts toward that goal, though, the Good News Movement found a more comprehensive mission within the United Methodist Church: reform of seminaries as the principal medium out of which the established intellectuals of the denominational hierarchy emerge. This allowed for identity formation as a prophetic, remnant witness in the midst of a denominational culture that the Good News Movement regards as busy wandering in the wilderness, stopping and worshiping the occasional golden calf, and all the time moving further and further from the Promised Land. Similarly, both the Presbyterian Lay Committee and the Community of Concern, while created initially to deal with specific denominational social policies and directions, have expanded their mandates and established their presence as the most recognizable voices for conservative reform in the PC(USA) and the UCCan, regardless of the particular circumstantial tension facing these churches.

Third, as a result of this, the expansion of a movement's conservative mandate increases its sensitivity to and, therefore, the availability of tension-producing issues and events, and concomitantly reinforces its movement identity as the remnant faithful. What began as concern over church involvement in social movements of which conservative members disapproved has develops into multifaceted concern clusters that include whatever precipitous moments, circumstantial tensions, or problems of practical life emerge in the context of denominational life. While the foundational message of mainline conservative reform has not changed appreciably over the past four decades, the manner in which reform and renewal movements have gone about the investigation of denominational problems and the theological, doctrinal, and practical analyses of circumstantial tensions have. Rather than simply reacting emotionally to the possibility of homosexual ordination, for example, many conservative reform movements—and, more importantly, the movement intellectuals who have shaped or attempted to shape the movement's cognitive praxis— have invested significant energy in examining biblical, historical, and doctrinal data in pursuit of more compelling presentations of their argument. Despite the unevenness of the articles they contain, for example, journals such as *Theological Digest & Outlook* (UCCan), *Theology Matters*, and *re-NEWS* (PC[USA]) are all attempts to present the conservative viewpoint in a more sophisticated fashion, to influence those segments of their denominational constituencies that are not moved either by emotional appeal or the journalistic sensationalism often found in popular reform magazines and broadsheets, and to make reform arguments that are divorced from the overt hostility and reproach that have so often characterized them in the past.

For example, in the context of debates over the place of homosexuality in the church, denominational opposition to reform movements has not infrequently framed its disagreement by characterizing the conservative-traditionalist response as little more than homophobia overlaid with a selective biblical literalism and an unreflective doctrinal intransigence. A favorite example of this is the criticism that if conservative reform movements were truly serious about the regard with which biblical injunctions ought to be held, then that regard ought to apply across the board, not simply to particular hot-button issues. That is, rather than continuously pointing to texts that condemn (or are interpreted as condemning) homosexual behavior, denominational conservatives are challenged to consider as well those Pentateuchal holiness code provisions regarding diet, dress, and the equitable treatment of refugees. In response, many reform movements have taken this criticism as an opportunity to deepen their approach to the issue, drawing on biblical, theological, and historical resources in order to strengthen the presentation of their argument. Dialectically, this has created a feedback loop of sorts, reinforcing movement identity and expanding the cognitive praxis that both stimulates and constrains movement development. Thus, as the availability of tension-producing circumstances expands, movement identity as the remnant faithful, denominational custodians of the remnant spirit, solidifies, and the public presentation of the conservative position becomes the established reform and renewal position.

ESCALATION OF TENSION AND PERCIPIENT DISSATISFACTION

It is important to remember that precipitous moments or circumstantial tensions do not bring reform and renewal conflict into being ex nihilo. There is a social history that both precedes and underpins the reform response. The precipitous moment, however, whether it is a particular event or event process, whether it unfolds all at once or over time, acts as a threshold across which latent conflict becomes manifest.

Latent Conflict: The Reform Movement in Embryo

Prior to the precipitous moment, the conflict within the denomination is latent. This is the *formation stage* for reform and renewal movement, the embryonic stage, as it were. How surprised were members of what became conservative reform movements by the precipitating moments that created them? The documentary evidence suggests that there was little wonder in any of the denominations considered, that the various contro-

Table 1
Conflict Escalation and Organizational Evolution

Character of Conflict	Stage of Reform Development	Nature of Percipient Dissatisfaction	Percipient Response
Latent Conflict	Formation	Vague, often unfocused dissatisfaction with denominational direction and policy.	Occasional protest of denominational policy and decision. At this stage, protest is ad hoc and unorganized. E.g., individual complaints to pastors, letters to denominational newspapers, vocal complaints or debates on the floor of denominational courts.
		Precipitating moment	
Manifest Conflict	Organization	Dissatisfaction often focused on specific issue.	Creation of self-identified reform groups, organized to contest either the realities or the possibilities represented by the precipitating moment. Denominational direction and/or policy has advanced to the point where systematic response is deemed necessary. Addresses the specific issue of moment in the denomination. Initial appearance of movement intellectuals, and publication of movement mandates and position statements. Ad hoc institutional structures emerge.
Escalating Conflict	Expansion	Dissatisfaction escalated as ability to stem, stall, or defeat the specific issue(s) represented by the initial precipitating moment is (or is regarded as) lost.	Extension of reform mandate from the specific issue to larger denominational problems. Creation of reform movements. Movement socialization expands mandate to address emergent issues within the larger context of denominational direction and conflict. Basic institutional structures emerge.
Entrenched Conflict	Institutionalization	Dissatisfaction with denominational direction and policy becomes a function of reform movement identity.	Reform movement is now capable of more complex organization, longer-term planning, and movement coalitioning. Permanent institutional structures emerge.

versies did not erupt ex nihilo, but escalated from latent dissatisfaction to manifest conflict after varying periods of incubation. At this stage, there is vague, often unfocused dissatisfaction with changing denominational directions, policies, and decisions. However, this dissatisfaction has not yet coalesced to the point where countermovement formation can occur. Social movements do not emerge in response to every social crisis. As Eyerman and Jamison note, they emerge when "there is a political opportunity, a context of social problem as well as a context of communication, opening up the potential for problem articulation and knowledge dissemination" (1991, 56). That is, there has to be something recognizable to talk about. The precipitous moment provides the catalyst for this conversation to take place, the point of argument around which reform and renewal movements can begin to converge.

Prior to this coalescence, though, at the embryonic stage, manifestations of dissatisfaction are ad hoc and usually unorganized. Limited to occasional protests of denominational policies and decisions, these manifestations include individual complaints to pastors from parishioners, letters to denominational newspapers and magazines, vocal complaints or occasional debates on the floors of the various denominational courts. Often, in the formation stage, there is a sense of unfolding isolation. Denominational members who are dissatisfied wonder whether they are the only ones, whether *their* perceptions of church processes and circumstances are somehow skewed. Thus, in 1966 when Charles Keysor wrote his brief plea for orthodoxy in the Methodist Church, he and his associates were amazed by the response from all across the church. They learned that they were *not* alone. That realization is important, for, without it, the ability to generate a sense of collective identity in opposition to denominational directions is significantly reduced.

Most often, though, there is a precipitous moment, a particular instant of crisis that catalyzes the environment in which reform movements can come together. While local church members may have been unhappy for years that some of the their favorite hymns were no longer being sung on Sunday morning, or that the words to old favorites were being changed at what they regarded as the politically correct whims of more liberal clergy, the precipitous moment comes when these hymns are omitted altogether from new editions of denominational hymnbooks. Or, while ongoing rumors and speculation that the church officials "at head office" (a phrase which is often a trope for the belief that denominational bureaucrats are disconnected from the reality of the local congregation) are considering changing the accepted standards of ordination to allow gay men and lesbians to be admitted to the ministry anger many church members, usually it is only when denominational initiatives make the possibility live that reform groups and movements are galvanized. This leads to manifest conflict.

Manifest Conflict: The Reform Movement Organizes

Once the line between latent and manifest conflict has been crossed, tension and dissatisfaction produce the critical mass necessary for an organized opposition to emerge. Often, as the various aspects of the circumstantial tensions become clear, there is a liminal period of increased communication among angry parishioners and clergy. As it did for organizations such as the UCCan's Church Alive, coffee shop meetings to discuss the current crisis evolve into strategy sessions about the level and manner of response required. These strategy sessions often disclose the length and breadth of denominational dissatisfaction and inspire the creation of organized protest. As the tension-producing circumstance becomes more real, as it moves from the denominationally abstract to the socially concrete, it begins to appear with greater frequency in denominational communications: magazines and newspapers, pastoral letters from denominational officials, and the various documentary stages of the denominational decision-making process. At this stage, latent dissatisfaction is able to coalesce around a particular problem of practical life.

It is important to remember that, like all metaphors, the precipitous moment covers a range of territory. It can be something quite sudden and unexpected—after a series of in-camera meetings, denominational officials vote to freeze clergy salaries. It can be something more processual—the various stages of discussion a major denominational change goes through before a final decision is made. At the early stages, among opponents there is often a sense of "they're just daft, it'll never happen," and the problem remains denominationally abstract. At those points, the potential change, while capable of producing tension, is less live for its opponents. At some point, though, and through the study of conservative reform movements we can identify some clear indicators about when this occurs, these abstract discussions gradually become live options in the church. Common moments of manifestation include the tabling of official intent to change denominational policy; actual publication of contentious denominational resources, including resources to facilitate discussion of proposed changes to church doctrine, polity, or practice; and public statements that are perceived to locate the denomination in opposition to dominant social forces and established interdenominational relationships.

Each of these generates conversation, a primary constituent in the process of social world-building. Church members who had to that point been able to ignore the potential conflict, or dismiss it as a dead option, suddenly find themselves faced with the possibility that their fears may come true. At this stage, denominational direction or policy has advanced to the point where systematic response is deemed necessary, and the creation of self-identified reform groups, organized to contest either the realities or the possibilities represented by the precipitous moment, take place. This stage includes the initial appearance of movement intellectuals and the publication of preliminary movement manifestos and position statements. These movement manifestos and position statements are useful data for understanding the official development of social movements. At this stage as well, ad hoc institutional structures emerge: steering committees, local organizations, and more formalized meetings. At this point, though, since the nascent movement is often organized around specific opposition to the issue of moment, there is little initial concern for an ongoing reform presence.

Escalating Conflict: The Movement Expands

The expansion stage is often marked by the emerging reform movement's inability to stem, stall, or defeat the specific issue(s) represented by the precipitous moment. As with the other stages, there are a number of ways in which this occurs. Sometimes, traditionalist groups believe that the initial outpouring of opposition will be sufficient to dissuade denominational officials from their proposed path. That is, once the bureaucrats at head office see how people really feel about this, they will back down.

Letters from now officially constituted reform groups, coherent statements of opposition drafted by emergent movement intellectuals, organized protests and lobbying at denominational meetings—all are part of this initial battle plan. As each tactic fails, however, and the denominational potential moves forward, the dissatisfaction increases, and the tension within the system builds.

Many denominations have statutory safeguards built into their organizational constitutions that prevent unilateral changes to doctrine, polity, and practice. In the case of Mary Elizabeth Blue Hull Memorial and Eastern Heights Presbyterian Churches, for example, the Georgia courts ruled that changes in the denomination breached the organizational agreement under which the two churches entered into the denomination. In the United Church of Canada, a change to the Basis of Union can only be made after a denominational consultation process, and a remit from the congregations and presbyteries of the church authorizing the change. Conservative reform groups often argue that the proposed changes to the denomination are sufficiently serious to warrant invoking this consultation and referendum process. This tactic proceeds on two fronts: first, it stalls the decision and allows the reform group time to organize its opposition further; and second, it forces the church into a position where the issue has to be placed before the various denominational stakeholders in ways that might not otherwise have occurred. However, in some instances, it also allows for greater denominational control of the discussion. In these case, those responsible for the production of denominational study materials often become the documentary Other against which countermovements contend.

At this stage, the development of reform and renewal proceeds on a more dialectic level. The cognitive praxis of the denomination directly affects the cognitive praxis of conservative reform. The manner in which relevant information is presented, the way information is chosen or represented as relevant, the directions in which denominational discussions are taken, the resources provided to facilitate and ground those discussions, and the questions denominational participants are asked to consider—all of these are mechanisms by which the nature of the conflict is framed, expressed, and managed. And all contribute to the social environment in which reform movements emerge and evolve. These periods of debate and consultation allow for opposition to develop both organizationally and intellectually. While the denomination processes the information necessary to make its decision, movement intellectuals within the reform camp produce materials designed specifically to counter denominational direction.

If the denomination makes the decision to proceed with whatever plan has occasioned the opposition and led to the emergence of a reform presence in the first place—the ordination of gay men and lesbians, the authorization of a new denominational position on ecumenism, or the publication of a new liturgical resource—that reform presence often expands, extending its mandate from the specific issue at hand to what it regards as the larger denominational problems of which specific issues are merely symptomatic. Rather than individual reform *groups,* which operate at varying levels of organizational and practical sophistication, this stage witnesses the emergence of reform *movements.* More complex institutional structures appear as movement socialization expands the reform commission to address a variety of different issues within the larger context of denominational direction and conflict. Movement intellectuals begin to consider the issues in more intentional ways, devoting more and more time and energy to the struggle. Staff are hired to coordinate and finance ongoing reform efforts. Ad hoc publishing is gradually replaced by more permanent media resources. Conferences appear, often organized to recruit members, showcase movement intellectuals, develop and promote the reform movement's agenda, and extend the movement's denominational impact. Offspring groups come into being as different movement participants decide which oppositional niche they fit best.

The ongoing conversation that takes place over the course of conservative reform's evolution from vague dissatisfaction to organized movement also invokes a sensitizing process, what I term the logical extension of a social movement's proximate thresholds of instability. Initially, the systemic instability to which nascent reform groups respond is the precipitous moment. As reform movements develop, and as a consequence of this development, these moments occur more frequently. Put differently, as a social movement comes into being, as its movement intellectuals consider the issues at hand with greater intentionality, as its cognitive praxis develops and matures, issues of systemic instability appear on its radar with greater frequency and regularity. It is as though the gain has been increased on a radio receiver. Signals that heretofore fell below the threshold of perception now surface and invoke the various processes of conservative response. What may not have appeared as a concern during the initial stages of movement development is now seen as an integral part of a much larger systemic problem. The issue of gay ordination, for example, is not the problem; it is a symptom of decaying social and ethical mores. Inclusive language is not the problem; it is symptomatic of a much deeper doctrinal degeneration in the church. Sensitivity to individual symptoms generates derivative issues, including the (declining) authority of Scripture in the life of the church, the (diminishing) significance of Jesus in an increasingly pluralistic world, and the (increasingly problematic) relationship between Christianity and other religious faith traditions. Occasionally, this sensitization process also results in anxiety about the motives of denominational officials and suspicion that opponents are being targeted for punishment by church authorities. This leads to the fourth stage: entrenched conflict.

Entrenched Conflict: Reform and Renewal as Denominational Institution

This stage is reached when ongoing dissatisfaction with denominational direction and policy has become an embedded function of reform movement identity. Here, all aspects of denominational perception and participation are organized in terms of the conflict between the denominational Other and reform traditionalists. With this identity and self-understanding in place, reform movements are now capable of more complex organization yet—movement coalitioning, for example—longer-term planning, and more permanent institutional structures. Rather than loosely connected interest groups seeking to influence denominational policy and direction on an ad hoc, reactionary basis, in the context of entrenched conflict—the struggle for the church's soul, as a number of commentators have put it— conservative reform movements become part of the institutional landscape of the church, whether all stakeholders recognize them as such or not. They become integral strands in the web of power relations according to which denominational positions are debated, established, confronted, and maintained. And, as different denominations recognize that they are dealing with similar problems, interdenominational coalitions—such as the Association for Church Renewal, an umbrella group of renewal movement executives from a number of different denominations—emerge.

As Michel Foucault demonstrated throughout his work, while power need not always be conceptualized in terms of an a priori repression, that social actors seek to exercise control over situations in which they participate demonstrates that power relations are never far from the center of social action (cf. 1988). Foucault went further than this, however. For him, it was not enough to ask who exercised power in given situations, but how that power was exercised. How control (or the attempted control) of a situation is established and maintained. How the discourse surrounding it is directed, regulated, and ultimately fixed. In the final chapter, I will consider some of the ways in which reform and renewal discourse is conducted as it attempts to shape and to control the direction in which respective denominations are moving.

CHAPTER 9

Dissent as Identity: Reform and Renewal Teleology

"I can't help but notice that the emblem you are wearing is not a religious but a political one," remarked Bob Harvey at the beginning of the *Ottawa Citizen* interview that was to haunt Bill Phipps for his entire term as leader of The United Church of Canada (UCCan). "Zero Poverty" read the button bluntly, though Harvey continued, "I would have expected a cross on the lapel of the moderator of the United Church. You haven't mentioned Jesus." Referring to the evangelical men's group Promise Keepers, Harvey opined that "it seems to me that a person who had a proper relationship with Jesus, who had opened his heart to believe in Jesus, would not engage in actions that harmed other people near or far" (1997a, A1). Revealing either a stunning lack of awareness about Christian history or a simple desire to bait the moderator, whose views on such issues as apartheid, urban and rural poverty, the marginalization of First Nations Peoples, and the apathy with which all too many members of his own denomination regarded these were well known, Harvey continued to press Phipps about his Christology, his belief about eschatology, and his regard for the literal word of the Bible. All of these issues Harvey framed in explicitly evangelical terms.

From his days as poverty lawyer to the moderator's office in the largest mainline Protestant denomination in Canada, Bill Phipps has never hidden who he is from those he serves. A man deeply committed to the social gospel and to the plight of the socially marginalized, over and over during his tenure as moderator he found himself explaining his views on various aspects of Christian theology, most often around issues of biblical authority and the person of Christ—viz., "No, I don't believe Christ was God."

In April 1999, Phipps responded to more conservative criticism of his social policies and the theological beliefs that underpin them. And still, nearly two years later, the fateful *Ottawa Citizen* interview echoed in the background of that criticism. "First of all," Phipps wrote (Phipps 1999) in a letter to the *National Post*, "I never said Jesus is not the son of God, rather, I said 'Jesus is not God.' There is a world of difference between these two statements and it is important that Coyne [the *Post* editorialist] get it right."

The clear difference between these two theological statements notwithstanding, this time Phipps was challenged by Ted Wigglesworth, another longtime critic of denominational policy and then-chairperson of the church's National Alliance of Covenanting Congregations. In a complaint filed through his lawyer, Wigglesworth (1999) charged that the moderator was now guilty of heresy, blasphemy, idolatry, false swearing, and "conduct unbecoming a Member, Minister and Moderator of the United Church of Canada and has harmed the well-being of the Church." As far as Wigglesworth and many other traditionalists in the Church were concerned, the membership hemorrhage that began years before had only increased as a result of Phipps's comments, and the church was once again in danger of bleeding out. Less than three weeks after Phipps's letter appeared, Wigglesworth faxed a three-page statement of charges to Calgary Presbytery, the church court in which Phipps's membership resided and which exercised pastoral authority over him.

Because they highlight the politics of religious identity and the manner in which that identity is asserted and controlled, Wigglesworth's allegations are worth quoting at length:

The aforesaid statement [that is, in Phipps's letter and, by implication, the *Citizen* interview] constitutes false teaching and the said Right Reverend Gentleman is thereby guilty of that offence; and the said statement is false in which the said Right Reverend Gentleman is guilty of false utterance; and the said statements are true in fact and thus deprive the Right Reverend Gentleman of his capacity to be a member of the United Church of Canada; and the said statements deprive him of his capacity to claim to be a member of the Universal Holy Catholic Church; and the said statements deprive him of his right to claim to continue to serve as a minister within the United Church of Canada inasmuch as he is no longer qualified or able to comply with his ordination vows; and the said statements deprive him of his right to claim to continue to serve as Moderator of the United Church of Canada inasmuch as he is no longer qualified or able to comply with his installation vows; and the said statement is heretical; and the said statement is blasphemous; and the said statement is idolatrous; and he is guilty of false swearing, all of which are contrary to Articles 2 and 2.1 and Article 15 of the Basis of Union. (Wigglesworth 1999; cf. Koch 1999; Legge 1999)

Ultimately, Wigglesworth requested a formal hearing at which these charges would be addressed, and Phipps presumably disciplined. Calgary

Presbytery declined to take any action, however, declaring that Phipps was still in essential agreement with the church's Basis of Union, and therefore no further action was warranted. When Wigglesworth appealed the decision to a higher court in the church, he was denied.

FROM TRADITION TO ORTHODOXY: CONSERVATIVE DISCOURSE AND THE POLITICS OF IDENTITY

In the context of denominational reform and renewal, I would like to suggest that Wigglesworth's formal charges are not primarily about beliefs, doctrine, or, in this case, the moderator's adherence to either. Rather, those are particular theological markers by which the real issue is delineated. Primarily, these allegations are about identity and authenticity, specifically, the *right* to call oneself a true Christian, and to challenge that claim when it is appropriated by those with whom one disagrees. While, obviously, not all disagreement will result in these kinds of accusations, in reform and renewal discourse issues of doctrinal integrity are regularly underpinned by this politics of authentic Christian identity. That is, who has the right to say, "I am a true Christian"? Who is bounded out of that claim by virtue of differing interpretations of everything from the nature of Scripture to the place of the Church in the world?

Even a cursory examination of Wigglesworth's charges reveals this division clearly. Wigglesworth and Phipps do not simply disagree on theological ephemera. Rather, Wigglesworth contends that Phipps's statements are so erroneous that they have placed him explicitly beyond the pale of the Christian faith. Ethically, Wigglesworth insists that Phipps is guilty of "false utterance" because the statement "Jesus is not God" is, according to Wigglesworth, not true. More directly, Wigglesworth argues that the converse statement "Jesus is God" is "true in fact." Thus, theologically, since Phipps denies what Wigglesworth regards as the constitutive declaration of the Christian faith, he has lost the right, not only to be the moderator of the United Church of Canada, but to claim any identity as a Christian at all—"the said statements deprive him of his capacity to claim to be a member of the Universal Holy Catholic Church." While, admittedly, this is an extreme example of the politics of identity, more subtle variants obtain throughout reform and renewal discourse.

During the first few years of its existence, for example, the Community of Concern (COC) usually referred to itself either as the guardian of traditional Christianity or of the historic Christian faith, both phrases that are open to varying interpretations. As the proximate thresholds of instability expanded, however, and the COC evolved from a single-issue lobby group to a more general theological watchdog, words like "traditional" and "historic" began to be replaced by a more concrete signifier of authentic identity: "orthodox." While "traditional" might be contrasted with "non-traditional," and "historic" with "contemporary," no necessary opprobrium attaches to either by virtue of the change. Not so with "orthodoxy."

Orthodoxy ("correct belief") exists only as a correlative of heterodoxy ("different belief"), or, as it is more colloquially understood, *incorrect* belief. "Objective truth is the plumb line," writes Presbyterian Church (USA) (PC[USA]) conservative Susan Cyre, executive director of Presbyterians for Faith, Family and Ministry, and editor of its bimonthly journal, *Theology Matters*, "which divides truth and falsehood creating a boundary" (1995, 1). "To affirm truth," she continues, "we must identify what is false. If we attempt to reaffirm orthodoxy without rediscovering heresy we deny the boundaries and we embrace the syncretism of pagan religions" (1995, 2).

The dubious nature of Cyre's final conclusion notwithstanding, what generally goes undiscussed in traditionalist appeals such as this is the crucial matter of who gets to decide what constitutes "objective truth," and on what grounds that decision is made. While Cyre herself contends that "the one who authoritatively defines truth is a god" (1995, 1), she misses the criticism of her own position implicit in that charge. She and other traditionalists regularly appeal to the objective authority of Scripture, the historic (but often ahistoricized) creeds of the Church, and in some cases denominational statements of faith, but they fail to acknowledge the necessarily interpretive and constructed nature of each of those appeals. Put differently, they have universalized their own particular interpretation, and in so doing obscured the fact that this universalization has taken place. Similarly, writing of the problem of Marcion and referring to the second-century heretic who believed that the gospel of love wholly superceded the gospel of law, Cyre's colleague, Randall Otto, declares that "there can be little question that Marcion's early foray into textual criticism was driven by hermeneutical interests sustaining his dualistic views" (1998, 6). This ignores, of course, the reality that (a) all of Marcion's writings have been lost and we have access to them only through the lens of his critics and (b) reform and renewal forays into textual criticism are driven by hermeneutical interests that sustain their traditionalist views of the Church and the faith.

Theologians as diverse as Sallie McFague (see 1989, 1997) and Thomas Merton (see 1967, 1968), and as far apart on the theological spectrum as Mary Daly (see 1973, 1984) and Leonardo Boff (see 1978, 1986), have long recognized that a wide variety of models exist to describe the nature of the relationship between humanity and the Divine. Even within Scripture, different metaphors attempt to communicate the mysterious character of that relationship. Because of their metaphoric nature, however, no model is ever complete or uniquely authoritative. Each privileges certain aspects of the relationship at the same time as it censors others. Each arises from a particular historical and sociological position within the Church and reflects in those positions the life experiences of the people from within which they arise. In virtually all respects, for example, the experience of Gaulic tribes converted to Christianity under the ministry of St. Martin of Tours in the late fourth century is worlds apart from that of Oklahoma farmers who walked the sawdust trail at the exhortations of a young Oral Roberts or middle-management executives who accept Jesus at a Billy Graham Crusade in Madison Square Garden. To suggest that there is a coherent orthodoxy obtaining between these two moments of the Christian faith, and across the 16 centuries that divide them, is to ignore the wide range of other factors that influence religious belief, development, and conversion (cf., for example, Fletcher 1997 on the barbarian conversions of the first Christian millennium).

By appropriating and deploying the language of correct belief, however, conservative reform groups such as the COC and Presbyterians for Faith, Family and Ministry have staked a normative claim to their own particular interpretation of the gospel message. Ignoring for the most part the long history of the concept, they have popularly equated "orthodox" with "conservative, evangelical Protestant." And, by defining their position as orthodox, these groups declare that theirs is the only authentic description of the mysterious relationship between humanity and the Divine. The importance of this conceptual shift ought not be understated because, as I have noted, while signifiers such as "traditional" and "historic" do not necessarily imply an inauthentic "Other," "orthodox" demands it. As a signifier of theological, doctrinal, or ethical authenticity, it only exists in opposition to heterodoxy or heresy. In fact, as illustrated by Cyre and Otto, orthodoxy demands heresy as the means by which its own boundaries are delineated, tested, and sharpened; these oppositional signifiers provide for orthodoxy's own identity. Thus, while the point is often glossed in the midst of denominational debates, the ability to lay claim to orthodoxy is as much a political assertion as it is theological. Those outside the orthodox camp are considered unorthodox at best, though just as often heretical. While few denominational traditionalists are as blunt in their charges as Wigglesworth or Cyre, and many claim not so much to be alleging heresy on the part of others but asserting orthodoxy for their own position, the practical difference is thin at best.

Reprising the history of the UCCan's denominational decline, for example, Ed McCaig contends that in its abandonment of traditionally held understandings of sexuality and of the nature of divinity the Church had "[broken] free from orthodoxy" (1995, 22). McCaig believes that the first step to becoming a "good (that is, effective) church" is "to reaffirm our orthodox Christian heritage in our Twenty Articles of Faith instead of continuing to distance ourselves from it" (1995, 23). Victor Shepherd, McCaig's UCCan colleague, concurs, writing about different groups of "almost Christians," those who believe their identity as authentic followers of Jesus hinges on something other than an explicitly evangelical profession of faith (1996). According to Shepherd, these almost Christians include "moralists who look upon the gospel as a trustworthy guide for personal morality"; "those who regard the gospel as a program for social improvement"; "those who recognize the gift of Christian inspiration to the arts" (1996, 16, 17). Included in this group would be such denominational luminaries as Bill Phipps, and virtually every church moderator for the last 30 years—a reality that is not lost on conservative reform movements.

And what bridges the gap between almost Christian and actual Christian? In language familiar to anyone versed in evangelical discourse, the answer is a conscious decision "to enter upon a living relationship with Jesus Christ" (Shepherd 1996, 17)—the well-known acceptance of Jesus Christ as one's personal savior. However well intentioned their faith might be, those who have not yet done so remain firmly beyond the pale of authentic Christianity. Of course, the ability to identify those who are almost Christians arrogates to conservatives such as Shepherd the concomitant ability to define actual Christians—surely a political feat as much as a theological one. This shift in reform and renewal discourse, interpreting any change in theological focus or Christological understanding as a decline, a de facto departure from orthodoxy, has not gone unnoticed by less conservative members of the church, many of whom take great offence at what they regard as the illegitimate co-optation of the term and the rhetoric of exclusion it implies.

A more pointed example of the politics of identity concerns the language of worship. In the UCCan, this debate heated up in 1999 with the release of a proposed new worship service book. In an article that has been widely distributed across the spectrum of reform and renewal groups in North American mainline Protestantism, Don Faris writes that "if this draft is approved, the United Church of Canada will cease to be an ecumenical Church and will become an emotionally-based, politically-correct cult" (1999, 23). A rather sensationalist statement, perhaps, but one that cuts to the heart of debate over the politics of identity. "Cult," of course, is well known in popular discourse for its profoundly negative connotation. In this instance, Faris regards the use of any language other than the traditional "God the Father" in the resource's printed prayers as a clear indication that the line between church and cult has been irrevocably crossed. "In the first 100 pages of over 500 prayers," he laments, "only one is addressed to the Father" (Faris 1999, 23). In place of the new resource, Faris recommends a service book similar to that published by the Uniting Church in Australia. "It is written for a Christian Church," he affirms, given that it "honours the Father, the Faith and the Family, . . . which is what our United Church is meant to be. Not a cult" (1999, 27).

Similar charges are appearing throughout the mainline Protestant reform movement. In *The Layman Online*, one angry PC(USA) member berated then-moderator Jack Rogers and declared that Rogers's " 'leadership' team led the elected representatives of our denomination to approve an overture that denies the sinful nature of immorality and the Lordship of Christ. In a mere week his team has reduced one of the most evangelical denominations in history to the level of a New Age cult" (Loftis 2001). Writing in *Good News Magazine*, and protesting the Re-Imagining Conference's Sophia liturgy, Lutheran pastor Sally Nelson summarizes the issue of Christian identity as many mainline Protestant traditionalists regard it.

In the very midst of their idolatry the conference participants still resist being known as heretics or pagans. A heretic is one who distorts the gospel. A pagan is one who casts it aside in favor of an idol. Sadly, these people have done both, and it is time for the Church to discipline those who still claim to be its own. It is time for pastors, bishops, presbyters, church councils, and religious orders to call to repentance those who worship false gods, and to remove from the clergy rosters and membership rolls those who refuse to repent. (Nelson 1994)

The politics of identity as they are expressed in the official language of worship do not only revolve around Christian versus non-Christian, true church or cult. For traditionalist members of the Anglican communion, in addition to its function as a repository of Anglican doctrine, the unadulterated liturgy as it was it is laid down in Thomas Cranmer's *Book of Common Prayer* (*BCP*) constitutes the sine qua non of Anglican identity. Here, the politics of identity are informed, not by the nature of the change that has been made to the language of worship, but by the fact that any change has been made at all.

In similar manner to Shepherd's almost Christians, the Prayer Book Society's (PBS-USA's) Peter Toon writes that there are "would-be orthodox" members within the Anglican communion who are seeking to respond to perceived crises in the denomination. While traditionalists such as Toon and the would-be orthodox agree that "there is a major crisis of faith, morals and worship in the Episcopal Church, USA" (Toon 2000b, 14), they disagree on the root of the crisis and the manner in which it ought to be addressed. For the PBS-USA, the vast majority of problems in the Episcopal Church, USA (ECUSA)—from the ordination of women to the celebration of same-sex marriages, from the teaching of liberal theology in Episcopal seminaries (cf. Breyer 2000) to the drastic decline in denominational numbers—finds its source in the abandonment of the *BCP* as the liturgical signifier of Anglican identity. According to Toon, the would-be orthodox want to solve the problem by protoschism, by introducing into the church a range of options from "flying bishops" (traditionalists specially consecrated for the care of parishes that are in open disagreement with denominational direction and policy) to the creation of a new episcopal province within the Anglican communion. While Toon sympathizes with those who feel such drastic measures are necessary, in his view they still do not represent a "long term solution to the rejection of traditional worship, doctrine and discipline within the ECUSA" (2000b, 14). In a metaphor common to mainline conservative rhetoric, unless the ECUSA mandates a return to the *BCP* as the only acceptable manner of Anglican worship, any other response to the crisis is simply rearranging deck chairs on the *Titanic*.

As well, in a manner similar to Faris's characterization of the UCCan as "an emotionally-based, politically-correct cult," as well as United Methodist Church (UMC) and PC(USA) criticism of Re-Imagining, Toon tells *Mandate* readers that there are not one but really two religions in the ECUSA (2000c). The "old religion" is that brought to North America by European colonists, who arrived in the seventeenth and eighteenth centuries bringing "their Bible [*The King James Version*] and their Prayer Book [*The Book of Common Prayer*]" (Toon 2000c: 3; glosses in the original). "The religion of the Anglican Way is supremely a revealed religion," Toon continues, although one wonders just what Thomas Cranmer would make of such a declaration. While abandonment of this supremely revealed religion is laid for the most part at the doorstep of alternative liturgy, Toon is clear that that is not the only problem. In the old religion, people recognized that they were sinners in need of a saving God; they knew that there were none who did not deserve eternal punishment at the hands of a just, if somewhat stringent Deity. Salvation, traditionally understood, was the raison d'être of Christ's church. In the shrinking domain of mainline Protestant (in this case, Anglo-Catholic) Christianity, however, this religion is increasingly rare. "One basic reason it is difficult to find this religion in a pure form anywhere today in the ECUSA," writes Toon, "is because the divorce/remarriage culture has invaded and affected virtually every parish, compromising the witness of the church to the claims of the Gospel of Christ. And this culture is one major door [another is the feminist movement and women's ordination] through which the new religion finds entrance into human hearts" (2000c, 4).

And what is this "new religion"? Like Faris's "emotionally-based, politically-correct cult," it "calls paganism Christianity and declares that immorality is morality. It is basically a form of pantheism or monism using a Christian vocabulary to cover a rejection of the basic dogmas and moral teachings of orthodox Christianity" (Toon 2000c, 4). As an example of this, given Toon's rejection of this other religion as paganism, the reception of controversial former Roman Catholic Father Matthew Fox into their communion as an Episcopal priest could hardly have been viewed as a positive development (cf. Fox 1996). Widely known for his liberal theological views—including his articulation of creation spirituality, the rejection of an "original sin" paradigm in Christianity in favor of a soteriological model based on original blessing (see Fox 1983)—since his reception into the ECUSA, Fox has been responsible for such liturgical innovations as rave and technocosmic masses, both of which blend modern technology with ancient forms of Christian ritual. According to a Catalog of Concerns recounted by the Concerned Clergy and Laity of the Episcopal Church, "Fox entered the Episcopal Church and then performed a 'Rave Mass' with its loud music, suggestive dancing and flashing images ending in a colloquial Eucharist exhortation to 'Eat God' " (Concerned Clergy and Laity of the Episcopal Church 1997). Not surprisingly, if the liturgical tradition of the *BCP* represents the epitome of Anglican orthodoxy and identity, then Fox's liturgical innovations exemplify the point furthest away, and only underscore the problems to which *BCP* traditionalists such as Toon seek to call attention.

While the various units of the Prayer Book Society may be said to operate with a certain degree of proper Anglican restraint and decorum, even they recognize that is not always the case in the often emotional domain of reform and renewal movements. "On occasion the Society has come perilously close to libelling a Bishop," writes Canadian Anglican bishop Anthony Burton (1992), "and more than once has interpreted a Bishop's actions in a less than generous light." Where the society has come "perilously close," other organizations come closer still.

The Concerned Clergy and Laity of the Episcopal Church (CCLEC), "a lay movement of concerned and faithful Episcopalians to renew and reform the Church," name their denominational problems with considerably less ambiguity than is evident in some other reform movements. "There are two religions in the Episcopal Church," reads the first sentence of their Web site (www.episcopalian.org/cclec/index.htm), recalling Toon's evaluation. "One remains faithful to the biblical truth and the received teachings of the Church, while the other rejects them." Here, slightly different language informs the CCLEC conceptualization than obtains in other reform groups. With a self-consciously evangelical tenor, for example, it speaks of the influence in church and society of "secular humanism" and its attendant "moral relativism." Numerous issues collect under these rubrics.

Much of the space on the CCLEC Web site is devoted to a series of "Episcopal Tracts for Our Times," written by George Burns, a traditionalist Episcopal priest in Florida. While he acknowledges that they are not intended as a restatement of Episcopal catechetics, they are "an answer to the erroneous teaching in the Episcopal Church in the United States in this day" (Burns 2000b). Burns's first tract, "The Sodomy Bishops," attacks the 1994 Koinonia Statement, written by the controversial bishop John Shelby Spong and signed by more than 90 of Spong's Episcopal and Anglican colleagues (see chapter 3). To recall, The Koinonia Statement declared the moral neutrality of both homosexuality and heterosexuality and acknowledged that loving ,committed relationships exist in both domains. Because of this, sexual orientation is neither a barrier to full church membership, nor to either priestly or episcopal ordination. The section that so offended Burns appears near the end of the document.

> But let there be no misunderstanding, both our lives and our experience as Bishops have convinced us that a wholesome example to the flock of Christ does not exclude a person of homosexual orientation, nor does it exclude those homosexual persons who choose to live out their sexual orientation in a partnership that is marked by faithfulness and life giving holiness (Spong 1994).

Burns is unequivocal in his denunciation of this statement, which he calls the "Sodomy Document." "These Bishops actually promote and encourage Sodomy, and even Ordain those who practice Sodomy. I therefore believe that they should be called by the Biblical name—THE SODOMY BISHOPS" (Burns 2000a). While it remains unclear where, precisely, one might find this in the Bible, Burns continues: "By signing the Sodomy Document, the Sodomy Bishops have committed acts of apostasy which will affect the eternal salvation of many souls, including their own." That is, the politics of identity have bounded out those with whom Burns and his CCLEC colleagues disagree. Other tracts attack the ordination of women ("Priestesses in the Church"), Bishop John Shelby Spong ("the Judas Iscariot of our generation"), and lay presidency at the celebration of the Eucharist, which "may cause faithful souls to lose the benefits of the saving grace of the Body and Blood of Christ."

As I have tried to demonstrate throughout the book, reform and renewal discourse is not a documentary point in space. In the public articulation of its cognitive praxis, only a portion resembles Burns's angry philippic. Indeed, many reform and renewal groups have recognized that bitter sloganeering, antipathetic rhetoric, and vague invective alleging high-level conspiracism often serve only to alienate denominational members—including some who might otherwise be sympathetic to the conservative cause. Indeed, other types of reform and renewal discourse represent more serious and significant efforts to engage denominational opponents in dialogue—either to persuade them of their error, or to articulate the conservative position more clearly and eloquently.

In the context of this discourse, a useful distinction can be made here between *rational* and *prerational* knowledge, that is, between knowledge that is worked out in some coherent, systematic fashion through an intentional process of investigation, reflection, articulation, and re-examination, and knowledge that, though perhaps held in common by members of a group, is apprehended apart from any systematic integration of that knowledge into a coherent framework or rationale. For example, a prerational statement common to Christian believers is: "Jesus died for my sins." A slightly more sophisticated version might read: "Jesus died to pay the price for my sins." Given the weight of tradition behind them, the fact that they are repeated throughout Christian hymnody, liturgy, and pedagogy, neither of these claims need adduce any more complex statement of a substitutionary atonement in order to be meaningful within the Christian community. They are *pre*-rational; that is, one need not work out a carefully articulated, theoretically coherent argument for the vicarious suffering and substitutionary death of an ontologically divine Christ in order to proclaim with full confidence: "Jesus died for my sins."

While, according to Karl Mannheim (1952, 40), "it cannot be gainsaid that religious experience, even though its mainsprings be of an irrational character, often finds expression through the most elaborate theoretical exercises" Peter Berger and Thomas Luckmann (1966, 87–88) maintain that "institutional meanings tend to become simplified in transmission, so that the given collection of institutional 'formulae' can be readily learned and memorized by successive generations." Indeed, they continue, it is the " 'formula' character of institutional meaning that ensures their memorability." Neither, obviously, is incorrect; rather, each complements the other. Neither, too, are there hard and fast dividing lines between rational and prerational statements; rather they are like endpoints on a continuum bounded on one hand by a fully integrated, coherent rationale, on the other by a simple adherence with little or no intentional reflection on the matter at hand. This is readily discernible in any number of congregational efforts to transmit the Christian story throughout the liturgical year. Consider, as just one example, the ubiquitous children's Christmas pageant, which is usually held during the first weeks of Advent, and which conflates aspects of the two birth narratives (Matthew and Luke) into one simplified, prerational theological transmission that is, paradoxically, true to both gospels at the same time as it is true to neither.

Or, in terms of movement intellectuals in the conservative reform domain, consider the response of former *Fellowship Magazine* editor Gail Reid, when asked to participate in a televised debate on the saving significance of Jesus. Reid writes that her "first response" was "No! . . . You have the wrong person," she told the producer. "I hate arguing and I don't know the theology to defend my perspective" (1997, 3). For Reid, there is no question that Jesus is the only way to God, but in the absence of a more fully articulated rationale for that belief—that is, "the theology to defend my perspective"—she adverts to a prerational, but no less powerful statement of faith. Reid, in fact, illustrates the reality that many believers feel ill equipped to defend their faith when challenged. That increasingly elaborate theoretical exercises have been marshaled in defense of Christian doctrine since the early years of the Church is not in dispute; neither, however, is the reality that these complex theoretical statements have grown increasingly unavailable to Christian believers who lack specialized theological training. Rather, through hymns, sermons, and Sunday School storyboards, they have been simplified and codified, rendered formulaic and, therefore, memorable.

One result of the ongoing dispute between reform and renewal groups and the denominations of which they are a part—a result that more often than not goes unrecognized by the less conservative members of the denomination—is that the anger and outrage over the various precipitous moments have forced conservative members to consider their theological, ethical, and political positions in substantially greater depth than had been, perhaps, the case. That is, they have recognized that their churches no longer accept at face value the formulaic doctrinal statements to which believers have adhered for centuries. In order to contest what they regard as the dilution of doctrine and the weakening of the church, a number of conservative reform groups have sought to articulate their traditionalist theological vision with more sophistication and intellectual rigor than has heretofore been the case. Among these efforts are *reNEWS* and *reFORM* (Presbyterians for Renewal); *Theological Digest & Outlook* (Church Alive); *The Machray Review* (Prayer Book Society of Canada); and *Theology Matters* (Presbyterians for Faith, Family and Ministry). For our purposes, let us consider the latter very briefly.

Theology Matters is the bimonthly journal published by Presbyterians for Faith, Family and Ministry. It collects articles ranging from those written by prominent academics to PC(USA) clergy and laypeople, and through them seeks to articulate this more sophisticated vision of traditionalist Presbyterian belief. Elizabeth Achtemeier, for example, then an adjunct professor at Union Theological Seminary (Richmond, Virginia), contributed a trenchant critique of gender-inclusive language to the first issue (1995). An article by Oxford theologian Alister McGrath on "Doctrine and Ethics" is reprinted from *The Journal of the Evangelical Theological Society* (1995). Academics and intelligent-design proponents Phillip Johnson (1999) and William Dembski (1999) both contributed articles to an issue considering various aspects of the evolution-creation controversy, a debate that *Theology Matters* editor, Sue Cyre, regards as central to the task of Christian theology.

Well aware that theological conservatives from all mainline Protestant denominations have been castigated by more liberal coreligionists for their rigid adherence to an exclusivist understanding of the nature of Christ, Bryan Burton, a PC(USA) pastor from New Jersey, contributed "Faithful Witness to the Uniqueness of Jesus Christ" (1995). Rather than simply repeat prerational appeals to the soteriological uniqueness of Christ, Burton delineates the major Christological positions currently available—that is, exclusivist, inclusivist, and pluralist—and then critiques each in the light of his own preferred position, the exclusivist. While he differs little theologically from his more immoderate compeers, Burton takes seriously the need to conceptualize and articulate matters of faith and belief that lie at the heart of many of the controversies in the PC(USA). Similarly, an entire issue is devoted to Randall Otto's "A Map for the Maze" (2001), a guide for traditionalist Presbyterians "through the maze of contemporary theologies" by which they are confronted on a regular basis. Otto, a Presbyterian pastor with a Ph.D. from Westminster Theological Seminary, outlines and critiques a number of proponents of well-known theological models and movements, including Karl Barth (neo-orthodoxy), Wolfhart Pannenberg (political theology), Jürgen Molt-mann (theology of hope), Paul Ricouer (narrative theology), James Cone (black theology), and Rosemary Radford Ruether (feminist theology). At the end of each section, Otto includes a series of discussion questions interested readers might ask of those who adhere to these different theological models. Designed not only to elicit answers, the questions are framed in such a way that readers are encouraged to articulate more clearly their own beliefs—an aspect of reform and renewal movements their opponents seem unwilling to acknowledge.

FEW VICTORIES: THE SCORECARD THUS FAR

In the ongoing battle for the soul of the mainline church, a characterization not uncommon on both sides of the field, how does the scorecard read thus far? What clear victories can conservative reform and renewal movements celebrate? In the PC(USA), on the one hand, a 2002 remit of presbyteries defeated a proposed amendment that would have changed the denomination's standards of ordination to allow for the full, acknowledged participation of gay men and lesbians in church ministry. On the other hand, conservatives perceive a singular unwillingness on the part of denominational authorities to enforce the current statutes of the church regarding canonically acceptable sexual behavior. Despite the best efforts of conservative reform groups, The United Church of Canada accepted the 1988 MMHS statement, reaffirmed it two years later, and seems unlikely to retreat from that position any time soon. Similarly, while the *Book of Common Prayer* remains in use in the ECUSA and the Anglican Church of Canada, other liturgical resources, other books of alternative services, are here to stay. While those in favor of more progressive directions might consider the pace of change exceedingly slow, that change away from more conservative positions is occurring is clear. Thus, it seems that conservative reform and renewal can claim few direct victories in denominational politics.

As well, simply because The *Layman* is mailed to half a million households in the PC(USA), does not necessarily translate into an active membership anywhere near that large. Where the Prayer Book Society was once regarded as "the largest voluntary association of laypersons in the history of the Episcopal Church" (Ralston 2001), now its membership is in decline as congregations adjust to the new liturgies and realize that the roof of the sanctuary has *not* fallen in.

For a variety of reasons, reform groups have not been successful in attracting the majority of their constituent denominations to their cause. First, while a significant number of denominational members might sympathize with the feelings that have led to the formation of these groups, the often vitriolic rhetoric and simplistic logic, the emphasis on emotionalized religious experience, and the perpetuation of an entrenched polarity keeps many from participating. Second, as the cognitive praxis of conservative reform has developed and solidified over the years, many denominational critics contend that the theology and doctrine of reform groups has moved so far beyond the historical boundaries of North American mainline Protestantism that they should be more appropriately (and honestly) located within the broader culture of evangelical-fundamentalist Protestantism. That is, if members of the Presbyterian Lay Committee or the Good News Movement are closer theologically to the Southern Baptist Convention, why don't they simply leave either the PC(USA) or the UMC and join a church that offers a better fit? Once again, though, while any number of mainline members might share the concerns that reform and renewal movements have for the church, they remain mainline. That is, they do not want to be identified as evangelicals or, worse, fundamentalists.

Third, much of the debate that takes place on the various precipitous moments in the church does so between competing interest groups, and at an ecclesiastical level far removed from the lives of the majority of church members. Of the hundreds of thousands of mainline members, only a small fraction participates in the various church courts where denominational decisions are made. Thus, if denominational direction has a certain momentum simply by virtue of its institutional character, reform movements are faced with the task of convincing the mainline middle that the direction is wrong. In this, it appears, they have not been directly successful.

Indirect success, however, the ability to frame church problems and processes in terms of one's identity as a Christian, has been more significant. While reform and renewal movements have to date been too small to effect significant change in denominational directions, and often too strident in their presentation to attract large numbers of recruits, they have contributed significantly to the creation of a religious discourse that locates issues of denominational faithfulness, Christian integrity, and biblical fidelity at or near the center of the debate. On the one hand, many denominational members who have grown weary of the seemingly endless debates over homosexual ordination, the constant harping on changes in liturgical language, or the inclusion of alternative spiritualities into the worship life of the church simply want the fighting to end. Whether they agree with the particular decisions or not, as long as they or their congregations are not directly affected, they would be just as happy if controversy over the Issue—whatever precipitous moment that happens to be in the life of a denomination—would just go away. Reform and renewal movements, on the other hand, have not permitted this to happen.

When denominational officials castigate conservatives for their perceived lack of decorum and good grace, traditionalists like Sue Cyre challenge the "cry for 'civility' and 'non-polarization' which permeates our church." She laments the fact that "we no longer pursue truth with vigorous debate and clear thinking" (1997, 10; on civility, or the lack thereof, cf. Haberer 2001; Kirkpatrick and Hopper 1997; Knight and Saliers 1999). And she is correct. While less conservative members remain content counting everyone among the company of the blessed, Cyre and her colleagues contest the right of some to claim any authentic identity as Christians.

This issue of authenticity is the central problem of practical life as it is experienced by those who adhere to narrowly defined, exclusive religious claims when they are confronted by theological or doctrinal formations that challenge the unique legitimacy of those claims. Put differently, if Bill Phipps is as authentic a Christian as Ted Wigglesworth, if the women who attend Re-Imagining Conferences are no less Christian than Sue Cyre, and if those who would deny pride of place to Cranmer's venerable *Book of Common Prayer* can count themselves every bit as Anglican as Peter Toon, then the ultimate authority of the interpretation claimed by theological exclusivists is in jeopardy. For many, perhaps most members in these denominations, these are matters of low priority. If the differences between competing groups are simply matters of interpretation, and nothing more, then there is little weight carried by either. If the debate can be successfully framed in terms of authentic identity, however, who is and who is not a true Christian, then the debate remains before the bar of the church and the reform cause remains alive.

A FINAL EXCURSUS: FRICTION, FRAGMENTATION, AND THE ROAD AHEAD FOR MAINLINE PROTESTANTISM

And what of the denominations themselves? What does the future hold for them in the midst of these continuing battles? To respond to these questions, I would like to step into the liminal space between social scientist and former pastor, the space between one who has asked questions about why certain things are happening in mainline Protestantism and one who has tried (though, I fear, in vain) to arrest the membership and participation slide that seems so very evident. I do so with one caveat, however.

Contrary to the opinion of some of my academic colleagues, I believe that a historical sociology is in the business of *explanation*, not *prediction*. Consider how surprised American scholars of religion were by the rise of the neo-Pentecostal charismatic movement (see Poloma 1982). Or, consider the astonishment with which the fall of the Berlin Wall and the collapse of communism were greeted by political scientists, historians, and sociologists around the world. Neither of these was—nor, many feel, could have been—predicted. As academics, then, our task is to examine the data and suggest reasonable explanations that can account for them. Any extrapolations from those data, especially where they concern such inherently complicated social dynamics as religious involvement, behavior, commitment, and attrition, can only be made in the broadest of terms. That is not to say, though, that there are not some broad strokes that we may fill in.

Over the years, in defense of the various precipitous moments and contentious decisions made by their churches, I have heard many clergy and laypeople suggest that "becoming a socially just church sometimes means that you get smaller." And that may very well be true. While the question of being socially just may be open to denominational debate, there is little doubt that these denominations are, indeed, getting smaller. And, while the range of factors involved in mainline denominational decline is considerably greater than either conservative or liberal members are often prepared to admit, few at either end of the theological spectrum contest the reality of that decline. At its height, the Presbyterian Church (USA) counted just over 4 million members; in 1999 it claimed 2.5 million—a loss of around 37 percent. The Episcopal Church posted roughly similar losses, dropping from 3.6 million in the mid-1960s to 2.3 million in 1999. And, in that same time frame, the United Methodist Church dropped from its pre-merger peak of just over 11 million to 8.4 million—a loss of roughly one-fourth of its membership. These are very raw figures, to be sure, and they only tell a part of the story. The real picture, it seems to me, is considerably darker yet, a situation that has not gone unnoticed by other researchers (for example, Bibby 1989; Finke and Stark 1992).

First, for example, there is the issue of national population growth during the period of decline, a component that factors into the equation as a loss of religious market share. As scholars such as Roger Finke, Rodney Stark, and Reginald Bibby have concluded, this demonstrates a considerably steeper drop than simple membership decline might otherwise indicate (see Finke and Stark 1992: 199–275; Bibby 1989). According to the U.S. Census Bureau, the population of the United States increased from 194.3 million in 1965 to about 273 million in 1999—a net increase of about 79 million, or just under 30 percent (U.S. Census Bureau 2001, 8). In Canada the situation was little different; between 1965 and 2000, the population increased from 19.6 million to 30.7 million—a growth of around 37 percent. Put differently, in the closing decades of the twentieth century, the mainline Protestant denominations were losing members at roughly the same rate the population in each country was growing. This means that as fast as denominational membership was declining, the denominational market shares were shrinking even faster.

Second, there is the denominational reality that the reported membership and adherence figures do not begin to reflect the actual level of participation in the church, whether active (that is, involved in congregational or denominational activities) or nominal (that is, those who claim membership, but exhibit little or no active involvement). Consider, for example, the United Church of Canada. According to the church's official 2001 statistics, when asked their religious affiliation by Statistics Canada more than 3 million Canadians—or about 10 percent of the population—identified themselves as "United Church." Spread out among just over 3,700 congregations, this might suggest an average church of about 800 members. Hardly. Those same church figures list 1.7 million "persons under pastoral care," a category the church defines as persons affiliated with the UCCan but whose names are not listed on official congregational rolls. Indeed, *those* rolls contain just over 650,000 full members—38 percent of the number under pastoral care. But that still isn't the end of the story. Of those 650,000 members, only 53 percent are "identifiable givers to the church," and only 270,000 average weekly attendance at worship.

Put differently, 3 million people claim affiliation with the United Church. Of those: a little more than half are sufficiently affiliated with a congregation to qualify being identified by the church as under pastoral care; slightly more than one-fifth are actually members of the church; slightly more than 11 percent can be identified as givers to the church; and less than 1 in 10 attend worship on a weekly basis. Finally, few people who have ever been involved in a congregation, I think, would challenge the suggestion that the actual work of keeping a church's doors open, its heat on, and a minister in its pulpit is relegated to a substantially smaller number than that.

So, given all of this, and even if the precise ratios in other mainline Protestantisms do not exactly match those of the United Church, it appears that these denominations are less in danger of splitting than they are of simply withering away. Certainly not if by "split" one means a major sectarian event on the order of the Protestant Reformation. First, it seems to me that such a schism would require far more energy than many of the mainline churches have to invest at the present time. Second, there is a considerably wider range of options available for disgruntled members short of schism. Third, as any number of congregations have found out in the wake of precipitous moments, the legal statutes under which congregational property is held in trust for the denomination as a whole make leaving without one's property a decidedly less attractive option.

Rather, I believe that the continued friction generated by denominational decisions that are regarded by many in the pulpits and the pews as unequivocally wrongheaded, by denominational avoidance of key theological issues implied in the question of irreconcilable differences, and by the evident membership and participation decline that is already well under way will continue to erode the great mainline Protestantisms, rendering them eventually mere shades of their former selves. Rather than split, unless they can do something to abate the demoralization of membership—both lay and clergy—and stem the demographic decline, they will continue to wither away, suffering instead from attrition and an occasional, spasmodic splintering.

At the end, we return to one of the principle questions by which my interest in conservative reform and renewal movements was piqued: "Why stay?" As Parker Williamson (1996, 194) puts it: "So what are evangelical members of mainline churches to do? Shall we shake the dust from our feet and depart from communions more amenable to Christian truth? Shall we abandon a sinking ship?" Certainly, there are not a few who would be quite happy to see this happen.

Some contend that conservatives remain because they want to take over the denomination, to return the church to less enlightened times. And I suspect this is true; reform movements do want to exercise some measure of control over denominational direction. They do want to take over and turn the ship around rather than abandon it. I disagree with critics such as Lewis Daly, however, that this potential for denominational conflict is necessarily a bad thing. Others remain because the denominational home in which they were raised (and in which, perhaps, they served for many years) is the only denominational home they know. However conservative they may be theologically, it makes no more sense to become a Southern Baptist than a Buddhist. Still others have become so wrapped up in the concept of the remnant faithful, of their identity as the few guardians of orthodoxy in a land overrun with heretics and apathetics, that to leave the church would be to leave their very identity behind—an unthinkable prospect.

A majority of mainline traditionalists, though, remain for a combination of these reasons. They do love their churches; they are outraged by their current direction and decline; they do see themselves as the few remaining faithful; and they have constructed their religious lives to embody their resistance, their fidelity, and their remnant spirit.

References

Abraham, William J. 1996. "Healing Our Doctrinal Dyslexia." *Good News* 29 (4), January-February: 12–16.

Achtemeier, Elizabeth. 1995. "Exchanging God for 'No Gods': A Discussion of Female Language for God." *Theology Matters* 1 (1): 1–7.

Adams, John H. 1998. "Assembly Ends Funding for College Women's Group." *The Layman* (June); online at www.layman.org/layman/general-assembly/general-assembly/june18.html, accessed October 10, 2002.

———. 2002. "Hundreds of Presbyterian Leaders Are Defying Constitution." *The Layman* (October): 1, 3.

Ahlstrom, Sydney E. 1972. *A Religious History of the American People*. New Haven and London: Yale University Press.

Aldersgate Renewal Ministries. n.d. "A Little about ARM;" retrieved online from www.aldersgaterenewal.org/background/aboutus.html, accessed March 20, 2002.

Allen, Todd W. 1966. "A Pastoral Letter to All Members of the Eastern Heights Presbyterian Church." April 13; photocopy of typescript.

———. 1973. "Can Two Walk Together Except They Be Agreed?" *Southern Presbyterian* 1 (1): 3–6.

Anderson, Robert M. 1979. *Vision of the Disinherited: The Making of American Pentecostalism*. New York: Oxford University Press.

Anderson, Terence R. 1983. "The Sexuality Report: Another View." *Touchstone: Heritage and Theology in a New Age* 1 (1): 22–30.

Assembly Committee on Theological Issues. 2000. "Report of the Assembly Committee on Theological Issues." *Journal of the 212th General Assembly of the Presbyterian Church (USA)*; retrieved online from horeb.pcusa.org/ga212/journals, accessed September 19, 2002.

Averill, Lloyd J. 1967. *American Theology in the Liberal Tradition*. Philadelphia: West-minster Press.

Averyt, Michael. 1992. "The BCP or BAS: Does It Matter?" *The Machray Review* 1; online at www.prayerbook.ca/machray/pbscmac2.htm, accessed November 2, 2002.

Barker, Kenneth S. 1988. "Declaration of Dissent: A Theological Background." *Theological Digest* 3 (2): 2–4 (May).

Bates, Stephen. 1993. *Battleground: One Mother's Crusade, the Religious Right, and the Struggle for Our Schools*. New York: Henry Holt and Company, Owl Books.

Bauer, Walter. 1971. *Orthodoxy and Heresy in Earliest Christianity*. 2d ed. Translated by Philadelphia Seminar on Christian Origins and edited by Robert A. Kraft and Gerhard Krodel. Mifflintown: Sigler Press.

Baulmer, Randall. 1996. *Grant Us Courage: Travels Along the Mainline of American Protestantism*. Oxford: Oxford University Press.

Becker, Penny Edgell. 1999. *Congregations in Conflict: Cultural Models of Local Religious Life*. Cambridge: Cambridge University Press.

Bellah, Robert N. 1967. "Civil Religion in America." *Daedalus* 96: 1–21.

Bellah, Robert N., ed.; Madsen, Richard; Sullivan, William M.; Swidler, Ann; Tipton, Steven M. 1996. *Habits of the Heart: Individualism and Commitment in American Life*. Rev. ed. Berkeley and Los Angeles: University of California Press.

Bennett, Dennis. 1970. *Nine O'Clock in the Morning*. Plainfield, NJ: Logos International.

Bennett, Dennis, and Rita Bennett. 1971. *The Holy Spirit and You*. Plainfield, NJ: Logos International.

Berger, Peter L. 1967. *The Sacred Canopy: Elements of a Sociological Theory of Religion*. New York: Doubleday, Anchor Books.

Berger, Peter L., and Thomas Luckmann. 1966. *The Social Construction of Reality: A Treatise on the Sociology of Knowledge*. London: Penguin Books.

Berghoef, Gerard, and Lester DeKoster. 1984. *Liberation Theology: The Church's Future Shock: Explanation, Analysis, Critique, Alternative*. Grand Rapids, MI: Christian's Library Press.

Berlinerblau, Jacques. 2001. "Toward a Sociology of Orthodoxy, Heresy, and *doxa*." *History of Religions* 40 (4): 327–51.

Berneking, Nancy, and Pamela Carter Joern. 1995. *Re-Membering and Re-Imagining*. Cleveland: Pilgrim Press.

Berry, Jason, and Andrew M. Greeley. 2000. *Lead Us Not Into Temptation: Catholic Priests and the Sexual Abuse of Children*. Urbana and Chicago: University of Illinois Press.

Bibby, Reginald W. 1989. *Fragmented Gods: The Poverty and Potential of Religion in Canada*. Toronto: Stoddart.

———. 1999. "On Boundaries, Gates, and Circulating Saints: A Longitudinal Look at Loyalty and Loss." *Review of Religious Research* 41: 149–64.

Bibby, Reginald W., and Merlin B. Brinkerhoff. 1973. "Circulation of the Saints: A Study of People Who Join Conservative Churches." *Journal for the Scientific Study of Religion* 12: 273–83.

———. 1983. "Circulation of the Saints Revisited: A Longitudinal Look at Conservative Church Growth." *Journal for the Scientific Study of Religion* 22: 253–62.

———. 1994. "Circulation of the Saints, 1966–1990: New Data, New Reflections." *Journal for the Scientific Study of Religion* 33: 273–80.

Biblical Witness Fellowship. 1999. *Uncloseting the Goddess: A Look at Emerging Feminist, Neo-Paganism in the Church through the Open Door of Re-Imagining."* Candia, NH: Biblical Witness Fellowship.

Biblical Witness Fellowship. N.d. *Seeking a Godly Pastor: A Guide to Finding Godly Leadership in Your Church.* Candia, NH: Pastoral Referral Network.

Bloesch, Donald G. 1982. *Is the Bible Sexist? Beyond Feminism and Patriarchalism.* Westchester, IL: Crossway Books.

———. 1984. *Crumbling Foundations: Death and Rebirth in an Age of Upheaval.* Grand Rapids, MI: Academic Books.

———. 1985. *The Battle for the Trinity: The Debate over Inclusive God-Language.* Ann Arbor, MI: Vine Books.

Boers, Arthur Paul. 1999. *Never Call Them Jerks: Healthy Responses to Difficult Behavior.* Bethesda, M.D.: The Alban Institute.

Boff, Leonardo. 1978. *Jesus Christ Liberator: A Critical Christology for Our Time,* Translated by Patrick Hughes. Maryknoll, NY: Orbis Books.

———. 1986. *Ecclesiogenesis: The Base Communities Reinvent the Church,* Translated by Robert K. Barr. Maryknoll, NY: Orbis Books.

Bowman, Tom. 1999. "Limits Sought on Navy Bombing Range." *The Baltimore Sun* (September 21), 3A.

Bowman, Tom, and Jonathan Weisman. 1999. "Puerto Rico a Threat to Big Guns." *The Baltimore Sun* (September 1), 1A.

Boyer, Paul, and Stephen Nissenbaum. 1974. *Salem Possessed: The Social Origins of Witchcraft.* Cambridge and London: Harvard University Press.

Bradfield, Cecil David. 1979. *Neo-Pentecostalism: A Sociological Assessment.* Washington, D.C.: University Press of America.

Brandt, Doug. 2000. "The Irony of the Debate." *General Assembly Gazette* 1 (4): 1, 3.

Breyer, Chloe. 2000. *The Close: A Young Woman's First Year at Seminary.* New York: Basic Books.

Briggs, Charles A. 1893. *The Defence of Professor Briggs before the Presbytery of New York, December 13, 14, 15, 19, and 22, 1892.* New York: Scribner.

Briggs, Robin. 1996. *Witches and Neighbors: The Social and Cultural Context of European Witchcraft.* New York: Penguin Books.

Bright, Rhea N. 1992. "The Dangers of Inclusive Language." *The Machray Review* 1; online at www.prayerbook.ca/machray/pbscmac2.htm, accessed November 2, 2002.

Brouwer, Arie. 1982. "Dr. Arie Brouwer." *Christianity, Democracy, and the Churches Today: Critique and Debate,* 19–22. Washington, D.C.: Institute on Religion and Democracy.

Brown, Harold O. J. 1988. *Heresies: Heresy and Orthodoxy in the History of the Church.* Peabody: Hendrickson Publishers.

Brown, Robert McAfee. 1988. *Spirituality and Liberation: Overcoming the Great Fallacy.* Philadelphia: Westminster Press.

———. 1993. *Liberation Theology: An Introductory Guide.* Louisville, KY: Westminster John Knox Press.

Bruce, Steve. 1998. "The Charismatic Movement and the Secularization Thesis." *Religion* 28: 223–32.

Burnett, Richard E. 2001. "Why a Confessing Church Movement?" *The Layman* 34: 3 (April); online at www.layman.org/layman/the-layman/2001/april01-special-report/why-a-confessing.htm, accessed October 12, 2002.

Burns, George. 2000a. "The Sodomy of Bishops"; online at www.episcopalian.org/cclec/tract-1.htm.

———. 2000b. "Tracts for Our Times: An Introduction"; online at www.episcopalian.org/cclec/tract-intro.htm, accessed December 2, 2002.

Burton, Anthony. 1992. "Sausages and the Potemkin Village: The Basic Problem with the B.A.S." Address delivered at the Annual General Meeting of the Prayer Book Society of Canada (May 23); online at www.prayerbook.ca/machray/pbscmr2d.htm, accessed November 8, 2002.

———. 1998. "The End of the Liturgical Movement and the Recovery of Biblical Worship: An Anglican Perspective." *Crisis in Common Prayer in the Anglican Church of Canada;* online at www.prayerbook.ca/crisis/crisis04.htm, accessed November 15, 2002.

Burton, Bryan D. 1995. "Faithful Witness to the Uniqueness of Jesus Christ." *Theology Matters* 1 (6): 1–8.

Cagney, Mary. 2000. "Signs, Wonders and St. Patrick." *Good News* 33 (5): 15–18 (March–April).

Carreker, Michael. 1994. "Balanced Language?" *The Machray Review* 4; online at www.prayerbook.ca/machray/pbscmac2.htm, accessed November 9, 2002.

Cauthen, Kenneth. 1962. *The Impact of American Religious Liberalism.* New York and Evanston: Harper & Row, Publishers.

Chalmers, Randolph Carleton. 1945. *See the Christ Stand! A Study in Doctrine in The United Church of Canada.* Toronto: Ryerson Press.

Chomsky, Noam. 1988. *The Culture of Terrorism.* Montréal: Black Rose Books.

———. 1993. *Year 501: The Conquest Continues.* Montréal: Black Rose Books.

———. 2000. *Rogue States: The Rule of Force in Foreign Affairs.* Cambridge, MA: South End Press.

Chomsky, Noam, and Edward S. Herman. 1979. *The Political Economy of Human Rights: Volume I, The Washington Connection and Third World Fascism.* Montréal: Black Rose Books.

Church Alive. [1974] 1989. "15 Affirmations," 2nd ed. *Theological Digest* 4 (2): 3–4.

Cimino, Richard. 2001. *Trusting the Spirit: Renewal and Reform in American Religion.* San Francisco: Jossey-Bass.

Clark, S. D. 1948. *Church and Sect in Canada.* Toronto: University of Toronto Press.

Clifford, N. Keith. 1984. "The United Church of Canada and Doctrinal Confession." *Touchstone: Heritage and Theology in a New Age* 2 (2): 6–21.

———. 1985. *The Resistance to Church Union in Canada, 1904–1939.* Vancouver: University of British Columbia Press.

Coalter, Milton J., John M. Mulder, and Louis B. Weeks. 1996. *Vital Signs: The Promise of Mainstream Protestantism.* Grand Rapids, MI: William B. Eerdmans Publishing Company.

Coalter, Milton J., John M. Mulder, and Louis B. Weeks, eds. 1990. *The Mainstream Protestant "Decline": The Presbyterian Pattern.* Louisville, KY: Westminster John Knox Press.

Coleman, Richard J. 1972. *Issues of Theological Warfare: Evangelicals and Liberals.* Grand Rapids, MI: William B. Eerdmans Publishing Company.

Coleman, Robert E. 1993. *The Master Plan of Evangelism.* 30th ann. ed. Grand Rapids, MI: Fleming H. Revell.

"Comments." 1969. "Constitutional Law—Church Property Disputes—First Amendment Prohibits Judicial Examination of Ecclesiastical Matters." *Iowa Law Review* 54: 899–914.

"Commissioning History." 1998. *The Layman,* editorial (November/December 18).

Community of Concern. 1988a. "Declaration of Conviction." Photocopy of typescript.

———. 1988b. "Declaration of Dissent." Photocopy of typescript.

———. 1988c. "Declaration of Intentions." Photocopy of typescript.

———. 1988d. "Declaration of Position." Photocopy of typescript.

———. 1989. "Survey Results." Photocopy of typescript.

———. 1990. "Articles of Concern." May 2; photocopy of typescript.

———. 1992. "An Awesome Responsibility." *Concern* 3 (5), August 15: 1–2.

Concerned Clergy and Laity of the Episcopal Church. 1997. "A Catalog of Concerns: The Episcopal Church in the U.S. under Edmond Lee Browning;" retrieved online from www.episcopalian.org/cclec/catalog-concerns.htm, accessed January 10, 2003.

Confessing Movement. 1995. "A Confessional Statement." The Confessing Movement within the United Methodist Church; online at www.confessingumc.org/statement.html, accessed September 22, 2002.

Copestake, David R., and H. Newton Maloney. 1993. "Adverse Effects of Charismatic Experiences: A Reconsideration." *Journal of Psychology and Christianity* 12: 236–44.

Corbett, Julia Mitchell. 1999. *Religion in America.* 4th ed. Upper Saddle River, NJ: Prentice-Hall.

Cowan, Douglas E. 2000. " 'What's in It for Us?' Notes on Membership and Commitment." *Touchstone: Heritage and Theology in a New Age* 18 (2): 7–21.

———. 2003. *Bearing False Witness? An Introduction to the Christian Countercult.* Westport, Conn.: Praeger Publishers.

Crouse, Robert. 1998. "Something to Sing About? The Assumptions Underlying the Theology of the New Hymn Book." *Anglican Free Press* 15 (1).

Cumming, Lloyd G. 1990. *The Uncomfortable Pew.* Barrie, Ont.: The United Church Renewal Fellowship.

Cuneo, Michael W. 1997. *The Smoke of Satan: Conservative and Traditionalist Dissent in Contemporary American Catholicism.* New York: Oxford University Press.

Cunningham, Jim. 1997. "Ministers Call on Moderator to Resign." *Calgary Herald,* November 9, A2.

Curry, David. 1996. "The Prayer Book and Revision." *Crisis in Common Prayer in the Anglican Church of Canada;* online at www.prayerbook.ca/crisis/crisis11.htm, accessed November 10, 2002.

———. 1998. "A Matter of Faith: A Matter of Doctrine." *Crisis in Common Prayer in the Anglican Church of Canada;* online at www.prayerbook.ca/crisis/crisis08.htm, accessed November 10, 2002.

———. 1999a. " 'Ethnic cleansing' Feared in Church." *The Anglican Journal* (September): 7.

————. 1999b. "Press Release . . . " (July); online at www.prayerbook.ca/pblam/
    pblam437.htm, accessed November 12, 2002.

Cyre, Susan. 1995. "Truth Creates Boundaries." *Theology Matters* 1 (2): 1–3.

————. 1997. "The Church Militant." *Theology Matters* 3 (1): 10–12.

Daly, Lewis C. 2000a. "A Moment to Decide for the PC(USA)"; online at
    www.witherspoonsociety.org/analysis_by_lew_daly.htm, accessed October
    19, 2002.

————. 2000b. *A Moment to Decide: The Crisis in Mainstream Presbyterianism.* Wash-
    ington, D.C.: Institute for Democratic Studies.

Daly, Mary. 1973. *Beyond God the Father: Toward a Philosophy of Women's Liberation.*
    Boston: Beacon Press.

————. 1984. *Pure Lust: Elemental Feminist Philosophy.* Boston: Beacon Press.

Danner, Mark. 1994. *The Massacre at El Mozote: A Parable of the Cold War.* New York:
    Vintage Books.

Davids, Peter H. 1995. "What is Biblical Revival?" *Good News* 28 (6): 16–20 (May–
    June).

Davis, Bob. 2000a. "Elephants in the Living Room." *General Assembly Gazette* 1 (5):
    4.

Davis, Bob. 2000b. "Unity: What Does It Mean?" *General Assembly Gazette* 1 (1): 4.

DeCamp, Jim. 2000. "School of the Americas: PCUSA Chaplain Refutes Criticism."
    The Layman 33: 3 (May–June); online at www.layman.org/layman/the-
    layman/2000/no3-may-jun00/school-of-the-americas.htm, accessed October
    15, 2002.

Deck, Allan Figueroa. 1995. " 'A Pox on Both Your Houses': A View of Catholic
    Conservative-Liberal Polarities from the Hispanic Margin." In *Being Right:
    Conservative Catholics in America,* eds. Mary Jo Weaver and R. Scott Appleby,
    88–104. Bloomington: Indiana University Press.

Dembski, William A. 1999. "Admitting Design into Science." *Theology Matters* 5
    (2): 7–13.

Demos, John Putnam. 1982. *Entertaining Satan: Witchcraft and the Culture of Early
    New England.* New York: Oxford University Press.

Dieter, Melvin E. 1975. "Wesleyan-Holiness Aspects of Pentecostal Origins: As
    Mediated through the Nineteenth Century Holiness Revival." In *Aspects of
    Pentecostal-Charismatic Origins,* ed. Vinson Synan, 55–80. Plainfield, NJ:
    Logos International.

————. 1980. *The Holiness Revival of the Nineteenth Century.* Metuchen, NJ: Scare-
    crow Press.

Dinges, William D. 1983. *Catholic Traditionalism in America: A Study of the Remnant
    Faithful.* Ph.D. dissertation, University of Kansas.

Dinges, William D., and James Hitchcock. 1991. "Roman Catholic Traditionalism
    and Activist Conservatism in the United States." In *Fundamentalisms Ob-
    served,* eds. Martin E. Marty and R. Scott Appleby, 66–141. Chicago: Uni-
    versity of Chicago Press.

Discipleship Resources. 1996. "Guidelines: The United Methodist Church and the
    Charismatic Movement." In *The Book of Resolutions of the United Methodist
    Church: 1996,* 696–709. Nashville, TN: United Methodist Publishing House.

Division of Ministry Personnel and Education. 1984. *Sexual Orientation and Eligibility for the Order of Ministry.* Toronto: The United Church of Canada.

Division of Mission in Canada. 1980. *In God's Image . . . Male and Female: A Study on Human Sexuality.* Toronto: The United Church of Canada.

Dobbelaere, Karel. 1981. *Secularization: A Multi-Dimensional Concept.* Current Sociology Series 29. Beverly Hills, Calif.: Sage Publications.

———. 1984. "Secularization Theories and Sociological Paradigms: Convergences and Divergences." *Social Compass* 31: 199–219.

———. 1989. "The Secularization of Society? Some Methodological Considerations." In *Secularization and Fundamentalism Reconsidered,* eds. Jeffrey K. Hadden and Anson Shupe, 27–44. Religion and the Political Order, vol. 3. New York: Paragon House.

———. 1999. "Towards an Integrated Perspective of the Processes Related to the Descriptive Concept of Secularization." *Sociology of Religion* 60 (3): 229–47.

Dooling, Silvia D. n.d. "Is It Just a Matter of Opinion?" retrieved online from www.vow.org/wulff.html, accessed October 21, 2002.

Dow, John. 1951. *Alfred Gandier: Man of Vision and Achievement.* Toronto: The United Church Publishing House.

Dwyer, James G. 1998. *Religious Schools v. Children's Rights.* New York: Cornell University Press.

Eastern Heights Presbyterian Church. 1966. "A Resolution Recommended by the Session and Pastor for Adoption by the Congregation of the Eastern Heights Presbyterian Church," April 17; photocopy of typescript.

Eastern Heights Presbyterian Church. n.d. "Church History;" photocopy of typescript.

Ehrman, Bart D. 1993. *The Orthodox Corruption of Scripture: The Effect of Early Christological Controversies on the Text of the New Testament.* New York: Oxford University Press.

Ellenby, Whitney. 1996. "Divinity vs. Discrimination: Curtailing the Divine Reach of Church Authority." *Golden Gate University Law Review* 26: 369–412.

Enman, Charles. 1997. "Moderator 'Undermines' Faith." *The Ottawa Citizen* (October 27): A1.

Enquiring Methodist. 1891. "Unscriptural Teaching." Letter to the editor, *The Christian Guardian* (June), n.p.

Eyerman, Ron, and Andrew Jamison. 1991. *Social Movements: A Cognitive Approach.* University Park: The Pennsylvania State University Press.

Faris, Donald L. 1989. *Trojan Horse: The Homosexual Ideology and the Christian Church.* Burlington, Ontario: Welch Publishing Company Inc.

———. 1993. *The Homosexual Challenge: A Christian Response to the Age of Sexual Politics.* Markham, Ontario: Faith Today Publications.

———. 1999. "From Church to Cult?" *Fellowship Magazine* 17 (4): 23, 27.

Fassett, Thom White Wolf. 1997. Letter to the editor. *Good News* 30 (5)l: 3 (March–April).

Fenn, Richard K. 1978. *Toward a Theory of Secularization.* Society for the Scientific Study of Religion Monograph Series 1. Storrs, Conn.: The Society for the Scientific Study of Religion.

Finke, Roger, and Rodney Stark. 1992. *The Churching of America, 1776–1990: Winners and Losers in Our Religious Economy*. New York: Routledge.

———. 2001. "The New Holy Clubs: Testing Church-to-Sect Propositions." *Sociology of Religion* 62 (2): 175–89.

First United Methodist Church Marietta. 1998. "Report on the Doctrinal Integrity of The United Methodist Church;" retrieved online from www.ucmpage.org/articles/report_on_doc_integrity.html, accessed December 3, 2002.

Five Members in Faith. 1990. "Regarding the 'Sexuality Reports' Emanating from General Council." Letter to all United Church of Canada congregations, February.

Fletcher, Joseph. 1966. *Situation Ethics: The New Morality*. Philadelphia: Westminster Press.

Fletcher, Richard. 1997. *The Barbarian Conversion: From Paganism to Christianity*. Berkeley and Los Angeles: University of California Press.

Foucault, Michel. 1988. *Politics, Philosophy, Culture: Interviews and Other Writings, 1977–1984*. Edited by Lawrence D. Kritzman. New York: Routledge.

Fox, Matthew. 1983. *Original Blessing: A Primer in Creation Spirituality Presented in Four Paths, Twenty-Six Themes, and Two Questions*. Santa Fe, N. Mex.: Bear & Company.

———. 1996. *Confessions: The Making of a Post-Denominational Priest*. New York: HarperSanFrancisco.

Francis, Leslie J., and Susan H. Jones. 1997. "Personality and Charismatic Experience among Adult Christians." *Pastoral Psychology* 45: 421–28.

Francis, Leslie J., and T. Hugh Thomas. 1997. "Are Charismatic Ministers Less Stable? A Study Among Male Anglican Clergy." *Review of Religious Research* 39: 61–69.

Fraser, Daniel James. 1915. "Recent Church Union Movements in Canada." *Harvard Theological Review* 7: 363–78.

Frozene, Glenn R. 1994. "Letter to the Editor." *Good News* 28 (3), November–December: 7.

Fry, John R. 1975. *The Trivilialization of the United Presbyterian Church*. New York: Harper & Row.

Gabel, Wesley J. 2000. "Catching the Wave of Spiritual Renewal: Unleashing the Church for New Life." *Good News* 33 (6): 12–15 (May–June).

Geertz, Clifford. 1973. *The Interpretation of Cultures*. New York: Basic Books.

General Convention. 1977. "Resolution 1976-A104: Adopt *The Draft Proposed Book of Common Prayer* [First Reading]." *Journal of the General Convention of the Protestant Episcopal Church of the United States of America, 1976*. New York: General Convention.

———. 1980a. "Resolution 1979-A133: Adopt *The Draft Book of Common Prayer* [Second Reading]." *Journal of the General Convention of the Protestant Episcopal Church of the United States of America, 1979*. New York: General Convention.

———. 1980b. "Resolution 1979-A121: Declare Guidelines for Worship from the 1928 Prayer Book." *Journal of the General Convention of the Protestant Episcopal Church of the United States of America, 1979*. New York: General Convention.

Gerstenblith, Patty. 1990. "Civil Court Resolution of Property Disputes among Religious Organizations." *American University Law Review* 39: 513–72.

Giambalvo, Carol, and Herbert L. Rosedale, eds. 1996. *The Boston Movement: Critical Perspectives on the International Churches of Christ.* Bonita Springs, FL: American Family Foundation.

Gibson, James A. n.d. "The Best Defense Is a Great Offense." *Josiah;* online at http://ucmpage.org/josiah_journal/, accessed November 20, 2002.

———. 1994a. "The Quadrilateral Quandary." *Josiah* (spring); online at http://umpage.org/josiah_journal/, accessed November 20, 2002.

———. 1994b. "A Time of Challenge, A Day of New Beginnings." *Josiah* (fall); online at http://ucmpage.org/josiah_journal/, accessed November 20, 2002.

———. 1995. "Drunk on the Wine of Diversity." *Josiah* (summer); online at http://ucmpage.org/josiah_journal/, accessed November 20, 2002.

———. 1996. "A Wesleyan Response to 'A Critical Challenge'." *Josiah* (winter); online at http://ucmpage.org/josiah_journal/, accessed November 20, 2002.

———. 1999. "The Errors of the Eminents." *Josiah* (March); online at http://ucmpage.org/josiah_journal/, accessed November 20, 2002.

Glock, Charles Y. 1964. "On the Role of Deprivation in the Origin and Evolution of Religious Groups." In *Religion and Social Conflict,* eds. Robert Lee and Martin Marty, 24–36. New York: Oxford University Press.

Glock, Charles Y., and Rodney Stark. 1965. *Religion and Society in Tension.* Chicago: Rand McNally.

Good News. 1997. "Editor's Comments." *Good News* 30 (5), March–April: 3–4.

Grant, John Webster. 1963. "Blending Traditions: The United Church of Canada." *Canadian Journal of Theology* 9 (1): 50–59.

Greeley, Andrew M. 1972. *The Denominational Society: A Sociological Approach to Religion in America.* Glenview, IL: Scott, Foresman and Company.

Green, Linda. 1997. "Good News Celebration Emphasizes Revival and Renewal." *United Methodist News Service* (July); online at http://umns.umc.org/News97/jul/ggoodnew.htm, accessed October 30, 2002.

Gualtieri, Antonio R. 1989. *Conscience and Coercion: Ahmadi Muslims and Orthodoxy in Pakistan.* Montréal: Guernica Editions.

Gunnemann, Louis H. 1999. *Shaping of the United Church of Christ: An Essay in the History of American Christianity.* Cleveland: United Church Press.

Gutiérrez, Gustavo. 1973. *A Theology of Liberation: History, Politics, and Salvation,* Translated and edited by Caridad Inda and John Eagleson. Maryknoll, NY: Orbis Books.

———. 1984. *We Drink from Our Own Wells: The Spiritual Journey of a People,* Translated by Matthew J. O'Connell. Maryknoll, NY: Orbis Books.

Gyertson, David J. 1995. "One More Divine Moment." *Good News* 28 (6): 12–14 (May–June).

———. 1997. "Whatever Happened to Holiness?" *Good News* 31 (1): 10–14 (July–August).

Haberer, John. 2001. *Godviews: The Convictions that Drive Us and Divide Us.* Louisville, KY: Westminster John Knox Press.

Habermas, Jürgen. 1984. *The Theory of Communicative Action, Volume One: Reason and the Rationalization of Society,* Translated by Thomas McCarthy. Boston: Beacon Press.

Hadaway, C. Kirk, and P. L. Marler. 1998. "Did You Really Go to Church this Week? Behind the Poll Data." *The Christian Century* (May 6): 472–75.

Hadaway, C. Kirk, and David A. Roozen. 1995. *Rerouting the Protestant Mainstream: Sources of Growth and Opportunities for Change.* Nashville, TN: Abingdon Press.

Hadden, Jeffrey K. 1969. *The Gathering Storm in the Churches.* Garden City, NY: Doubleday.

———. 1989. "Desacralizing Secularization Theory." In *Secularization and Fundamentalism Reconsidered,* eds. Jeffrey K. Hadden and Anson Shupe, 3–26. Religion and the Political Order, vol. 3. New York: Paragon House.

Hadden, Jeffrey K., and Douglas E. Cowan, eds. 2000a. *Religion on the Internet: Research Prospects and Promises.* London: JAI Press/Elsevier Science, Inc.

———. 2000b. "The Promised Land or Electronic Chaos? Toward Understanding Religion on the Internet." In *Religion on the Internet: Research Prospects and Promises,* eds. Jeffrey K. Hadden and Douglas E. Cowan, 3–21. London: JAI/ Elsevier Science, Inc.

Hadden, Jeffrey K., and Charles F. Longino Jr. 1974. *Gideon's Gang: A Case Study of the Church in Social Action.* Philadelphia: Pilgrim Press.

Hailson, Donna F. G., and Karelynne Gerber. 1998. "Cooking Up Gotterdamerung: Radical Feminist Worship Substitutes Self for God." *Theology Matters* 4 (4): 1–8.

Harper, Steve. 1995. "Do We Need a Confessing Movement?" *Good News* 28 (5), March–April: 12–15.

Harvey, Bob. 1997a. " 'I Don't Believe Jesus Was God': United Church's New Moderator Rejects Bible as History Book." *The Ottawa Citizen,* October 24, A1–2.

———. 1997b. "Phipps Must Go, Two Area Churches Demand." *The Ottawa Citizen,* October 30, A1–2.

Hatch, Carl E. 1969. *The Charles A. Briggs Heresy Trial: Prologue to Twentieth-Century Liberal Protestantism.* New York: Exposition Press.

Haugk, Kenneth C. 1988. *Antagonists in the Church: How to Identify and Deal with Destructive Conflict.* Minneapolis: Fortress Press.

Heelas, Paul. 1996. *The New Age Movement: The Celebration of the Self and the Sacralization of Modernity.* London: Blackwell Publishers.

Heidinger, James, II. n.d. "30 Years of Vision for United Methodist Reformation and Renewal." In *The Ministry of Good News,* 13–17. Wilmore, KY: Good News.

———. 1987. "The United Methodist Church." In *Evangelical Renewal in the Mainline Churches.* Edited by Ronald H. Nash, 15–39. Westchester, IL: Crossway Books.

Henderson, John B. 1998. *The Construction of Orthodoxy and Heresy: Neo-Confucian, Islamic, Jewish, and Early Christian Patterns.* Albany, NY: SUNY Press.

Hillis, Bryan V. 1991. *Can Two Walk Together Unless They Be Agreed? American Religious Schisms in the 1970s.* Chicago Studies in the History of American Religion. Brooklyn, NY: Carlson Publishing Inc.

Hocken, Peter D. 1988. "Charismatic Movement." In *Dictionary of Pentecostal and Charismatic Movements,* eds. Stanley M. Burgess and Gary B. McGee, 130–60. Grand Rapids, MI: Zondervan.

Hoge, Dean R. 1976. *Division in the Protestant House: The Basic Reasons behind Intra-Church Conflicts.* Philadelphia: The Westminster Press.

Hoge, Dean R., Benton Johnson, and Donald A. Luidens. 1994. *Vanishing Boundaries: The Religion of Mainline Protestant Baby Boomers.* Louisville, KY: Westminster/ John Knox Press.

Hoge, Dean R., Kenneth McGuire, and Bernard F. Stratman. 1981. *Converts, Drop-outs, Returnees: A Study of Religious Change among Catholics.* Washington, D.C.: United States Catholic Conference, New York: Pilgrim Press.

Hoge, Dean R., and David T. Polk. 1980. "A Test of Theories of Protestant Church Participation and Commitment." *Review of Religious Research* 20: 315–29.

Hoge, Dean R., and David Roozen. 1979. *Understanding Church Growth and Decline, 1950–1978.* New York: Pilgrim Press.

Horton, Douglas. 1962. *The United Church of Christ: Its Origins, Organization, and Role in the World Today.* New York: T. Nelson.

House, H. Wayne. 1997. "With an Apology to Arius: When and How Should We Deal with Heresies and Heretics?" *Journal of Christian Apologetics* 1 (1): 29–47.

Hunt, Dave. 1990. *Global Peace and the Rise of Antichrist.* Eugene, Oreg.: Harvest House.

———. 1994. *A Woman Rides the Beast: The Catholic Church and the Last Days.* Eugene, Oreg.: Harvest House.

Hunter, George G. III. 2000. "Barbarians in Our Midst: How the Irish Spread the Gospel." *Good News* 33 (5): 19–22 (March–April).

Hunter, James Davison. 1991. *Culture Wars: The Struggle to Define America.* New York: Basic Books.

Hutcheson, Richard G., Jr., and Peggy Shriver. 1999. *The Divided Church: Moving Liberals and Conservatives from Diatribe to Dialogue.* Downers Grove, IL: InterVarsity Press.

Hutchinson, William R. 1971. "Cultural Strain and Protestant Liberalism." *The American Historical Review* 76 (2): 386–411.

Hutchinson, William R., ed. 1989. *Between the Times: The Travail of the Protestant Establishment in America, 1900–1960.* Cambridge, England: Cambridge University Press.

Iannaccone, Laurence. 1994. "Why Strict Churches Are Strong." *American Journal of Sociology* 99: 1180–1211.

Institute on Religion and Democracy. 1982. *Christianity, Democracy, and the Churches Today: Critique and Debate.* Washington, D.C.: Institute on Religion and Democracy.

———. 2001. "Methodist Bishops Make Poor Case against Missile Defense." Press release (May 9); online at www.ird-renew.org/News/, accessed October 17, 2002.

———. n.d. "Mission Statement;" retrieved online from www.umc-renew.org, accessed December 10, 2002.

Jensen, Paul Rolf. 1998. "Multi-Cultural Event Celebrated." *The Layman* (June); online at www.layman.org/layman/general-assembly/general-assembly/june14.html, accessed September 10, 2002.

Johnson, Benton, Dean R. Hoge, and Donald A. Luidens. 1993. "Mainline Churches: The Real Reason for the Decline." *First Things: A Journal of Religion and Public Life* 31: 13–18; online at www.firstthings.com/ftissues/ft9303/johnson.html, accessed August 25, 2002.

Johnson, Phillip E. 1999. "The Wedge in Evolutionary Ideology: It's [sic] History, Strategy, and Agenda." *Theology Matters* 5 (2): 1–7.

Jones, Preston. 1997. "The Place of the Prayer Book Society of Canada in Canadian History." *The Machray Review* 6; online at www.prayerbook.ca/machray/ pbscmac2.htm, accessed November 12, 2002.

Kelley, Dean M. 1977. *Why Conservative Churches Are Growing: A Study in the Sociology of Religion*. ROSE—Reprints of Scholarly Excellence. Macon, GA: Mercer University Press.

Kelly, Herbert. 1917. "The United Church of Canada." *The Constructive Quarterly* (September): 435–52.

Keysor, Charles W. 1966. "Methodism's Silent Minority: A Voice for Orthodoxy." *New Christian Advocate* (July 14); reprinted in *The Ministry of Good News*, 10–12. Wilmore, KY: Good News.

———. 1973. "Tongues-Speaking: Good or Bad?" *Good News Magazine* (fall–winter); online at www.goodnewsmag.org/renewal/tongues.htm, accessed October 2, 2002.

———. 1977. "Good News and Charismatics." *Good News Magazine* (September–October); online at www.goodnewsmag.org/renewal/gncharismatics.htm, accessed October 2, 2002.

Kieckhefer, Richard. 1979. *Repression of Heresy in Medieval Germany*. Liverpool: Liverpool University Press.

Kincaid, Paula R. 1998. " 'Coming Out Day' Service Held at Columbia Seminary." *The Layman* 31(November–December): 6; online at www.layman.org/layman/ the-layman / 1998 / nov-dec / comingout-service / coming-out-day-columbia. htm, accessed October 30, 2002.

Kinghorn, Kenneth Cain. 1989. "A Foundation for Theological Education." *Challenge to Evangelism Today* 22 (2): 4.

———. 1994. "Is the UM Church a Confessional Denomination?" *Good News* 28 (3): 12–16 (November–December).

Kirkpatrick, Clifton, and William H. Hopper. 1997. *What Unites Presbyterians: Common Ground for Troubled Times*. Louisville, KY: Geneva Press.

Kjos, Berit. 1997. "From Father God to Mother Earth: The Effect of Deconstructing Christian Faith on Sexuality." *Theology Matters* 3 (5): 1–9.

Knight, Henry H., and Don E. Saliers. 1999. *The Conversation Matters: Why United Methodists Should Talk with One Another*. Nashville, TN: Abingdon Press.

Knippers, Diane. 1989. "Social and Political Values on Our Theological Seminary Campuses: A New Orthodoxy or a Macedonian Call?" *Challenge to Evangelism Today* 22 (2): 6–7, 12.

Koch, George. 1999. "United Church Moderator Charged with Blasphemy." *Calgary Herald*, April 25, A7.

Kraft, Robert A. 1975. "The Development of the Concept of 'Orthodoxy' in Early Christianity." In *Current Issues in Biblical and Patristic Interpretation*, ed. Gerald F. Hawthorne, 47–59. Grand Rapids, MI: Eerdmans.

Kuhn, Thomas S. 1970. *The Structure of Scientific Revolutions*. Chicago: University of Chicago Press.

Kurtz, Lester R. 1983. "The Politics of Heresy." *American Journal of Sociology* 88 (6): 1085–1115.

Leas, Speed, and Paul Kittlaus. 1973. *Church Fights: Managing Conflict in the Local Church.* Philadelphia: The Westminster Press.

Legge, Gordon. 1999. "Phipps Responds to Heresy Claim." *Calgary Herald,* May 20, A1.

Leith, John H. 1997. *Crisis in the Church: The Plight of Theological Education.* Louisville, KY: Westminster John Knox Press.

Lenski, Gerhard. 1961. *The Religious Factor.* Garden City, NY: Doubleday.

LeoGrande, William. 2000. *Our Own Backyard: The United States in Central America, 1977–1992.* Chapel Hill: University of North Carolina Press.

Loftis, Gary. 2001. "Moderator is Vilifying Faithful Congregations." Letter to the editor, *The Layman* (August 7); online at www.layman.org, accessed October 10, 2002.

Looper, Patricia B. 1995. "There Is No Other Name . . . "; *Josiah* (Summer); online at http://ucmpage.org/josiah_journal/, accessed September 22, 2002.

Lüdemann, Gerd. 1995. *Heretics: The Other Side of Early Christianity.* Translated by John Bowman. Louisville, KY: Westminster John Knox Press.

Lüdemann, Gerd, and Martina Janssen. 1997. *Suppressed Prayers: Gnostic Spirituality in Early Christianity.* Translated by John Bowden. Harrisburg, PA: Trinity Press International.

Luidens, Donald A. 1990. "Numbering the Presbyterian Branches: Membership Trends Since Colonial Times." In *The Mainstream Protestant 'Decline': The Presbyterian Pattern,* eds. Milton J. Coalter, John M. Mulder, and Louis B. Meeks, 29–65. Louisville, KY: Westminster John Knox Press.

Mann, W. E. 1963. "The Canadian Church Union, 1925." In *Institutionalism and Church Unity: A Symposium,* eds. Nils Ehrenstrom and Walter G. Muelder, 171–193. New York: Association Press.

Mannheim, Karl. 1952. "On the Interpretation of *Weltanschauung.*" In *Essays on the Sociology of Knowledge,* ed. Paul Kecskemeti, 33–83. London: Routledge & Kegan Paul.

Marshall, David B. 1992. *Secularizing the Faith: Canadian Protestant Clergy and the Crisis of Belief, 1850–1940.* Toronto: University of Toronto Press.

Martin, Walter R. 1985. *The Kingdom of the Cults.* 3rd rev. ed. Minneapolis: Bethany House.

Martin, Walter R., and Norman Klann. 1974. *Jehovah of the Watchtower.* Rev. ed. Minneapolis: Bethany House.

Mawdsley, Ralph D. 2000. *Legal Problems of Religious and Private Schools.* 4th ed. New York: Cornell University Press.

McCaig, Ed. 1995. "Now that We Have the Answers, What Was the Question?" *Fellowship Magazine* 13 (2): 22–23.

McCartney, Michael J. 1998. "Letter to the Editor." *Fellowship Magazine* 16 (1): 30.

McCook, John J., comp. 1893. *The Appeal In The Briggs Heresy Case Before The General Assembly Of The Presbyterian Church In The United States Of America.* New York: J. C. Rankin.

McDonnell, Kilian. 1976. *Charismatic Renewal and the Churches.* New York: Seabury Press.

McFague, Sallie. 1989. *Models of God: Theology for an Ecological, Nuclear Age.* Minneapolis: Fortress Press.

———. 1997. *Metaphorical Theology: Models of God.* Minneapolis: Fortress Press.

McGrath, Alister E. 1995. "Doctrine and Ethics." *Theology Matters* 1 (4): 1–7.

Merton, Thomas. 1967. *Mystics and Zen Masters*. New York: Noonday Press.

———. 1968. *Faith and Violence: Christian Teaching and Christian Practice*. Notre Dame: University of Notre Dame Press.

Midelfort, H. C. Erik. 1972. *Witch Hunting in Southwestern Germany, 1562–1684: The Social and Intellectual Foundations*. Stanford, Calif.: Stanford University Press.

Mills, C. Wright. [1959] 2000. *The Sociological Imagination*. New York: Oxford University Press.

Mills, David. 1999. "The Flatlanders' Creed." *Mandate* 18 (6): 7–8.

Mills, Robert P. 1998. "NNPCW Funding Is Restored." *The Layman* (June); online at www.layman.org/layman/general-assembly/general-assembly/june20.html, accessed October 13, 2002.

———. 1999a. "Enforcing Inclusive God-Language." *The Layman* 32: 3 (May–June); online at www.layman.org/layman/news/news-from-pcusa/overture99-24.htm, accessed October 13, 2002.

———. 1999b. "Overture Attempts to Mandate Use of Inclusive God-Language." *The Layman* (June); online at www.layman.org/layman/news/news-from-pcusa/ga99-topten-03.htm, accessed October 13, 2002.

Miranda, José Porfirio. 1974. *Marx and the Bible: A Critique of the Philosophy of Oppression*, Translated by John Eagleson. Maryknoll, NY: Orbis Books.

———. 1982. *Communism in the Bible*. Translated by Robert K. Barr. Maryknoll, NY: Orbis Books.

Moir, John S. 1975. *Enduring Witness: A History of the Presbyterian Church in Canada*. N.p.: Bryant Press.

Moir, John S., ed. 1966. *The Cross in Canada*. Toronto: Ryerson Press.

Morgan, James M. 1994. "Letter to the Editor." *Good News* 28 (1), July–August: 3–4.

Morris, Alan O. N.d. *The Church in Bondage: Problems and Trends in the United Methodist Church;* online at http://ucmpage.org/bondage/index.html, accessed October 30, 2002.

Morrow, E. Lloyd. 1923. *Church Union in Canada: Its History, Motives, Doctrine, and Government*. Toronto: Thomas Allen.

Morrow, Quintin. 2001a. "Cranmer's Two-edged Sword." *Mandate* 20 (5): 14.

———. 2001b. "St. Andrew's, Fort Worth and Her Rector." *Mandate* 20 (4): 5.

———. 2001c. "Why '28 in '01?" *Mandate* 20 (4): 4.

Morton, Arthur S. 1912. *The Way to Union: Being a Study of the Principles of the Foundation and of the Historic Development of the Christian Church as Bearing on The Proposed Union of the Presbyterian, Methodist, and Congregational Churches in Canada*. Toronto: William Briggs.

Nash, Ronald H. 1987. "The Presbyterian Church." In *Evangelical Renewal in the Mainline Church*. Edited by Ronald H. Nash, 87–103. Westchester, IL: Crossway Books.

National Alliance of Covenanting Congregations. 1990. "Articles of Association for Member Congregations of The United Church of Canada Wishing to Maintain the Historic Faith;" photocopy of typescript.

National Coordinating Group. 1988. *Toward a Christian Understanding of Sexual Orientation, Lifestyles and Ministry*. Recommendations and Report to the 32nd General Council from the Division of Ministry Personnel and Education and the Division of Mission in Canada. Toronto: The United Church of Canada.

Nelson, Sally. 1994. "Theology Should Start with God, Not Women's Lives." *Good News;* online at www.goodnewsmag.org/library/articles/cyre-ma94.htm, accessed October 20, 2002.

Nelson-Pallmeyer, Jack. 1997. *School of Assassins: The Case for Closing the School of the Americas and for Fundamentally Changing U.S. Foreign Policy.* Maryknoll, NY: Orbis Books.

Neuhaus, Richard John. 1981. "Christianity and Democracy: A Statement of the Institute on Religion and Democracy." Washington, D.C.: The Institute on Religion and Democracy.

———. 1982. "Pastor Richard John Neuhaus." *Christianity, Democracy, and the Churches Today: Critique and Debate,* 1–3. Washington, D.C.: Institute on Religion and Democracy.

Niagara Conference v. Truax. 1893a. "Findings and Decisions of the Committee of Trial of Rev. A. Truax." November 29; photocopy of handwritten manuscript.

———. 1893b. "Preference of Charges." November 11; photocopy of typescript.

———. 1893c. "Truax Trial: Summary of Evidence Presented." November 27; photocopy of typescript.

Nietzsche, Friedrich. 1974. *The Gay Science: With a Prelude in Rhymes and an Appendix in Songs.* Translated by Walter Kaufmann. New York: Vintage Books.

Novak, Michael. 1978. *Ascent of the Mountain, Flight of the Dove: An Invitation to Religious Studies.* Rev. ed. New York: Harper & Row, Publishers.

———. 1991. *Will It Liberate? Questions about Liberation Theology.* Rev. ed. Lanham, Md.: Madison Books.

Oden, Thomas C. 1995. *Requiem: A Lament in Three Movements.* Nashville, TN: Abingdon Press.

Ogilvie, Margaret H. 1992. "Church Property Dispute: Some Organizing Principles." *University of Toronto Law Journal* 42: 377–400.

———. 1996. *Religious Institutions and the Law in Canada.* Scarborough, Ont.: Carswell.

Oliver, Edmund H. 1930. *The Winning of the Frontier: A Study of the Religious History of Canada.* Toronto: The United Church Publishing House.

Otto, Randall. 1998. "The Problem with Marcion: A Second-Century Heresy Continues to Infect the Church." *Theology Matters* 4 (5): 1–8.

———. 2001. "A Map for the Maze: Finding Your Way through Contemporary Theology (A) Guide for PNC's)." *Theology Matters* 7 (3): 1–16.

Outerbridge, Ian W.; Ross, C. Gonoon; Kary, Joseph H. 1994. *Ecclesiastical Minefields: A Guide, Casebook and Materials, Including a Criticism of Certain Portions of the* Manual *and the* Sexual Abuse Guidelines *of the United Church of Canada, for Use by Students, Both Laity and Clergy.* N.p.: Or Emet Publishing.

Overture 00-37. 2000. "On Establishing a Task Force to Conduct a Study of Abortion Forcused Solely on Explicating the Biblical Witness in a Manner Faithful to the Scriptures and Consistent with the Confessional Standards." *212th General Assembly of the Presbyterian Church (USA);* retrieved online from horeb.pcusa.org/ga212/overtures/ovt00-37.htm, accessed September 19, 2002.

Overture 00-5. 2000. "On Declaring That There Exists in the PC(USA) an Irreconcilable Impasse Regarding Biblical Authority, Biblical Interpretation, Jesus Christ, Salvation, Ethics, Leadership. Sanctification. and the Church." *212th General Assembly of the Presbyterian Church (USA)*; retrieved online from horeb.pcusa.org/ga212/overtures/ovt00-5.htm, accessed September 19, 2002.

Overture 01-9. 2001. "On Entering a Process of Churchwide Spiritual Discernment Considering the Current Division Within Our Denomination." *213th General Assembly of the Presbyterian Church (USA)*; retrieved online from horeb.pcusa.org/ga213/business/OVT019.htm, accessed September 24, 2002.

Page, Owen H. 1967. "A Message to Our Church." *News and Events Report*. November 29; photocopy of typescript.

———. 1968. Letter to Todd Allen, March 6; photocopy of typescript.

Pannenberg, Wolfhart. 1997. "Homosexuality and the Scripture." *Good News* 30 (5): 26–27 (March–April).

Perkins, Bonnie J. 2000. "In pursuit of a burning passion." *Good News* 34 (3): 14–17 (November–December).

Peters, Robert S. 1969. "Limitations on the Power of Courts in Resolving Church Property Disputes." *Tennessee Law Review* 36: 549–65.

Phipps, Bill. 1999. "God and the Market [letter]." *National Post* (April 3): B9.

Pidgeon, George C. 1950. *The United Church of Canada: The Story of Union*. Toronto: Ryerson Press.

Politzer, Jerome F. 2001. "The Prayer Book Society's Thirtieth Birthday (1971–2001)." *Mandate* 20 (4): 2.

Poloma, Margaret. 1982. *The Charismatic Movement: Is There a New Pentecost?* Boston: Twayne Publishers.

Prayer Book Society of Canada (PBSC). 1991. "Submission to the *Book of Alternative Services* Evaluation Commissioners"; online at www.prayerbook.ca/articles/ pbscbasx.htm, accessed December 2, 2002.

Prayer Book Society of Canada. n.d. "Welcome;" retrieved online from www.prayerbook.ca/pbscmain.htm, accessed December 15, 2002.

Prayer Book Society of Canada—Nova Scotia/Prince Edward Island (PBSC-NS/ PEI). 1999. *Something to Sing About? Scripture and the New Hymn Book of the Anglican Church of Canada*. Chester, Nova Scotia: Prayer Book Society of Canada—Nova Scotia/Prince Edward Island.

Presbyterian Church (USA). 1999. *Book of Confessions: Study Edition*. Louisville, KY: Geneva Press.

Presbyterian Coalition. 1998. "Union in Christ: A Declaration for the Church;" retrieved online from www.presbycoalition.org/union.htm, accessed October 11, 2002.

Presbyterian Coalition. 1999a. "Historical Context;" retrieved online from www.presbycoalition.org/HistoricalContext.htm, accessed October 11, 2002.

Presbyterian Coalition. 1999b. "Turning Toward the Mission of God: A Strategy for the Transformation of the PC(U.S.A.)" retrieved online from www. presbycoalition.org/strategy.htm, accessed October 10, 2002.

Presbyterian Forum. n.d. "The Certain Trumpet;" retrieved online from www. pforum.org/trumpet.html, accessed October 22, 2002.

Presbyterian Lay Committee. 1997. "The History of the Presbyterian Lay Committee"; online at www.layman.org/layman/the-lay-comm/plc-history.htm.
———. 1998. "Slain Missionaries Defining Moment for *Layman* Editor"; online at www.layman.org/layman/the-lay-comm/williamson-parker.htm, accessed October 4, 2002.
Presbyterians for Faith, Family and Ministry. 1996. "Masthead." *Theology Matters* 2 (2): 16.
Presbyterians for Renewal. n.d. "Our History;" retrieved online from www.pfrenewal.org, accessed September 9, 2002.
Price, Clive. 2000. "An Ancient Fire: The Ever-Burning Truth of Celtic Christianity." *Good News* 33 (5): 12–14 (March-April).
Quebedeaux, Richard. 1976. *The New Charismatics: The Origins, Development, and Significance of Neo-Pentecostalism.* Garden City, NY: Doubleday & Company.
Ralston, William H., Jr. 1992. "Gender and God." *The Machray Review* 1; online at www.prayerbook.ca/machray/pbscmac2.htm, accessed November 12, 2002.
———. 2001. "Thirty Years Ago in Tennessee: The Origins of the Prayer Book Society." *Mandate* 20 (3): 2.
Rediger, G. Lloyd. 1997. *Clergy Killers: Guidance for Pastors and Congregations under Attack.* Louisville, KY: Westminster John Knox Press.
Reed, David A. 1991. "From Movement to Institution: A Case Study of Charismatic Renewal in the Anglican Church of Canada." *American Theological Library Association: Summary of Proceedings* 45: 173–94.
Reeves, Thomas C. 1996. *The Empty Church: Does Organized Religion Matter Anymore?* New York: Touchstone.
Reid, Gail. 1997. "Editor's Note." *Fellowship Magazine* 15 (1): 3.
Reverend B. 1996. "Priestess and Pastor: Serving between the Worlds." In *Living Between Two Worlds: Challenges of the Modern Witch,* ed. Charles S. Clifton, 61–86. St. Paul, Minn.: Llewellyn Publications.
Righter, Walter C. 1998. *A Pilgrim's Way.* New York: Alfred A. Knopf.
Riordan, Michael. 1990. *The First Stone: Homosexuality and the United Church.* Toronto: McLelland and Stewart.
Robb, Edmund W. 1986. "An Open Letter to My Moderate Friends." *Challenge to Evangelism Today* 19 (2): 4, 9.
———. 1989. "The Crisis of Theological Education in the United Methodist Church." *Challenge to Evangelism Today* 22 (2): 1, 11.
———. 1990. "A Holy Crusade for Freedom." *Challenge to Evangelism Today* 23 (1): 1.
———. 1991. "A Call to Commitment." In *The World Forever Our Parish,* ed. Dean S. Gilliland, 107–122. Lexington, KY: Bristol House.
———. 1998. "The Spirit Who Will Not be Tamed: Can the Mainline Denominations be Part of a Holy Spirit Revival?" *Good News* 31 (4), January–February: 10–15 (January–February).
Robb, Edmund W., and Julia Robb. 1986. *The Betrayal of the Church: Apostasy and Renewal in the Mainline Denominations.* Westchester, IL: Crossway Books.
Robb, Julia. 1987. "A Tale of Two Priests." *Challenge to Evangelism Today* 20 (1): 3, 9.
Robinson, Thomas A. 1988. *The Bauer Thesis Examined: The Geography of Heresy in the Early Christian Church.* Lewiston, NY: The Edwin Mellen Press.
Rogers, Max Gray. 1964. *Charles Augustus Briggs: Trial of a Conservative Heretic.* Ph.D. dissertation, Columbia University.

Roof, Wade Clark. 1987. "The Church in the Centrifuge." *The Christian Century* (November 8): 1012–1014.

———. 1993. *A Generation of Seekers: The Spiritual Journeys of the Baby Boom Generation.* New York: HarperSanFrancisco.

———. 1999. *Spiritual Marketplace: Baby Boomers and the Remaking of American Religion.* Princeton: Princeton University Press.

Roof, Wade Clark, and William McKinney. 1987. *American Mainline Religion: Its Changing Shape and Future.* New Brunswick, NJ: Rutgers University Press.

Ross, C. Gordon. 1990a. Letter to Richard Moffatt. January 22; photocopy of typescript.

———. 1990b. "An Open Letter to the Executive of General Council." January 31; photocopy of typescript.

———. 1999. "Remembering Church Alive: An Historical Memoir." *Theological Digest & Outlook* 14 (2), September: 3–5.

Ross, C. Gordon, and John H. Trueman. 1990. "Letter to Rt. Rev. Sang Chul Lee." *Concern: A Voice at General Council* 5 (August 23): 1.

Rutledge, Kathleen K. 2000. "The Courage to Be Free." *Good News* 34 (2): 14–20 (September–October).

Ruzicka, Marilyn K. 2001. "Faith of Our Fathers." *Mandate* 20 (2): 10.

Salvidar, Ernest. 1997. "Letter to the Editor." *Good News* 31 (1), July–August: 5.

Schirmer, Jennifer. 2000. *The Guatemalan Military Project: A Violence Called Democracy.* Pennsylvania Studies in Human Rights. Pittsburgh: University of Pennsylvania Press.

School of the Americas (SOA) Watch. 2001. "Still a School of Assassins;" online at www.soaw.org/Articles/legislative/talking_points_feb_01.htm, accessed August 10, 2002.

Schooley, S. Alan. 1997. "What to Believe?" *Calgary Herald,* November 9, A18.

Scott, Ephraim. 1928. *"Church Union" and the Presbyterian Church in Canada.* Montréal: John Lovell & Son.

Scott, Graham A. D. 1989. "History of the Community of Concern." *Theological Digest & Outlook* 4 (1), January: 5–9 (January).

———. 1997. "Statement of the Rev. Dr. Graham Scott, President, Church Alive, on Published Remarks by Moderator Bill Phipps in October 1997"; photocopy of typescript.

Seamands, David A. 1998. "Blessing the Unblessable." *Good News* 31 (6): 19–22 (May/June).

Semple, Neil. 1996. *The Lord's Dominion: The History of Canadian Methodism.* Montréal and Kingston: McGill-Queen's University Press.

Schneider, Howard. 1997. "Letter from Canada." *The Washington Post* (December 25), A36.

Schrader, Elizabeth H. 1994. "Letter to the Editor." *Good News* 28 (1), July–August: 5.

Shelley, Marshall. 1994. *Well-Intentioned Dragons: Ministering to Problem People in the Church.* Minneapolis: Bethany House.

Shepherd, Victor. 1996. " 'Almost' Christian." *Fellowship Magazine* 14 (4): 16–18.

———. 1998. "Bermuda Testimony"; online at http://www.victorshepherd.on.ca/ BermudaTrial/bermuda1.htm, accessed November 17, 2002.

Shriver, George H., ed. 1966. *American Religious Heretics: Formal and Informal Trials.* Nashville, TN: Abingdon Press.

Shupe, Anson D., William A. Stacey, and Susan E. Darnell, eds. 2000. *Bad Pastors: Clergy Misconduct in Modern America.* New York: New York University Press.

Silcox, Claris Edwin. 1933. *Church Union in Canada: Its Causes and Consequences.* New York: Institute of Social and Religious Research.

Small, Joseph D. 1999. "Signs of a Postdenominational Future." *The Christian Century* (May 5): 506–09.

Smart, James D. 1968. *The Confession of 1967: Implications for the Church's Mission.* Significant Papers, no. 17. New York: Commission on Ecumenical Mission and Relations, The United Presbyterian Church in the USA.

Smelser, Neil. 1962. *Theory of Collective Behavior.* New York: Free Press.

Smith, Alexa. 1999. "Despite Frustrations, Presbyterian Evangelicals Say They'd Rather Fight Than Switch." Presbyterian News Service (September 24); retrieved online from www.pcusa.org/pcnews/oldnews/1999/99315.htm, accessed October 9, 2002.

Smith, Frank J. 1999. *The History of the Presbyterian Church in America.* 2nd ed. Lawrenceville, GA: Presbyterian Scholars Press.

Smith, Sam. 1994. "Letter to the Editor." *Good News* 28 (1), July–August: 5.

Socarides, Charles W. 1994. "The Erosion of Heterosexuality: Psychiatry Falters, America Sleeps." *Good News* 28 (2): 19–21 (September–October).

Spong, John Shelby. 1994. "Statement of Koinonia;" retrieved online from newark. rutgers.edu/~lcrew/koinonia.html, accessed January 20, 2003.

Stackhouse, Reginald. 1999. "One Church—One Book." *The Anglican Journal* (September); online at www.anglicanjournal.com/125/07/oped03.html, accessed November 2, 2002.

Stallsworth, Paul T. 1994. "Doctrine, Not Theology." *Josiah* (fall); online at www.ucmpage.org/josiah_journal/, accessed November 20, 2002.

———. 1997. "Truthful worship and truthful preaching." *Josiah* 3 (2); online at www.ucmpage.org/josiah_journal/, accessed November 20, 2002.

Stanton, James C., et al. v. Righter. 1995a. "Brief in Support of Presentment"; photocopy of transcript.

———. 1995b. "Official Response to the Presentment"; photocopy of transcript.

———. 1995c. "Presentment"; photocopy of transcript.

———. 1996a. "The Accusers' Position on Doctrine in the Heresy Trial of Walter Righter"; photocopy of transcript.

———. 1996b. "Motion to Strike Improper, Immaterial and Scandalous Matters and to Limit the Argument of the Church Attorney"; photocopy of transcript.

———. 1996c. "Notice Concerning an Appeal to the Decision of the Court"; photocopy of transcript.

———. 1996d. "Opinion of the Court for the Trial of a Bishop"; photocopy of transcript.

———. 1996e. "Statement of Exceptions"; photocopy of transcript.

Stark, Rodney. 1984. "The Rise of a New World Faith." *Review of Religious Research* 26 (1): 18–27.

———. 1999. "Secularization, R.I.P." *Sociology of Religion* 60 (3): 249–73.

Stark, Rodney, and Roger Finke. 2000. *Acts of Faith: Explaining the Human Side of Religion.* Berkeley and Los Angeles: University of California Press.

Stark, Rodney, and William Sims Bainbridge. 1987. *A Theory of Religion*. New Brunswick, NJ: Rutgers University Press.

Starkey, Marion L. 1949. *The Devil in Massachusetts: A Modern Inquiry into the Salem Witch Trials*. Alexandria, VA: Time-Life Books.

Stirling, Andrew. 1999. "The Trinity: Irrelevant or Essential?" *Fellowship Magazine* 17 (1): 4–7.

Stoll, David. 1990. *Is Latin America Turning Protestant? The Politics of Evangelical Growth*. Berkeley and Los Angeles: University of California Press.

"Summary of Cases." 2002. *The Layman* (October): 3.

Summit Presbyterian Church. 2001. "Summit Presbyterian Church's Confessional Statement;" retrieved online from www.confessingchurch.homestead.com/ resolutionbutler.html, accessed October 31, 2002.

Sykes, C. Powell. 1998. "Rosemary Radford Ruether gives 1998 Sprunt Lectures; says 'Flesh became Word not Word became Flesh;." *The Layman* 31:2 (March–April); retrieved online from www.layman.org, accessed October 10, 2002.

Synan, Vinson. 1997. *The Holiness-Pentecostal Tradition: Charismatic Movements in the Twentieth Century*. 2nd ed. Grand Rapids, MI: William B. Eerdmans Publishing Company.

Thomas, Ernest. 1919. "Church Union in Canada." *The American Journal of Theology* 23 (3): 257–73.

Tooley, Mark. 1997. "Should We Send More Money to the Board of Church and Society?" *Good News* 30 (4), : 43 (January–February).

———. 1999a. "Cold War Double Standards Still Underlie Debate over Terrorism." UM*Action* News Report (September 20); online at http://umaction.org/ mtooley50.htm, accessed October 10, 2002.

———. 1999b. "UM Bishops Condemn U.S. Military Action in Yugoslavia." UM*Action* News Report (May 14); online at http://umaction.org/mtooley34. htm, accessed October 10, 2002.

———. 2000a. "Castro-Friendly National Council of Churches Is Not a Neutral Arbiter in Dispute over Displaced Cuban Boy." UM*Action* News Report (January 12); online at http://umaction.org/mtooley64.htm, accessed October 10, 2002.

———. 2000b. "The Church Council and Little Elian." UM*Action* News Report (January 27); online at http://umaction.org/mtooley67.htm, accessed October 10, 2002.

———. 2000c. "Church Leaders Repeat Mistakes over Nuclear Weapons." UM*Action* News Report (August 29); online at http://umaction.org/mtooley96. htm, accessed October 10, 2002.

———. 2000d. "Churches, Little Elian and Greg Craig." UM*Action* News Report (April 27); online at http://umaction.org/mtooley81.htm, accessed October 10, 2002.

———. 2000e. "Labyrinths Are Latest Fad for Spiritual Seekers." UM*Action* News Report (April 13); online at http://umaction.org/mtooley80.htm, accessed October 10, 2002.

———. 2000f. "Liberal Churches Condemn Israel, Back Palestinians." UM*Action* News Report (October 24); online at http://umaction.org/mtooley107.htm, accessed October 10, 2002.

———. 2000g. "The Mythology of the Jesus Seminar." UM*Action* News Report (March 14); online at http://umaction.org/mtooley75.htm, accessed October 10, 2002.

———. 2000h. "UM Agency Opposes Missile Defense for U.S." UM*Action Briefing* (Christmas); online at http://umaction.org/umaction_christmas2000.htm, accessed October 10, 2002.

———. 2000i. "UM Church Agency Defends Funding for Lawyer Greg Craig in Elian Case." UM*Action* News Report (May 8); online at http://umaction.org/mtooley84.htm, accessed October 10, 2002.

———. 2000j. "UM Leader Defends Funding for Greg Craig in Elian Case; IRD Responds." UM*Action* News Report (May 10); online at http://umaction.org/mtooley84b.htm, accessed October 10, 2002.

———. 2000k. "UM Missions Board Condemns Israel, Sides with Palestinians." UM*Action* News Report (October 16); online at http://umaction.org/mtooley105.htm, accessed October 10, 2002.

———. 2000l. "U.S. Church Leaders Fight U.S. Navy Facility at Vieques." UM*Action* News Report (January 11); online at http://umaction.org/mtooley65.htm, accessed October 10, 2002.

———. 2000m. "U.S. Churches Showing Bias in Middle East Conflict." UM*Action* News Report (November 2); online at http://umaction.org/mtooley109.htm, accessed October 10, 2002.

———. 2001a. "11 U.S. Religious Leaders Ask Bush to Get Navy Out of Vieques." UM*Action* News Report (April 18); online at http://umaction.org/mtooley152.htm, accessed October 10, 2002.

———. 2001b. "D.C. Thinktank Fails to Understand Mainline Church Problems." UM*Action* News Report (N.d.); online at http://umaction.org/mtooley141.htm, accessed October 10, 2002.

———. 2001c. Personal communication with author, June 21.

———. 2001d. "UM Missionary Urges Solidarity with Palestinian 'Liberation Movement'." UM*Action* News Report (April 26); online at http://umaction.org/mtooley158.htm, accessed October 10, 2002.

Toon, Peter. N.d. "The American Book of Common Prayer"; online at www.episcopalian.org/pbs1928/ Articles/whatis.htm, accessed November 29, 2002.

———. 1992. *Knowing God through the Liturgy*. Largo, FL: The Prayer Book Society Publishing Company.

———. 1999a. *Proclaiming the Gospel through the Liturgy: The Common Prayer Tradition and Doctrinal Revision*. Largo, FL: The Prayer Book Society Publishing Company.

———. 1999b. "A Statement for Discussion." *Mandate* 18 (5): 13–14.

———. 2000a. "Apology & Olive Branch." *Mandate* 19 (5): 2.

———. 2000b. "Differing Solutions to the Crisis in the ECUSA." *Mandate* 19 (6): 14–15.

———. 2000c. "Two Religions of the Episcopal Church of the USA Visible at General Convention." *Mandate* 19 (5): 3–4.

———. 2001a. "Lent and Selfish Autonomy." *Mandate* 20 (2): 3, 6.

———. 2001b. "Our Thirtieth Anniversary (1971–2001)." *Mandate* 20 (3): 3.

Toy, E. V., Jr. 1969. "The National Lay Committee and the National Council of

Churches: A Case Study of Protestants in Conflict." *American Quarterly* 21 (2): 190–209.

Truax, Albert. 1893. Letter to John Wakefield. November 25, photocopy of handwritten manuscript.

Trueman, John. 1990a. Letter to Chairpersons of Official Boards. May 2; photocopy of typescript.

———. 1990b. "Oh! If Only You Had Been There." *Concern: A Voice at General Council* 5 (August 23): 4.

Tuttle, Robert G. N.d. "The Charismatic Movement: Its Historical Base and Wesleyan Framework." In *The Book of Resolutions of The United Methodist Church: 1996*, 703–09. Nashville, TN: United Methodist Publishing House.

Tymchak, Michael. 1969. "A Pluralist Church?" *The Small Voice* 1: 8–10.

UM*Action*. N.d. "The United Methodist Church Is in Crisis!" Information leaflet.

United Church of Canada. 1928. *The Manual of The United Church of Canada: Constitution and Government*. Toronto: The United Church of Canada Publishing House.

———. 1984. *Record of Proceedings of the 30th General Council of The United Church of Canada*. Toronto: United Church Publishing House.

———. 1988. *Record of Proceedings of the 32nd General Council of The United Church of Canada*. Toronto: United Church Publishing House.

———. 1990. "33rd General Council on Membership, Ministry and Human Sexuality," open letter to The United Church of Canada; photocopy of typescript.

United Church Renewal Fellowship. 1975. *Our Inheritance*. Barrie, Ont.: The United Church Renewal Fellowship.

———. 1984a. "A Critique of the Division of Ministry Personnel & Education Task Force Report." Photocopy of typescript.

———. 1984b. *We Have an Anchor: A Searching Study of the Basis of Union of The United Church of Canada*. Barrie, Ont.: The United Church Renewal Fellowship.

United Methodist *Action*. N.d. "UM*Action* Reform Agenda for United Methodists." Washington, DC: The Institute on Religion and Democracy.

U.S. Census Bureau. 2001. *Statistical Abstract of the United States*. Washington, D.C.: U.S. Census Bureau.

Valentin-Castagnon, Eliezer. 2001. Personal communication with author (June 25).

Voices of Orthodox Women. 1999. "The VOW Survey: Findings;" retrieved online from www.vow.org/survey.html, accessed October 21, 2002.

———. 2001. "Vow Board Recommends Againsts Using Horizons' Bible Study;" retrieved online from www.vow.org/esther.html, accessed October 20, 2002.

———. N.d. [a] "Statement of Faith;" retrieved online from www.vow.org/statementoffaith.html, accessed October 19, 2002.

———. N.d. [b] "Voices of Orthodox Women;" retrieved online from www.vow.org/orthodoxy.html, accessed October 19, 2002.

Wainwright, Geoffrey. 1992. "Seminaries in Crisis." *Challenge to Evangelism Today* 25 (1): 5, 11.

Wakefield, Walter L., and Austin P. Evans. 1991. *Heresies of the High Middle Ages: Selected Sources Translated and Annotated*. Records of Western Civilization Series. New York: Columbia University Press.

Wales, Gary. 1998. "The Authority of Scripture." *Good News* 31 (5); online at www.goodnewsmag.org/library/articles/wales-ma98.htm, accessed October 2, 2002.

Walker, D. P. 1981. *Unclean Spirits: Possession and Exorcism in France and England in the Late Sixteenth and Early Seventeenth Centuries.* Philadelphia: University of Pennsylvania Press.

Walker, Robert, and Gordon Legge. 1997. "Repent or Resign, Church Leader Told." *Calgary Herald*, November 17, A1.

Warner, R. Stephen. 1988. *New Wine in Old Wineskins: Evangelicals and Liberals in a Small-Town Church.* Berkeley and Los Angeles: University of California Press.

Watts, A. M. 1983. "The Sexuality Report: Two Years Later." *Touchstone: Heritage and Theology in a New Age* 1 (1): 15–21.

Weaver, Mary Jo, and R. Scott Appleby, eds. 1995. *Being Right: Conservative Catholics in America.* Bloomington: Indiana University Press.

Weber, Max. 1951. *The Religion of China: Confucianism and Taoism.* Translated and edited by Hans H. Gerth. New York: The Free Press.

Wesleyan Methodist Trustees et al. v. Lightbourne and Lightbourne. 1996. Supreme Court of Bermuda 280/1996 and 282/1996.

Wigglesworth, Edward. 1999. *"Wigglesworth v. Phipps."* Charge to the Calgary Presbytery of the United Church of Canada. Photocopy of typescript.

Wilke, Richard B. 1986. *Are We Yet Alive? The Future of the United Methodist Church.* Nashville, TN: Abingdon Press.

Williamson, Parker T. 1996. *Standing Firm: Reclaiming Christian Faith in Times of Controversy.* Lenoir, N.C.: PLC Publications.

———. 1998a. "Building Community—Denying Jesus' Lordship." *The Layman* RealVideo; online at www.layman.org/layman/audio-slideshow-files/feb video.rm, accessed September 15, 2002.

———. 1998b. "John Leith: A Theologian in the Service of the Church." *The Layman* 31: 3 (May–June); online at www.layman.org/layman/the-layman/1998/may-june/john-leith-theologian.htm, accessed September 15, 2002.

———. 1998c. "Nine Presbyterians Arrested at School of the Americas." *The Layman* 31: 1 (January-February); online at www.layman.org/layman/the-layman/1998/january-feb/school-of-americas.htm, accessed September 15, 2002.

———. 1998d. "Union Seminary Receives Accreditation Warnings." *The Layman* 31: 1 (January–February); online at www.layman.org/layman/the-layman/1998/january-feb/union-receives-warning.htm, accessed September 15, 2002.

———. 1998e. "Unwatchful Gargoyles at Union Theological Seminary." *The Layman*. RealVideo; online at www.layman.org/layman/audio-slideshow-files/gargoyles.rm, accessed September 15, 2002.

———. 1999. *Essays from Zimbabwe.* Lenoir, N.C.: PLC Publications.

Willimon, William H., and Robert L. Wilson. 1987. *Rekindling the Flame: Strategies for a Vital United Methodism.* Nashville, TN: Abingdon Press; online at http://cmpage.org/rekindling/, accessed October 2, 2002.

Wilson, Bryan. 1966. *Religion in Secular Society.* London: C.A. Watts.

———. 1975. "The Debate over Secularization: Religion, Society, and Faith." *Encounter* 45: 77–84.

———. 1985. "Secularization." In *The Sacred in a Secular Age,* ed. Philip Hammond, 1–20. Berkeley and Los Angeles: University of California Press.

Wilson, John. 1971. "The Sociology of Schism." *A Sociological Yearbook of Religion in Britain* 4: 1–19.

Wilson, Robert L. N.d. *Biases and Blindspots: Methodism and Foreign Policy Since World War II;* online at http://cmpage.org/biases/, accessed October 2, 2002.

Wishart, Vernon R. N.d. "Some Misrepresentations and Rationalizations by Our Leadership." Photocopy of typescript.

Wolf, David. 1994. "Letter to the Editor." *Good News* 28 (3), November–December: 7.

Wood, David J. 2001. "Where Are the Younger Clergy?" *The Christian Century* 118 (12): 18–19.

Wuthnow, Robert. 1988. *The Restructuring of American Religion: Society and Faith Since World War II.* Princeton: Princeton University Press.

———. 1989. *The Struggle for America's Soul: Evangelicals, Liberals, and Secularism.* Grand Rapids, MI: William B. Eerdmans Publishing Company.

Young, Amos. 1998. "Interpreting Charismatic Experience: Hypnosis, Altered States of Consciousness, and the Holy Spirit?" *Journal of Pentecostal Theology* 13: 117–32.

Young, Lawrence A., ed. 1997. *Rational Choice Theory and Religion: Summary and Assessment.* New York: Routledge.

Zito, George V. 1983. "Toward a Sociology of Heresy." *Sociological Analysis* 44 (2): 123–30.

INDEX

About the Author

DOUGLAS E. COWAN is Assistant Professor of Religious Studies and Sociology at the University of Missouri, Kansas City. He is the co-editor of *Religion on the Internet: Research Prospects and Promises.*